OCCUPATIONAL CRIME

Nelson-Hall Series in Law, Crime, and Justice
Series Editor: Howard Abadinsky, St. Xavier University, Chicago

OCCUPATIONAL CRIME

Gary S. Green
Albany State College

Foreword by Gilbert Geis
University of California, Irvine

nh Nelson-Hall, Chicago

Project Editor: Richard Meade
Copy Editor: James Cambias
Text Design: Claudia von Hendricks
Photo Research: Stephen Forsling
Composition: Precision Typographers
Manufacturer: Bookcrafters
Cover Art: *The White Defendant,* Marcia Danits

Library of Congress Cataloging-in-Publication Data

Green, Gary S.
  Occupational Crime / Gary S. Green
    p.   cm. — (Nelson-Hall series in law, crime, and justice)
  Includes bibliographical references.
  ISBN 0-8304-1196-8
  1. Crime. 2. White collar crimes. 3. Criminal behavior
I. Title. II. Series.
HV6030.G69 1990
364.1'68—dc   2089-29234
                                                          CIP

Manufactured in the United States of America

10 9 8 7 6 5 4 3 2 1

For Jennia, with love

CONTENTS

ACKNOWLEDGMENTS

Fifteen years ago, I enrolled in a "White Collar Crime" course taught by Gilbert Geis during my senior year at the University of California, Irvine. Little did I know then that I would be writing a book related to that subject more than a decade later. Since my Irvine days, Gil has been a wonderful mentor, colleague, and friend. I deeply thank him for providing constant encouragement for this project, and for the comprehensive bibliographies and hard-to-find materials. He has made insightful editorial and substantive comments thoughout the book—many of the better ideas that appear in the following pages are his. The score of Dr. Geis's works that I have cited represent only a small portion of his contributions to the area of occupational crime. I owe him a debt I know I can never repay.

I thank several other colleagues for their input: John Braithwaite, Frank Cullen, James A. Fox, Paul Jesilow, Ron Kramer, Henry Pontell, Darrell Steffensmeier, Jay Albanese, Paul Tracy, and Austin Turk. Ted Philbin and Sandra Jackson, my student assistants at Albany State College, scurried around trying to find books and articles for me to use. I thank my supervisors at Albany State College for allowing me release time to complete this project: Hugh Phillips, James Hill, Ernest Benson, and Billy Black. Doug Brogden of the Food and Drug Administration and Hester Donziger of the Internal Revenue Service helped in securing information from their respective agencies. The library staffs at Albany State College, Darton College, and Florida State University were extremely helpful. Elisa Fowler was particularly adroit at running down government annual reports. Stephen Ferrara and the staff at Nelson-Hall gave me this opportunity, and I appreciate their confidence and support. I also thank Richard Meade, general manager, and Jim Cambias at Nelson-Hall, who allowed me freedom, time, and expert editorial help to complete the project.

I want to express my love and appreciation to my wife, Konnie, who often put up with cancelled dinners, late-night trips to the library, and *ad nauseam* narrations of various drafts during the past two years—and she did it all with a smile.

Gary S. Green

FOREWORD

The study of occupational crime involves an understanding of a considerable number of different fields of knowledge. Law defines the nature of the kinds of behavior that can result in penalties. Legislative histories, court decisions, statutory interpretations, and the litigation of individual cases are among the range of sources of data that shed light on the occupational crime issue. The informed student of occupational crime has to comprehend such diverse sources as the Sherman Antitrust Act, the regulations of the Securities and Exchange Commission, and the vast array of consumer protection statutes. Distinctions among administrative, civil, and criminal law processes must be appreciated. Such matters as these often necessitate forays into specialized law libraries, familiarity with the way to shephardize (that is, to use special reference books to locate citations to laws and court decisions), and skill in the variety of other information-gathering techniques unique to legal research.

The legal literature includes shelves-full of law reviews, with each law school issuing its own publication, usually on a bi-monthly or quarterly basis. These reviews often carry material on diverse jurisprudential aspects of occupational crime. Such pieces inevitably are embedded with an armory of citations, given the notoriety of law review writers to support statements with footnotes that often occupy much more of a page than the text above. Today, the *American Criminal Law Review* devotes one entire issue each year to a review of legal developments in the field of occupational crime.

Besides law, occupational crime students have to be familiar with criminology and criminal justice, and with those social sciences that provide a good deal of the underpinning of contemporary criminology—especially sociology. Most work in occupational crime finds its roots in sociological soil; and the theoretical statements are almost exclusively the product of sociologists. Criminal justice, a new and burgeoning discipline since the 1950s, now offers special focus on the police, the court processes, and the punishment system. It also examines the system of law-making and law-enforcing from a more multidisciplinary perspective than that found in earlier studies.

Contributions from other arenas of scholarly work also must be scrutinized to obtain satisfactory control over the information necessary for an adequate understanding of occupational crime. Anthropology offers cross-cultural perspectives of how different social structures define and regulate exploitative activities that we categorize as occupational crime. Political science has been especially concerned in regard to occupational crime with the operation of the new regulatory agencies and questions about the influence exerted over them by pressure groups, both within the regulated businesses and within the consumer constituency. History tells us how earlier societies dealt with such phenomena, and psychology offers insights about the manner in which people introject attitudes that underlie the kinds of behaviors that end up as violations of statutes regulating occupational activity.

Finally, economics (and such adjacent fields as public management, accounting, and business) possesses an impressive body of knowledge that can inform our understanding of occupational crime. Surprisingly, of all the relevant disciplines, these probably have made the least direct contribution to what we know about occupational crime. Economists in particular have a tendency to write off criminal consequences of law-breaking by businessmen as nothing but a factor that must be taken into account in cost-benefit analyses. Virtually no article in a major economics journal in the past decade has directly addressed the subject of criminal activity by major businesses or their executives, though popular forums, such as *Fortune*, attend rather often to the subject.

Similarly, business school scholars tend to use more lulling terms, especially "ethics," to camouflage what essentially are considerations of criminal behavior. They may anguish in print over whether company ethical stands are likely to inhibit deviant behavior by employees, but they steadfastly ignore the question of whether tough law-enforcement might be a good deal more inhibiting than what sometimes are little more than pious abstract dicta about how things ought to be done.

Given the vital need to encompass so disparate an array of fields of knowledge in order to comprehend the phenomena of occupational crime adequately, it is particularly gratifying to be able to introduce a book by a scholar who so uniquely possesses the academic qualifications for such a job. Gary Green did his undergraduate work in the Program in Social Ecology at the University of California, Irvine. That program had been formed only a few years before he arrived, and it brought together in an interdisciplinary setting persons with training in criminology and criminal justice, urban studies, and public health, as well as in environmental, social, clinical, and developmental psychology. Several faculty members also possessed law degrees and taught courses in criminal law and criminal procedure.

After leaving Irvine, Professor Green took his master's degree at Rutgers University in its highly regarded criminal justice program. Following this, he did his doctoral work in the prestigious criminology program at the University of Pennsylvania, a program then located in the Department of Sociology, and now established in the Wharton School of Business.

It would be difficult to find a person with educational training more suitable than Professor Green to handle the demanding interdisciplinary rigors required for an understanding of the breadth and nuances involved in occupational crime. This book provides the student with insights gathered from a uniquely specialized educational background.

Besides the challenge of mastery of parts of a variety of different subject areas, the study of occupational crime offers the student an opportunity to attend to matters that truly bear upon the kind of society we have produced and the kind of society that we would like to see. Occupational crime is without a doubt more dangerous, both in physical and in fiscal terms, than street crime. Nuclear control failures, produced by criminal negligence, can wipe out more people in a single day than all the murderers have slain in centuries. Occupational crime can also be regarded as more abominable. It can be argued that muggers, burglars, and drug addicts typically suffer from the slings and arrows of social circumstances that allow them less than a decent share of what the society has to offer. To be poor may be no excuse for committing a crime, but the crimes of poor people have to raise concerns about such ills as prejudice and the unequal distributions of wealth. To deal with the offenders and not with the social ailments can create a certain uneasiness in criminologists.

There is much less moral ambivalence associated with the phenomena of occupational crime. People who commit such crimes often need not do so in terms of what most of us would regard as reasonable motives. The doctor who earns $100,000 a year and steals $20,000 more by unnecessary surgery or the Congressman who uses his or her office to extort a bribe from a building contractor seem more deplorable to many of us than street offenders, because they seem to have so little excuse for what they do. In this regard, the study of occupational crime highlights philosophical questions of justice, of fairness and equity.

It is only recently—most notably since the Watergate scandals and the unnerving experiences of the Vietnam War—that scholarly and public attention has fixedly focused on occupational crime, its explanation and its control. The present textbook by Professor Green offers to the student an outstanding and interesting inventory and interpretation of these developments.

Gilbert Geis

OCCUPATIONAL CRIME

Investigators examine helicopter wreckage during the 1982 filming of *Twilight Zone: The Movie*. Director John Landis was later indicted for manslaughter as a result of the accident, in which veteran actor Vic Marrow and two Vietnamese child actors were killed. Although Landis was acquitted, homicide charges have marked a growing number of cases involving occupational crime in recent years. (AP/Wide World Photos)

O N E

THE CONCEPT OF OCCUPATIONAL CRIME

The commission of crime through occupational opportunity is hardly a new phenomenon.

More than three thousand years ago, for instance, Horemheb, a pharaoh in the fourteenth century B.C., passed what was probably the first law carrying a secular penalty for judicial bribetaking. Horemheb's edict called for capital punishment for those who committed such a "crime against justice" (Noonan, 1984:11). In ancient Greece, there were the Alcmaenoids, a leading family, who are reported to have contracted to build a solid marble temple, but instead used concrete, veneering it with marble (Geis 1968a). In ancient Persia, bakers who short-weighted bread or adulterated it with straw were executed in their own ovens (Schafer and Schafer, 1974:8). Henry III (1216-1272) passed laws against "forestalling," which outlawed the practice of buying up large amounts of foodstuffs, and thereby controlling prices (Geis, 1988:10). In the sixteenth century, Franz Schmidt (1973:111), the notorious executioner of Nuremberg, noted in his diary that a commercial defrauder was one of his victims at the gallows: Wastel Pennas, a butcher, had ". . . sold dog's flesh as mutton." By 1812, England had adopted complex legal regulations regarding labor practices. And in 1890, the United States Congress passed the Sherman Antitrust Act which outlawed unfair competition resulting from practices such as price-fixing.

These are but a few examples along the historical road of crime in the course of occupation. Such crime has aroused public and official indignation for many centuries. During the past two decades, however, the level of attention and indignation has increased dramatically. Every day's newspaper usually has some item about occupational crime. The stories may involve political bribery, embezzlement, child molestation in day care centers, income tax evasion, insider trading in the stock market, environmental pollution, or police brutality—each episode an example of occupationally related criminal behavior.

Some of the more infamous cases of occupationally related behavior during recent years have concerned charges of criminal homicide. Ford

Motor Company was charged by the State of Indiana in 1978 with reckless homicide because it allegedly willfully allowed unsafe Pinto automobiles to be marketed. In 1983, Hollywood movie director John Landis was indicted for manslaughter because of his alleged recklessness in filming a helicopter stunt for *Twilight Zone: The Movie*, during which three persons, including actor Vic Morrow, were killed. In New Jersey, two corporate managers of the Great Adventure amusement park were charged with manslaughter in 1984 after part of the park burned down, causing loss of life, because they allegedly failed to heed warnings that the park contained known fire hazards. In yet another on-the-job death, three executives of Film Recovery Systems Corporation were convicted of murder in 1985 for having "knowingly created a strong probability of death" (*Newsweek*, 1985a) by allowing employees to work around highly toxic chemicals used to recover silver from film. Although only the film recovery case ended in conviction, the fact that criminal homicide charges were brought against the other defendants as well demonstrates that occupationally related violence evokes some of the same public indignation as conventional street violence.

THE DISCOVERY OF OCCUPATIONAL CRIME

According to Merton and Zuckerman (1973:507), "codification" refers to the consolidation of knowledge into succinct and interdependent theoretical formulations. The various sciences differ in the extent to which they are codified. The intellectual organization of more codified sciences, such as physics and chemistry, differs from that of the less codified sciences, such as economics and criminology, in the extent to which particulars are knit together with general ideas. In less codified sciences, investigators must deal with a large block of descriptive facts and unrefined theories whose implications are not well understood. In the more codified fields, theoretical structures are more comprehensive and precise.

Bertrand Russell's (1929) distinction between "hard" and "soft" data bears a strong resemblance to the concept of codification, with the softer data being found in less codified sciences. Norman Storer (1967) uses the terms "hard" and "soft" to refer to, respectively, sciences possessing more or less ability to measure (or quantify) the phenomena under study. The concept of "discovery" in science is usually associated with an individual in the "harder" physical or biological sciences who was the first to obtain knowledge of an existing phenomenon. As examples, Marie Curie is credited with the discovery of radioactivity and the geneticists James Watson and Francis Crick are credited with the discovery of the double helix, which helps form the building blocks of life. In the "softer" social sciences (and some zoological sciences such as animal behavior), however, the term "discovery" is not as easily applied because the phenomena under study are behavioral rather than physical, and therefore cannot be observed in the same manner as a physical object. More accurately, behavioral scientists "construct" or "interpret" the realities they work with, rather than discover them.

Nevertheless, in the historical context of criminology, Edwin Hardin Sutherland (1883-1950) is officially credited with the discovery of occupational criminality (although his initial contribution focused only on "respected" occupations). The term "discovery" is used here in regard to Sutherland because crime in the course of occupation, though it had existed for a long time, had not been systematically identified until Sutherland. In his 1939 presidential address to the American Sociological Society (which will be discussed in the next section), Sutherland depicted as the "White Collar Criminal" any person of higher socioeconomic status who commits a legal violation in the course of his or her occupation. The speech was later published under the title "White-Collar Criminality" (Sutherland, 1940). Although Sutherland is most directly associated with the origin of the concept of occupational crime, his ideas were anticipated by at least three other criminological scholars during the early twentieth century—Charles R. Henderson, Edward Alsworth Ross, and Albert Morris.

Henderson probably had the most telling intellectual influence on Sutherland's interest in occupational crime. Henderson, using a textbook he had written, taught a correspondence course at the University of Chicago in which Sutherland was enrolled in 1905. Sutherland was teaching at Sioux Falls College at the time (Geis and Goff, 1983:xxiv). In that text, Henderson (1901:250) wrote:

"The social classes of the highest culture furnish few convicts, yet there are educated criminals. Advanced culture modifies the form of crime; tends to make it less coarse and violent, but more cunning; restricts it to quasi-legal forms. But education also opens up the way to new and colossal kinds of crime, [such] as debauching of conventions, councils, legislatures, and bribery of the press and public officials. The egoistic impulses are masked and disguised in this way, the devil wearing the livery of heavenly charity for a cloak of wrong. Many of the 'Napoleons' of trade are well named, for they are cold-blooded robbers and murderers, utterly indifferent to the inevitable misery which they must know will follow their contrivances and deals. Occasionally eminent legal ability is employed to plan raids upon the public in ways which will evade the penalties of the criminal code, and many a representative of financial power grazes the prison walls on his way to 'success'."

In 1907, Edward Ross also anticipated Sutherland by writing about the "criminaloid," referring to those who prosper by criminal practices in the course of their occupation, yet who have not come under adverse public opinion. Ross named as examples of criminaloids corporate executives, dishonest bank inspectors, food adulterators, corrupt judges, and labor leaders involved illegally in financial speculation, bribery and kickback schemes. For Ross, the key to the criminaloid was not evil impulse, but moral insensibility. The criminaloid prefers to victimize an anonymous public, and, when accused, he or she willingly makes restitution. The criminaloid is not antisocial by nature, often holding positions of high repute in the local community. Criminaloids have a double standard of morality, demonstrating high virtues in the family and unethical practices in the commercial and civic worlds. And the criminaloid is often piously religious, practicing a "protective mimicry of the good." The criminaloid "counterfeits the good citizen"— on the one hand being patriotic and donating to worthwhile charities, while on the other hand dodging taxes and corrupting government officials. For Ross, the criminaloid will flourish until the "growth of morality overtakes the growth of opportunities to prey" (Ross, 1968: 25-33).

Third, four years prior to Sutherland's address, Albert Morris's *Criminology* described "criminals of the upperworld," referring to "that numerous but never clearly identified group of criminals whose social position, intelligence, and criminal technique permit them to move among their fellow citizens virtually immune to recognition and prosecution as criminals" (Morris, 1968:35). Included among the twenty-three examples of criminals of the upperworld offered by Morris were bankers, stock brokers, manufacturers, politicians, contractors, and law enforcement officials. Morris further states:

"In many instances, the complexity and privacy of their dealings makes a fair identification of [the criminals of the upperworld] difficult. It is not always easy to evaluate their motives and methods. This is especially true if our general ethical notions are befogged or dulled by the near universality of sharp, if not illegal, business practices. Yet it needs to be emphasized that the criminals of the upperworld are genuine, not metaphorical criminals . . . . [Criminals of the upperworld] differ from their upright brethren only in being ethically less sensitive at certain points . . . . It is doubtful that they look upon themselves as criminals . . . . Failure to be caught and brought to account keeps many of them from being jolted out of their complacency. Their conduct becomes apparent in its true light only when a crisis reveals the details of their methods . . . . [T]he criminals of the upperworld are real, numerous, and near at hand" (Morris, 1968: 37-38).

This triumvirate—Henderson, Ross, and Morris—shared a pair of common ideas, both of which are bases for Sutherland's conception of the problem of occupational crime: (1) the most serious type of such criminality is found among the wealthy and respectable; and (2) these offenders do not see themselves as criminals nor are they perceived to be criminals by society or the criminal and regulatory justice systems.

SUTHERLAND'S HISTORIC SPEECH

Sutherland's (1940) presidential address, "The White Collar Criminal," was presented at the thirty-fourth annual meeting of the American Sociological Society in Philadelphia on 27 December 1939. Sutherland was fifty-six years old at the time and had been collecting information on occupational criminality since 1928. He had three main objectives for his address. First, Sutherland (1940:12) wanted to emphasize to the field of criminology the idea that "[w]hite-collar criminality is real criminality. . . ." because it is in violation of law; and the only major difference between white collar criminality and lower class criminality is that the former is primarily in violation of administrative law enforced by regulatory agencies while the latter is primarily in violation of statutory law enforced by the criminal justice system.

Second, Sutherland wanted to emphasize that poor people are not the only ones who commit crime. Therefore, according to Sutherland (1940:12), approaches that equate poverty with crime (that is, virtually all of the theories popular at the time of the speech) are biased with respect to socioeconomic status and "do not even explain the criminality of the lower class, since the [poverty factor is] not related to a general process characteristic of all criminality."

Third, Sutherland wanted to announce that his theory of "differential association," which he had first advanced a little over a decade earlier, constituted an approach that explained a general process characteristic of all criminality (differential association will be discussed in Chapter 3). Indeed, a theory that could explain crime in the lower class as well as it explains crime in the upper class would be a tremendous breakthrough in knowledge about the causes of crime. The speech was an iconoclastic strike by Sutherland.

Geis and Goff (1982:180) have examined the reviews of Sutherland's historic speech. The *Philadelphia Inquirer* (1939) reported that Sutherland's academic contribution was revolutionary, because it could throw "scores of sociological textbooks into a wastebasket." One infers from the *New York Times* coverage (1939), on the other hand, that its reporter believed that Sutherland might be going beyond social scientific inquiry by attempting to use science as a muckraking political tool in his battle against big business.

An academic interest and a desire for social decency, coupled with Sutherland's upbringing as the son of a Nebraska Baptist minister, lay behind his ground-breaking presidential address. The monumental importance of Sutherland's contribution to the area of occupational criminality was summed up by Professor Hermann Mannheim (1965:470) twenty-five years after the speech, when he wrote that Sutherland's discovery would have been given a Nobel Prize, were one awarded in the field of criminology. Mannheim's hindsight is probably correct, because Sutherland's (1949) *White Collar Crime* was the third most often nominated book by respected criminologists in their choice of the twenty best works ever published in the field through the first part of the 1970s. Sutherland's 1945 work, entitled "Is White-Collar Crime 'Crime'?," tied for fifth among articles nominated (Wolfgang, Figlio, and Thornberry, 1978:95-96).

In the decade that followed Sutherland's address, however, the question of whether his concept of "white collar crime" actually dealt with "real crime" was the subject of heated intellectual debate.

IS WHITE COLLAR CRIME "CRIME"?: THE SUTHERLAND-TAPPAN-BURGESS DEBATE

Sutherland's idea of white collar crime—crime by respected persons in the course of their occupation—was severely questioned by several of his colleagues, particularly Paul Tappan (1911-1964), who had earned a doctorate in both sociology and law. In a piece entitled "Who is the Criminal?," which appeared in the *American Sociological Review* in 1947, Tappan (1968:372) asserted that ". . . crime, as legally defined, is a sociologically significant province of study." Accordingly, actions that are not against the law are not crimes and persons who have not been convicted of criminal charges are not criminals. Sutherland (1945) agreed with Tappan that actions that are not against the law are not crimes, but insisted that white collar "crimes" could involve any violation of statutory or administrative law.

Adminstrative law violations are not criminal convictions *per se*. They most often result in court-imposed injunctions, consent decrees, and desist orders. An *injunction* is a judicial remedy awarded for the purpose of requiring a party to refrain from doing a particular act or behavior; it guards against future injuries rather than affording a remedy for past violations. A *consent decree* is an agreement between parties (usually the violator and an administrative agency) made under the sanction of the court. It is not a result of any judicial determination; rather, it is an agreement to be bound by certain stipulated facts. A *desist order* is a command from an administrative agency that is similar to an injunction. Sutherland (1945) argued that because these administrative orders result from violations of law and include government-imposed penalties, then such censured acts were equivalent to "crimes." The debate centered upon Tappan's assertion that criminologists must use only persons convicted of criminal charges as a sample of law violators.

Tappan believed that criminally convicted offenders represent the closest possible approximation to those who have in fact violated the law. Sutherland disagreed, maintaining that convicted offenders contain a gross overrepresentation from the lower class and that those few convicted of white collar crimes do not in any way closely approximate the totality of white collar criminals. Sutherland's position is consistent with Thorsten Sellin's (1951:490) dictum that "the value of criminal statistics as a basis for the measurement of criminality . . . decreases as the procedures take us farther away from the offense itself." Thus, Sutherland believed that Tappan's criterion of legal conviction is too far removed from the offense itself because: (1) criminals may operate undetected by various law enforcement and regulatory agencies; (2) if detected, the criminal may not be prosecuted; and (3) if prosecuted, the criminal may not be convicted. These three attrition stages between the offense and conviction render Tappan's conviction criterion too incomplete for determining the number and kinds of white collar offenders. For Sutherland, persons who committed legal violations were criminals, independent of whether they were officially detected, criminally charged, or criminally convicted.

Whereas Tappan opposed the concept of white collar crime because it was sociological rather than legalistic, Ernest W. Burgess opposed the concept because it was legalistic rather than sociological. Burgess, rooted deeply in the sociological school of "symbolic interaction," asserted that if individuals do not conceive of themselves as criminal or are not so considered by the public, then they should not be treated as such by social scientists. For Burgess (1950), a lack of public outrage, stigma, and official punishment attached to social action indicates that such action is not a violation of society's rules, independent of whether it is legally punishable. Burgess's conception could eliminate even more persons from the ranks of "criminals" than did Tappan's, because Burgess deletes from Tappan's already incomplete pool of law violators those who do not conceive of themselves as criminal. Burgess's further reduction in "who is the criminal" would be substantial, because many occupational offenders are otherwise quite respectable and have noncriminal self-images. Unlike Sutherland, Tappan's and Burgess's conceptions of "crime" omit a vast array of behaviors which are in violation of law. However, as broad as Sutherland's conception of crime might seem, it is still limited because it includes only behavior that has an illegal basis.

On the contrary, more recent scholars have attempted to go beyond legal violation in determining a perimeter of study. For instance, Douglas and Johnson (1977) conceptualized "official deviance," Quinney (1964) and Clark and Hollinger (1977) discuss "occupational deviance," Simon and Eitzen (1982) speak of "elite deviance," and Ermann and Lundman (1978) discuss "corporate and governmental deviance." These concepts have the benefit of breadth and flexibility, yet, depending upon who is defining the word, "deviance" could include a large array of behaviors that are not criminal and could exclude behaviors that are criminal. As Coleman (1987:407) notes,

> "There are . . . a vast number of groups with their own unique norms defining what is and is not deviant. Not only are many of those definitions contradictory, but, because most groups have no direct knowledge of the . . . activities that have come to be labeled as deviant, their definitions are also subject to erratic changes in response to vicissitudes of media coverage and public mood. Because of the absence of clearly formulated public standards for . . . behavior, sociologists using the deviance approach must often rely on their own values and prejudices to define the parameters of their work. In so doing, they not only threaten the integrity of the research process but also undermine the credibility of the entire effort to bring the problem . . . into the arena of public debate."

By including all and only criminal behavior, as legally defined, in the term "white collar crime," Sutherland's initial conception still seems to be the most useful and criticism-free approach, and it will provide the basis for our definition of "occupational crime."

A DEFINITION OF OCCUPATIONAL CRIME

Although Sutherland's idea about which *behaviors* constitute "crime" in the phrase "white collar crime" is well conceived, his concept of which *persons* are the "white collar" ones is considerably more problematic. In its original form, a white collar crime is any crime committed in the course of one's occupation by persons of respectability (Sutherland, 1940). For Sutherland, the respectability of the offender and the occupational opportunity for the offense are the two major criteria that determine whether a crime is a white collar one.

Respectability was an important criterion for Sutherland because it emphasized the strong influence that the respectable and privileged had on undercutting official censure against their behaviors. However, because perceptions about the respectability of persons and their occupations are relative to each individual and cannot be clearly demarcated, respectability as a criterion lacks concreteness and therefore adds interpretational problems to the term "white collar crime." Although the respectability notion in Sutherland's definition of white collar crime is important because of its emphasis on privilege and influence, it detracts from the precision of the definition.

Since Sutherland, there have been several attempts to hone his original conception of white collar crime. Edelhertz (1970:3) considers as white collar crime any "illegal act or series of illegal acts committed by nonphysical means and by concealment or guile, to obtain money or property, to avoid the payment or loss of money or property, or to obtain business or personal advantages." Similarly, the *Dictionary of Criminal Justice Data Terminology* (Bureau of Justice Statistics, 1981:215) defines white collar crime as "nonviolent crime for financial gain committed by means of deception by persons whose occupational status is entrepreneurial, professional or semi-professional and utilizing their special occupational skills and opportunities; also nonviolent crime for financial gain utilizing deception and committed by anyone having special technical and professional knowledge of business and government, irrespective of the person's occupation." These definitions are of little value in refining Sutherland's concept because they would include a virtually unlimited number of offenses that are not occupationally related and exclude offenses of a physical nature (e.g., illegally subjecting employees to unsafe working conditions, illegally distributing physically unsafe consumer products).

Other attempts at refining Sutherland's definition include that of Biderman and Reiss (1980:xxviii), who consider white collar crime to comprise "those violations of law to which penalties are attached and that involve the use of a violator's position of significant power, influence, or trust in the legitimate economic or political institutional order for the purpose of illegal gain, or to commit an illegal act for personal or organizational gain." And Coleman (1985:5; 1989:5) defines white collar crime as "a violation of the law committed by a person or group of persons in the course of their otherwise respected and legitimate occupation or financial activity." The concepts of "respectable" and "significant power, influence or trust" are no less controversial in these definitions than in Sutherland's, because they are terms relative to the definer of "respectable" and "significant." Moreover, Coleman's idea of crime in the course of respected or legitimate "financial activity" could include an essentially unlimited number of offenses that are unrelated to occupation, such as filing a fraudulent insurance claim or knowingly writing a check on an account that has insufficient funds. By including the concepts of respectability and nonoccupational activity, Edelhertz, Biderman and Reiss, and Coleman add little concreteness to a criminological area of study that should be conceptually precise.

There is another fundamental concern with the concept of white collar crime that goes beyond the difficulties in delineating exactly which offenses and offenders are to be so denoted. Unfortunately, "white collar crime" can also complicate explanation with description (Biderman and Reiss, 1980:xxvii). A major problem in using socioeconomic (vertical) status as the characteristic defining white collar crime is that the element cannot be utilized at the same time as an explanatory characteristic, since it is not allowed to vary independent of the definition. In other words, socioeconomic status cannot be an explanatory variable in white collar crime because only higher status persons, by definition, can commit such offenses. This could be a significant problem, because socioeconomic status has often been considered to be an important variable in the explanation of crime.

Others who have attempted to set perimeters on the kinds of behaviors falling within this area of criminology have restricted the definition to include only offenses in the course of one's job or occupation. For instance, Clinard and Quinney (1973) have abandoned the term "white collar crime" and offered the dichotomy of corporate and occupational crime. However, corporate crime is almost always within the course of one's occupation and therefore the term occupational crime would encompass corporate legal offending. Gross (1980) and Vaughan (1980) have suggested various ideas about "organizational" criminality to describe occupational crimes committed by members of organizations, but such an approach may be seen as rather limited for the purposes at hand because it excludes occupational crimes committed by persons who are not members of organizations. Albanese (1987:7) has conceptualized "organizational crime" by emphasizing planning and deceit, but does not limit the concept to occupationally related offenses. Horning (1970) has proposed the concept of "blue collar" crime to denote employee crimes by persons in occupations that are not traditionally considered among the most respectable. But, like "white collar," Horning's is a term relative to the definer.

The overall link between occupational opportunity and crime has been continually emphasized by criminologists, and it can be utilized as a concrete demarcation point for defining a unique area of study in criminology. For the purposes of this book, "occupational crime" refers to *any act punishable by law which is committed through opportunity created in the course of an occupation that is legal.* The concept of occupational crime seeks only to identify a general source of criminal opportunity.

The foregoing definition of "occupational crime" includes two major components: (1) an act punishable by law; and (2) one that is committed through opportunity created by an occupational role that is legal. Acts punishable by law are those to which a governmental penalty is attached (e.g., fine, imprisonment, injunction, consent decree, desist order; see Sutherland, 1945). Opportunity for crime arising in an occupation that is legal, however, is not as easily explained.

There have been several very broad definitions of "occupation" advanced by sociologists, most of which are too far-reaching for our conception of the term. For instance, Everett Hughes (1965:445) maintains that "an occupation, in essence, is not some particular set of activities; it is the part of an individual in any ongoing set of activities." Anne Roe (1956:3) defines an occupation as "whatever an adult spends most of his time doing . . . the major focus of a person's activities and usually of his thoughts." And Richard Hall (1969:5-6) defines occupation as ". . . the social role performed by adult members of society that directly and/or indirectly yields social and financial consequences and that constitutes a major focus in the life of an adult." These definitions, however, include non-income related criteria such as age, leisure activity, and an individual's major life and thought foci, which are beyond the scope of what is meant by occupation in our use of the term "occupational crime."

The concept of occupation used in this book refers more to what Robert Dubin (1958:4) has defined as "work": ". . . employment, in the production of goods and services, for remuneration." "Occupational" opportunities for crime come from any role in legal employment, job, or activity by which a person earns funds or has the potential to do so.

The criterion of *legal* occupation is necessary because without it the term "occupational crime" could conceivably include all crimes (criminals are always "occupied" during the commission of their offenses). A legal occupation is simply one that does not, in itself, violate any laws. Only persons who have a legal occupation can commit "occupational crime" according to our definition. Thus, the term would exclude persons with occupations which are illegal to begin with, such as bank robbers, organized crime figures who make money through illegal channels, or the professional "confidence man."

Crimes unrelated to one's legal occupation, in which previously learned skills from a legal occupation are used (e.g., a metal worker who "torches" into a bank safe, a computer operator employed by a manufacturer who steals money from a bank by accessing its computer, an automobile mechanic who "hotwires" a car on the street), should not be considered occupational crimes, because opportunities to commit such offenses are not accessed directly through roles in a legal occupation.

Occupational crime need not take place during working hours or at a given place of employment. For instance, personal (as opposed to corporate) income tax evasion is not directly undertaken in the course of one's occupation. However, the income derived from the occupation creates the opportunity to commit income tax evasion. Similarly, the investment landlord who allows illegally unsafe housing conditions or who racially discriminates against qualified tenant applicants is an occupational criminal, because although the income derived from the housing is, in income tax vernacular, "unearned," it is still legally derived income. A chambermaid who steals valuables from a hotel guest's luggage or a repairman who pilfers property after gaining legitimate access to a home are not stealing from their employers, but the opportunity for the crime was created by the job role and therefore these individuals can be considered occupational criminals. A parking lot attendant who duplicates customers' keys for later burglaries or an employee who uses legally possessed keys to burgle the workplace after working hours would not be committing crimes while on the job, but, again, it can be argued that these opportunities for burglary were created through roles in their legal occupations. A psychiatrist who learns of a patient's discreditable behavior through therapy sessions and then uses the information for blackmail is also an occupational criminal, because without access to that information, the offense would not be possible.

What about persons who seek or remain in legitimate occupational roles for the primary purpose of committing illegal acts? It could be argued that such offenders have *de facto* illegal occupations, and therefore their offenses would not fall within the confines of our concept of "occupational crime." However, even though such offenders may have illegal purposes in mind for their legal employment, they are nevertheless committing crimes in the course of a legal occupation. For instance, a person who continues employment at a bank in order to embezzle its funds is an occupational criminal according to the usage here, because, were it not for the opportunity created by the legal occupation of bank employee, that particular offense would not be possible. Similarly, the child molester at a day care center commits crime in the course of a legal occupation, even though such employment may have been gained in order to have access to children. Moreover, persons who are in legitimate occupations for the purposes of illegal gain should be included within the term "occupational crime" simply from a practical standpoint. To exclude them based on their intent to use an occupation for criminal activity would involve knowing the point at which legal employment for the purpose of employment changed to legal employment for the purpose of committing occupational crimes, assuming such a point even exists. Of course, such a determination would often be impossible, and would be fraught with subjective error possibilities.

Pinpointing exactly what constitutes occupational crime will, at times, become overly technical. For instance, a person who cheats at cards during an illegal game is not an occupational criminal, because the activity itself is against the law. However, anyone who cheats at cards in a legal poker game in Las Vegas is technically an occupational criminal, because both professional and amateur gamblers must declare any net winnings as ordinary income on their taxes. Including the Nevada amateur cheaters as occupational criminals not only represents a technical distinction, it also demonstrates how the definition's criterion of potential to earn money legally can encompass some leisure activites unrelated to the spirit of "occupation" or "work" (in this case amateur legal gambling). On the other hand, the definition's criterion that the activity must have a potential for income could also exclude instances that probably should be included, such as the unsalaried minister who peculates from the offering plate.

Whether certain offenses should be included under the definition of occupational crime may be a matter of opinion. Some critics will demand an exact demarcation between occupational crimes and nonoccupational ones, and it may not be possible to satisfy them completely by adjudicating unequivocally the relatively few borderline issues. In any case, the idea of "occupational" crime seems much less nebulous than previous conceptualizations, such as "white collar" crime.

FOUR CATEGORIES OF OCCUPATIONAL CRIME

There are criminal opportunities inherent in any occupation. Some offenses are possible in almost all occupations (e.g., employee theft, income tax evasion), while other offenses are unique to certain occupations (e.g., only physicians can falsify medical insurance claim forms and only politicians can accept bribes in exchange for political influence). Some occupational crimes benefit the offender directly (e.g., embezzlement), while others benefit directly entities other than the offender (e.g., price fixing for one's employer). Occupational crime can victimize one person (or organization) or many. Occupational crime can affect the community at large, such as in the case of illegal pollution. Employers, employees, competitors, customers, patients, consumers, political constituencies, and innocent bystanders are all subject to victimization by occupational crime. To cross-categorize all of these dimensions of occupational crime in an exhaustive typology, however, would require a vast and unworkable number of different categories.

In the interests of simplicity, the following four categories of occupational crime will be used in this book: (a) crimes for the benefit of an employing organization (organizational occupational crime); (b) crimes by officials through the exercise of their state-based authority (state authority occupational crime); (c) crimes by professionals in their capacity as professionals (professional occupational crime); and (d) crimes by individuals as individuals (individual occupational crime).

First, occupational crimes for the benefit of an employing organization (adapted from Geis, 1968a:16) denotes offenses in which employers, rather than offenders themselves, benefit directly. Although offenders may benefit indirectly from these crimes through employer organizational systems which allocate rewards (e.g., promotions, bonuses, salary raises), the major beneficiaries of such offenses are the owners of the organization for which one works. Price fixing by managers, falsification of product tests by technicians, theft of others' trade secrets by employees, and fraud by salesmen not working on commission are examples. The differentiation here between organizational occupational crime and the other three types of occupational crime is not idiosyncratic. Over a decade ago, for instance, Shover (1976:8) called for an adequate distinction "between [crimes in] occupations which individuals pursue as individuals and [occupations] which they pursue . . . as employees."

The next two categories are occupationally specific. That is, only persons in particular kinds of occupations have the opportunity to commit them. Occupational crimes through the exercise of state-based authority, the second category, requires offenders to be legally vested with governmental powers to make or enforce laws or to command others. This category would exclude criminal acts in the course of a state official's occupation which are unrelated to the exercise of these legal powers (e.g., employee theft, false expense reports, income tax evasion). Police who steal controlled substances confiscated as evidence or who illegally assault a suspect would be embraced under this second type, because opportunities for these activities are accessed through a police officer's legally vested powers. A Senator who takes bribes in exchange for political influence would be committing crime in his or her capacity to exercise state-based power. Military personnel who commit crime through their power to command others are also state authority occupational criminals. One may also want to include under this category notary publics who falsify documents, for they would do so through the official power vested in them.

Third, occupational crime by professionals in their professional capacity are also occupationally specific, because they arise out of opportunities from legal and professional trusts given only to an elite group of occupations (e.g., physicians, attorneys, psychologists, veterinarians). Certain professional oaths and trusts call for an ethical commitment to do what is in the best interests of the client or patient. And the legal system trusts professionals to be honest (e.g., signing of death certificates, distribution of controlled substances, filing insurance forms and claims). Examples include sexual assault of patients during examinations by physicians, unnecessary treatments and surgeries by physicians and veterinarians, illegal distribution of prescription drugs by doctors, and use of confidential information for personal gain by lawyers. Professional occupational crime would exclude offenses committed by professionals in the course of their occupation that are unrelated to the trusts given them as professionals (e.g., income tax evasion, discrimination in hiring).

Fourth, occupational crimes by individuals as individuals would encompass all remaining offenses—those in which opportunities are not based upon any governmental authority or the profession of the offender, and in which offenders themselves benefit directly. Examples of occupational crimes by individuals as individuals are personal income tax evasion, employee theft of goods (e.g., office supplies, scrap material, merchandise) and services (e.g., personal long distance telephone calls or photocopying), sexual molestation of children by nonprofessionals at day care centers, driving public transportation while intoxicated, fraud by salesmen working on commission, and filing a false expense claim to an employer.

Additionally, if the owners of an organization (e.g., the majority stockholder in a corporation, partners in a medium-sized firm, the owner of a small mom-and-pop business) were to commit offenses for the benefit of that organization, then they, too, would be committing crime as individuals (rather than organizational crime) because the potential gains from the offense would accrue directly to them (rather than accruing through an indirect organizational reward system). Indeed, of the four categories, individual occupational crime comprises the largest number of possibilities for occupational crime.

In certain cases, there will undoubtedly be some disagreement about which offenses belong under each of the four types. For instance, are occupational crimes by salaried professionals, such as a physician working for a hospital or a lawyer who is not a partner of his or her firm, committed by professionals or by individuals for the benefit of their employing organization? Are pharmacists "professionals," or are they merely the same as other persons given control over items regulated by the government (e.g., firearms, liquor, tobacco)? Some occupations, such as the clergy, may encompass all four types of occupational crime, depending upon the role in which it is committed. Ministers can be considered officials (during official acts such as marriage ceremonies), professionals (because of the confidential trusts they are given), individuals working for an employer (because they are supported by a denominational affiliation), or simply individuals. Are employees who own stock in their employer's firm committing crime for the benefit of their employer or for their own benefit? How much stock must be owned before one is considered an "owner" of a firm? Are soldiers who commit war crimes doing so in an official capacity, an individual capacity, or for the benefit of their employer? As in the case of any typology, problems will be encountered when trying to pigeonhole certain peripheral or overlapping cases. The four categories are not meant to be exclusive; they have been constructed only to help organize the vast array of occupational offenses into manageable topics.

PUBLIC VIEWS ABOUT OCCUPATIONAL CRIME

Before previewing the remainder of this book, it is appropriate to discuss the current public ideas about occupational crime. Edward Ross pointed out over eighty years ago that a major reason why many forms of harmful occupational behavior were not against the law (or laws against them were not enforced) was a lack of public sentiment against such behavior. Many occupational criminals "prosper by flagitious practices which have not yet come under the effective ban of public opinion" Ross (1968:26) wrote. Public sentiment was not sufficiently strong to enact criminal laws prohibiting socially irresponsible business behavior. Nor was it sufficiently strong to enact enforcement of existing codes, for as Ross (1968:26) also noted: "The law-makers may make their misdeeds crimes, but so long as morality stands stock-still in the old tracks, [occupational criminals] escape both punishment and ignominy." Sutherland (1940:11), too, in his historic 1939 speech, asserted that white collar occupational criminals are seldom censured because "the community is not organized solidly against the behavior." More recently, a President's Commission (1968:158) on crime noted that "the public tends to be indifferent to business crime or even to sympathize with the offenders who have been caught."

According to Cullen, Mathers, Clark, and Cullen (1983:482), however, "many of the attempts to blame tolerant public attitudes for the [occupational] crime problem have been based on impressionistic rather than on [hard] evidence." Cullen, et al. (1983) cite several surveys of public attitudes to support this claim. For instance, Newman (1968) found that 78 percent of his sample believed businessmen violating pure food laws should be given harsher punishments than those usually accorded. Gibbons's (1969) research reported that 88 percent of the public recommended prison terms for embezzlers, 70 percent for antitrust violators, and 43 percent for false advertisers. At about the same time, a Louis Harris (1969) poll showed that the public judged a manufacturer of unsafe automobiles worse than a mugger (68 percent to 22 percent) and a price-fixer worse than a burglar (54 percent to 28 percent). After reviewing several public surveys, Braithwaite (1982a:732-733) found that "contrary to a widespread misconception, there is considerable evidence to support the view that ordinary people subjectively perceive many types of [occupational] crime as more serious than most traditional crime." Similarly, Conklin (1977:27) concluded that there is a "greater degree of public condemnation of business violations than is thought to exist by those who claim that the public is apathetic or tolerant of business crime." Studies of public attitudes about occupational crime, then, generally demonstrate that it is perceived to involve sometimes very serious and costly kinds of behavior, and that the apathetic public attitude toward business crime portrayed by Ross, Sutherland, and the President's Commission no longer exists, if it ever did.

In a more recent study, Cullen, et al. (1983) reported information from three surveys conducted in the Midwest during 1979-1982. They found that about nine in ten subjects agreed that many occupational criminals "have gotten off too easily for too many years; they deserve to be sent to jail for their crimes just like everyone else." Almost the same proportion agreed that occupational criminals should be punished "just as severely as we punish people who steal money on the street." These results should be interpreted with some reservation, however, because only about one in three responded in two of the surveys.

Another dimension on which to measure public attitudes toward occupational crime is in regard to perceived costs. In one of the three surveys conducted by Cullen, et al. (1983), which took place in Galesburg, Illinois during 1981 (response rate = 38 percent), it was found that three of four respondents (75 percent) believed the amount of money lost through occupational crime is "more than that lost as a result of street crimes such as robberies, burglaries, and thefts." "Costs" can also be of a moral nature, and about half (55 percent) agreed that some occupational crimes "do more to undermine the morality in our society than do regular street crimes." However, while this strong indication of an intolerance for many kinds of occupational criminality exists, a clear majority of the Galesburg respondents perceived "street crime" to cause more fear and be more dangerous than occupational ones. This latter fact is shown more clearly in the discussion at the end of Chapter 2 concerning public attitudes about the relative "seriousness" of occupational crimes—they are regarded as serious, but not as serious as some street crimes, particularly violent offenses.

PREVIEW OF THE BOOK

Determining the incidence of crime and the distribution of criminals is exceedingly difficult. Establishing this information for occupationally related offenses is especially complicated. Chapter 2 addresses this issue and applies general methods for obtaining information on crimes and criminals to the area of occupational crime. That chapter also examines public perceptions about the gravity of occupationally related offenses, especially as compared to more traditional "common crime." Chapter 3 explores general criminological theories as they relate to occupational crime, including explanations of the creation and application of occupational criminal law, and explanations of the individual behavior of occupational criminals.

The next four chapters detail instances of occupational crime. Chapter 4 will address organizational occupational crime, followed by discussions of state authority crime (Chapter 5), professional occupational crime (Chapter 6), and individual occupational crime unrelated to official authority or professional status (Chapter 7). Additionally, the methodological approaches to counting set out in Chapter 2 and the theoretical approaches set out in Chapter 3 are applied selectively to the case material in these four chapters. Last, Chapter 8 looks at occupational offenses from a criminal justice system perspective, and considers various strategies to reduce occupational crime.

QUESTIONS FOR DISCUSSION

1. Identify all stories about occupational crime that are included in your local newspaper during the next seven days, and place each story into one or more of the four categories of occupational crime. Be prepared to explain why each example qualifies as an occupational crime and why you have relegated it to one or more particular categories.

2. It was noted that several scholars "anticipated" Sutherland's seminal work in white collar crime by writing about the same kinds of offenders that Sutherland did. This is one example of how advances in science are sometimes dependent upon previous work in the field (rather than arising independently). What are some other examples from the physical, biological, and social sciences where famous theories were anticipated by earlier thinkers?

3. Sutherland saw his theory of differential association as superior because he believed that it could explain crime in the upper classes as well as in the lower ones, whereas other theories of his day could not.

Should criminologists strive for a single theory to explain the different kinds of criminality? Why? Or why not?

4. According to Tappan, persons cannot be considered criminals unless they have been so defined by a conviction or its equivalent. Should a shoplifter who steals without being caught and convicted be considered a criminal? Why? Or why not?

5. List eight examples from each of the four categories of occupational crime without referring to the examples in this book.

Wall Street speculator Ivan Boesky arrives at Federal court after being convicted of using confidential information to profit in securities trading. Boesky paid the Securities and Exchange Commission a fine of $100 million and pleaded guilty to one felony count of insider trading. He was sentenced to a three-year prison term. (UPI/Bettman Newsphotos)

T W O

COUNTING AND RECORDING OCCUPATIONAL CRIMES AND CRIMINALS

To obtain the most reliable information on the incidences of crimes and criminals, sources should be used which are both accurate and closest to the scene of the crime. Unfortunately, these criteria are difficult to achieve simultaneously. Data from criminals and victims are close to the offense itself, but can be inaccurate because of a reluctance to provide satisfactory information. Data from police, court, and prison records may reflect accurately the criminality with which the agencies come into contact, but because the sources are removed from the offense itself, they cannot include information about the criminality of which the agencies are unaware.

The two major recorders of crimes and criminals are government agencies and criminology researchers, and the two groups often collaborate to determine how the records should be gathered. The difference between the actual number of crimes committed (the "universe of offenses") and the number of crimes documented by recorders is known as the "dark figure" of crime. Similarly, the difference between the actual number of criminals (the "universe of criminals") and the number of persons recorded as criminal is known as the "dark figure" of criminals. The universes of crimes and criminals are not necessarily equal for a given offense type because one person can commit several crimes and several persons can commit a single crime.

Each recording focus has its own dark figures. Consider the following example. In a given jurisdiction, a universe of, say, one thousand employee thefts are committed by a universe of three hundred fifty thieves (fifty, in Group A, committed ten crimes each; two hundred, in Group B, committed two crimes each; and one hundred, in Group C, committed one crime each). Of the one thousand crimes actually committed, seven hundred fifty become known to the criminality recorders. Of the seven hundred fifty offenses that are known, recorders can attribute four hundred of them to one hundred seventy persons caught (twenty from Group A; fifty from Group B, and all one hundred from Group C). Here the dark figure of crime is two hundred fifty ($1,000 - 750 = 250$), or 25 percent. The dark figure of criminals is one hundred eighty ($350 - 170 = 180$), or 51 percent.

Because these dark figures are not known, there is no way for recorders to ascertain the number of crimes and criminals that are not discovered by the methods they use (unless they attempt to employ another recording method to estimate dark figures). Naturally, the student of occupational crime wants to utilize the counting and recording methods that seem to produce the lowest dark figures.

There are four general methods employed to determine the incidences of crimes and criminals (each with its own strengths and weaknesses), and all of them are applicable to the area of occupational crime: (1) use of agency-based records (e.g., criminal complaints, arrest records, agency-written violations); (2) use of victim-based records (asking representative samples of persons whether they have been victimized and for any details about those victimizations); (3) use of criminal-based records (asking representative samples of persons whether they have committed any crimes and for any details about those crimes); and (4) records of crime and criminals based on direct observation.

AGENCY-BASED RECORDS

Agency-based records offer information about the numbers of crimes and criminals that are dealt with by authorities such as the police, regulatory agencies, courts, and prisons. Use of such records to tabulate criminality dates back to at least 1842, when Adolphe Jacques Quételet (1972:27) asserted in his *Treatise on Man* that "[T]here is a ratio, nearly invariably the same, between known and tried offenses and the unknown sum total of crimes committed."

According to Sellin's (1951) dictum, noted in Chapter 1, the best agency-based crime and criminal data would come from enforcement agencies (e.g., the police and regulatory agencies). Enforcement agency information is closer to the offense than adjudication agency-based criminality data (e.g., from the courts). And records from adjudication agencies are closer to the offense than those from penal agencies. However, during the stage between the commission of offenses and the recording of offenses and offenders by the enforcement authorities, the attrition of information becomes quite high. Therefore, even enforcement agency information is likely to have substantial dark figures of crimes and criminals.

There are probably no agency-based records of crimes and criminals that have a dark figure equalling zero. However, as Quételet indicated, even if an agency-based record does have a high dark figure, it is still possible that crimes and criminals recorded are *representative* of all crimes that occur and criminals that exist (the universes of offenses and offenders).

For example, consider the following question about the representativeness of agency-recorded *crimes*: If employee thefts known to the agency have increased by 20 percent, can one then assume that the universe of employee theft has increased by 20 percent overall? Other questions, this time regarding agency records' representation of the universe of *criminals*, could be: If 30 percent of employee thieves recorded by agencies are responsible for 60 percent of the employee thefts known to the agency, can the assumption be made that 30 percent of all employee thieves are responsible for 60 percent of all employee thefts? or, If 20 percent of employee thieves known to an agency are female, can the assumption be made that 20 percent of all employee thieves are female? Whether the answers to these questions about the representativeness of agency-based records are "yes" depends upon several factors.

Assumptions About Agency-Based Records

For each offense type, the most critical question about the representativeness of agency-based records centers on the extent to which enforcement groups' discoveries of offenses and offenders are uniform. That is, by using agency-based records as a representative indicator of crimes that occur, it is assumed that, *within* each category of crime in the records, offenses have similar chances of being discovered by the authorities. And by using agency-based records as a representative indicator of criminals that exist, it is assumed not only that a given crime type has similar chances of being discovered, but also that criminals in that crime category have similar chances of being discovered. These assumptions are incorrect for the vast majority of offense and offender categories. Enforcement agencies are not likely to put forth equal enforcement efforts against a given crime (or those who commit it), and citizens are not equally likely to contact authorities when they have been a victim of that crime.

Occupational crime enforcement authorities (police and regulatory agencies) do not uniformly conduct audits of financial records, inspections of products and premises, or "stings." Unlike being robbed, burgled or assaulted, many victims of occupational crime do not even know that they have been victimized. For example, in cases of sexual molestation of unconscious patients by physicians, unnecessary medical treatment, theft of trade secrets, and exposure to unsafe working conditions or consumer products, persons often remain unaware that they have been a victim of a crime. Even if victimization is perceived, not everyone responds in the same manner; some will contact the authorities while others will not.

Only in very rare instances can the assumption be made that there are equal probabilities of an agency discovering a given offense or a particular type of offender. In the area of occupational crime, embezzlement from a national bank may be about as close as one can come to such an instance. Here, legal requirements for periodic audits lead to equal efforts at discovering embezzlements. It also seems likely that victims of this kind of embezzlement will equally contact authorities about it, because according to *Orlando vs. United States* (377 F.2d 667, 1967), failure to report a theft of funds from a national bank would constitute aiding and abetting the offense. Therefore, agency-based records of embezzlement from a national bank probably reflect very large (and therefore very representative) portions of the universes of such embezzlements. Embezzlements other than from a national bank, however, are much less likely to come to the attention of the authorities because the victim (or the victim's insurance company) often agrees not to press charges if the money is repaid. For the great bulk of occupational and other crimes, one cannot assume equal discovery by the authorities (either of offenses or offenders), and therefore the assumption of representativeness becomes unwarranted.

Problems With Agency-Based Records

Even if it is assumed that authorities are equally likely to discover a particular type of occupational crime, assumptions about agency record representativeness are still problematic. First, some crimes may not be recorded properly, and second, some criminals may not be discovered.

Regarding offense recording, even if a representative sample of offenses becomes known to an enforcement agency, disparate definitions of offenses and violations, overlapping jurisdictions, and erroneous or incomplete recording practices may render recorded offenses unrepresentative of the universe. If an occupational crime occurs and is reported to an enforcement agency, the offense may not be recorded because it is considered unfounded. If a crime is considered to be founded, the agency may record it erroneously (e.g., embezzlement mistakenly recorded as larceny or vice versa), it may be recorded correctly by the agency but never submitted for inclusion in overall statistics, or it may be ignored. Because of differences in definition across jurisdictions, the occupational crime may be recorded as one thing in one jurisdiction (e.g., fraud) and as something else in another jurisdiction (e.g., larceny by trick). Or a single offense episode may be double-counted across two jurisdictions, if, say, it is recorded by local and federal enforcement agencies.

The Uniform Crime Reports, published annually by the Federal Bureau of Investigation, are usually taken to portray America's overall crime and criminal trends. The data in the UCR are based upon records kept by thousands of police agencies around the United States and submitted to the FBI. Four theft categories in the UCR (larceny, fraud, forgery, embezzlement) are likely to include in their totals some amount of occupationally related stealing, but the UCR does not disaggregate its statistics according to that variable. Of these four categories, the UCR publishes offense counts only for larceny, which is the one category that is least likely to contain a substantial proportion of occupationally related thefts.

Criminal statistics (arrestees) are published in the UCR for fraud, forgery, and embezzlement. However, studies which have analyzed local fraud and forgery arrests have generally concluded that most of them (as much as 98 percent) do not involve occupationally related offenders (Giordano, Kerbel, and Dudley, 1981; Daly, 1986; Steffensmeier, 1980; 1987). Rather, they mostly involve passing bad checks, theft of services, welfare fraud, small confidence games, and credit card fraud. Regarding embezzlement, although many persons arrested for that offense (probably a majority of them) have been involved in occupational thefts, the category is still "impure" because it comprises some amount of nonoccupational embezzlements. Moreover, even if we were to use the UCR data on embezzlement arrests to answer questions about occupational crime, the frequency of such arrests is so uncommon and the amounts involved are usually so small that the statistics would reflect an insignificant part of overall occupational crime patterns (Steffensmeier, 1989). The Uniform Crime Reports, then, are essentially useless (in their current form) for the study of occupational offending, although they have been used for that purpose (Simon, 1981; Hirschi and Gottfredson, 1987).

The purest agency-based occupational crime and criminal statistics are produced by state and federal regulatory agencies. The annual reports of these agencies often contain the numbers of criminal, civil, and administrative actions against firms and individuals for violation of occupationally related laws (e.g., unsafe working conditions, pollution, unsafe consumer products, antitrust, fraudulent advertising). At various points throughout the book, the reader will encounter many such statistics generated by these regulatory agencies (e.g., Federal Trade Commission, Occupational Safety and Health Administration, Securities and Exchange Commission, Environmental Protection Agency).

However, the tabulations of violations kept by regulatory agencies are subject to all of the previous criticisms: multiple counting from overlapping jurisdictions, conflicting definitions of crimes, and failures to record incidents properly. Regulatory enforcement agency records also tend to treat complex organizations (rather than individuals) as offenders, so individual rates of offending are difficult to determine. Moreover, because discovery of occupational crime by many regulatory agencies is often due primarily or solely to their irregular efforts at enforcement, their counts are often a reflection of these efforts rather than a reflection of true increases or decreases in the numbers of violations and violators. Furthermore, regulatory compliance and enforcement agencies generally are not particularly likely to discover many offenses and offenders, because violators often use sophisticated efforts to obscure their crimes from the authorities.

Even if a representative sample of a given offense type becomes known to the authorities, they may nevertheless fail to detect certain offenders. To illustrate, if there are one hundred known but unsolved employee thefts, there is no way to ascertain how many criminals committed them nor the characteristics of these unknown criminals. A failure to discover occupational criminals uniformly will cause statistics to be unrepresentative of the universe of occupational criminals. Moreover, the inaccuracies associated with recording crimes also can be a problem with the recording of known criminals (disparate definitions of the crime category to which an apprehended criminal belongs, double-counting of criminals, failures to record criminals properly once they are discovered).

Errors in agency-based records discussed above can be random or systematic. Random error is when error is present once in a while, and the usual assumption is that random errors cancel each other. For example, random counting error would mean that, for a given offense type, some offenses or offenders are sometimes overcounted in the records and others are sometimes undercounted, but, by assumption, the over- and undercounting nullify each other. On the other hand, systematic error, which is of much greater concern, occurs when there is a constant error throughout the records. Systematic counting error in agency-based records is caused by agencies having an overall higher or lower probability of discovering or counting offenses or offenders of a particular type.

Agency-based criminality recorders want as little error as possible in order to keep representativeness at its maximum. Some degree of error always exists, but random error is better than systematic error because one cannot account for the effects of random error (as it is present haphazardly), whereas when one accounts for the effects of systematic error, there is a known bias throughout the data. To illustrate, if females or teenagers were generally less likely to be reported to authorities as employee thieves, there would be a systematic underrepresentation of them in the records. Victim-based records (to be discussed in the next section) are used to discover the existence of random and systematic errors in the recording of offenses (Ennis, 1967:67; Hindelang, 1976: Chapter 3) and offenders (Hindelang, 1978; 1979; Green, 1985a) in agency-based records such as the *UCR*. Unfortunately, the offenses studied in these analyses are street crimes and therefore the results cannot be generalized to occupational crime.

Improving Agency-Based Information

In delineating the requirements of an optimally integrated federal agency-based crime and criminal recording system, Biderman and Reiss (1980) note the following requisites (which have been adapted here for occupational crime):

1. That the statistics encompass administrative, civil, and criminal matters.
2. That the changes related to overlapping and concurrent jurisdiction are monitored for their potential impact on the records.
3. The adoption of standard definitions and classification procedures for events regarded as occupational crimes to overcome statutory and administrative variability in defining them.
4. That ways be found to estimate or account for multiple counts of the same event.
5. That there be a clear definition of the totality of occupational crime with decision rules stipulating which occupational crimes are to be counted, whether the totality is to be defined by jurisdiction over events, by the territory of jurisdiction, or by special qualifications regarding the population of a jurisdiction.
6. That there be provisions obligating agencies to report information about occupational crime in ways that permit its merging from different sources.
7. That provision be made for central coordination of the processing and reporting of information and for control to insure uniformity and compliance.
8. That relevant violations of law, regulations, or standards be systematically and regularly reported by each and every agency, whether or not it has a mandate for law enforcement, regulation, or adjudication.
9. Although a uniform system of statistical reporting does not require that all agencies follow the same rules for deciding referrals, it does require that there be explicit criteria for defining referrals and their sources so that referral information can be merged among agencies and their sources of variability investigated.
10. That there be provision for standardization among agencies of data collection, analysis and reporting.

These suggestions are excellent, but there should be some concern about the inclusion of civil and administrative cases in a statistical reporting system about "crime" (see number 1 above). Administrative regulation encompasses the authority of administrative judges to act in executive and judicial matters. The volume of regulatory violations handled by administrative judges far exceeds those decided by civil or criminal court judges. And the volume of noncompliance matters that are detected and decided upon by regulatory agents is often larger than the violations detected by criminal enforcement divisions and adjudicated as criminal matters. Biderman and Reiss (1980:xxxii-xxxiii) use these rationales, as did Sutherland (1945), to argue that civil and administrative cases should be included—to exclude them would force a great many transgressions to lie outside the statistical reporting system. However, the inclusion of civil and administrative cases may contribute to overreporting in these "crime" statistics because the burden of proof required by such proceedings (preponderance of the evidence) is much less than that required in a criminal case (beyond a reasonable doubt). Further, it is usually necessary to establish a person's (or organization's) *mens rea*, or intent, in order to prove that a crime occurred; proving intent is not necessary for a judgment in a civil case or administrative law case. Thus, these lesser burdens of proof may tend to overincriminate and thereby overcount legal violations, but the alternative of excluding civil and administrative decisions presents the far greater danger of massively undercounting them. Biderman and Reiss suggest that occupational crime violations can be differentiated in agency-based data according to whether the case was decided through administrative, civil, or criminal jurisdictions, as long as the system of statistical reporting includes all three. When a regulatory agency convicts an entity on criminal charges and also gives a civil penalty for the same action, or if there is another overlap (e.g., same case involving several agencies, several charges in the same case), care must be taken not to double-count the event.

Even if the criteria suggested by Biderman and Reiss are met, there still must be an assumption of uniform discovery of a given offense type and its perpetrators before it could be said that agency-based records are truly representative of crimes that occur and criminals that exist. Currently, enforcement, adjudication, and penal agency-based records are generally unrepresentative measures of the universes of occupationally related offenses and offenders. However, as with many things, a little bit is better than nothing, and at least for the moment (that is, until records are integrated in a form something like that suggested by Biderman and Reiss, and the assumption about uniform discovery of offenses and perpetrators can be made), the student of occupational crime must depend upon agency-based records and acknowledge the weaknesses the records may have.

VICTIM-BASED RECORDS

Victim-based records comprise information about crimes and criminals solicited from the victims themselves. Typically, in victim-based records representative samples of persons are asked whether they have been victimized and, if so, are requested to provide details about such victimizations. Victimization for a population as a whole is then estimated from information gathered from the representative samples. Victim-based records are intuitively more appealing than agency-based data as a source of information about crime and criminals because victims are close to the offense; in fact, you cannot get much closer.

Victim-based records of crime were sought to fill in the dark figures of crime associated with agency-based records and to discover any random and systematic biases in such records. The first major victimization survey was conducted in the United States by the President's Commission on Law Enforcement and Administration of Justice (Ennis, 1967). About thirty-three thousand persons in the general population were selected for their representative characteristics and were asked whether they had been a victim of a given crime. If they had been victimized, then specific questions were asked about the details.

In addition to information on offenses unknown to agency-based records, victim-based information can yield data on the characteristics of criminals (e.g., number of offenders in a given offense; age, gender, and race of offenders), the time and location of an offense, the victim-offender relationship (e.g., relative, stranger, employee-employer), the effects of the offense on the victim (e.g., cost of property stolen, extent of injury, time lost from work because of physical injury, medical expenses associated with injury), the reasons for reporting (or not reporting) the offense to the authorities, and individuals' probabilities of being victimized by a given offense.

Problems With Victim-Based Records of Occupational Crime

There are three basic kinds of problems associated with any sample survey data: sampling error, response error, and measurement error.

Sampling error arises when persons in the sample do not accurately represent the population as a whole. If persons in a sample survey of occupational crime victimization over- or underrepresent certain categories of victims in the population (e.g., in terms of gender, age, race, or size of organization), then the estimates based on those samples will be inaccurate. The fewer the respondents who are asked about victimization, the higher the sampling error is likely to be (asking five thousand people is better than asking five hundred). Moreover, the fewer responses about previous victimization experience, the higher the sampling error for particular information about those relatively few experiences (surveyors who know the gender of one hundred employee thieves can make more reliable gender estimates than surveyors who know the gender of ten employee thieves). This latter point is especially important to occupational crime victim surveys. As will be shown in the following discussion of response error, victims of occupational crime are generally less likely than victims of street crime to perceive that they have been a victim, and therefore high sampling error attributable to small groups of victim respondents becomes a particular problem associated with victim surveys of occupational crime.

Further, as Biderman and Reiss (1980:xlii) point out, even if respondents are aware that they have been victimized by an occupational crime and are willing to tell an interviewer about it, some occupational crimes occur so seldom or victimize only a few persons or organizations that very large samples must be employed in order to include enough victims to obtain reliable statistical results. Therefore, economically feasible occupational crime victim surveys must be limited to the investigation of offenses which occur commonly (e.g., consumer fraud, housing violations, employee theft). Biderman and Reiss (1980:xlii) also point out that it may be difficult even to devise adequate sampling techniques that encompass representative proportions of organizations which have been victims (e.g., size, age, potential for exposure to certain victimizations).

Response error in victim surveys occurs when persons give inaccurate responses to surveyers. Several response errors have been found to be associated with street crime victim surveys (Hindelang, 1976), and there is no reason to believe that those problems would not exist in a survey of victims of occupational crime. In terms of overreporting victimization, respondents may exaggerate or fabricate their answers. Or they may inadvertently misinterpret facts to the point of stating a victimization when, in fact, none occurred. For instance, Ennis (1967:108) found that victimization by consumer fraud has been overreported by respondents in victim surveys because of misinterpretation of fact (e.g., a person who purchases a used car may claim fraud when the vehicle simply turns out to be a "lemon").

Because of the nature of occupational crime, however, there would probably be more underreporting response error than overreporting error. Victims of occupational crime, as noted, usually are less likely to be aware of their victimization than victims of street crime such as robbery, assault, and burglary. Victims of consumer fraud are not likely to know that they have been duped when, say, a used car salesman turns an odometer back several thousand miles. Patients are not likely to realize that they have been assaulted by a physician through unnecessary surgery. Victims of an unsafe consumer product (e.g., pharmaceuticals, automobiles) are not likely to be aware of the potential danger of the product. When a miner dies from a lung disease, it is difficult to appreciate that the death occurred because the employer violated mine safety regulations many years earlier. Persons exposed to poisonous living environments (e.g., toxic waste dumping, water and air pollution) may go for many years before the cumulative effects of exposure manifest themselves, and even then the symptoms may not be traced to the exposure. Retailers are often unaware that their inventory "shrinkage" is due to employee theft rather than to shoplifting. Corporations victimized by unfair competition or theft of trade secrets may not be aware of the offenses. In political corruption cases, the victim is the public, but because of the covert nature of the offense (the briber and bribee do not want the transaction known), the public is not cognizant of it. Therefore, using victim-based records to measure occupational crime is much more problematic than using them to measure the more traditional kinds of offenses.

Victim-based surveys of occupational crime tend to have underreporting biases other than those associated with an inability to perceive victimization. Respondents may have perceived a victimization at the time it occurred but have forgotten it by the time they are questioned, because "memory decay" has been shown to increase when the interim between a street victimization and the survey interview increases (Green, 1981:33). Further, victims of crime are often too embarrassed to report a victimization to an interviewer. They may not, for instance, want to admit that they were gullible. And victims of occupational crime such as employee theft may know that they have been victimized, but may not know other information associated with the offense (e.g., offender characteristics, loss per theft).

The third bias associated with victim surveys, *measurement error*, involves the inability of a respondent to understand survey questions properly. Measurement error also comprises mistakes in editing, processing, and recording data. Results from an interview can be lost, the wrong key can be punched when the information is entered into a computer, or the wrong figures can be printed when the survey is published. Careful questionnaire wording and recording of data reduces the amount of measurement error, but controlling response error and sampling error are often outside the powers of the researcher.

As with agency-based records, victim-based records can have random or systematic errors. It is response error that seems to pose the greatest potential for unknown error in victim-based surveys. To estimate both systematic and random errors in victim-based responses regarding street crime, recorders employ what is known as "reverse record checks." In these checks, *known* victims are selected from enforcement agency files, contacted, and asked questions about any victimization they may have suffered to determine if they will mention the offense that is already known to the police. Optimally, reverse record checks should use a "double-blind" approach in which neither the interviewer or victim is aware that the victim's name had been selected from police files. The "double-blind" procedure seeks to prevent eliciting more information than would otherwise be gathered. If the participants (interviewers and known victims) are aware that there was, in fact, a previous documentation of the victimization in enforcement agency files, they are more likely to produce information that would not turn up in a normal interview.

The following illustrates how a reverse record check would work for consumer fraud. First, police files would be searched for complaints from citizens who believe that they had been duped in such a fraud. Those persons' addresses would be extracted, unbeknownst to the survey interviewer, and included on the daily roster of persons to contact. The interviewer will carry out a normal interview with the person at that address. The response will be checked to determine whether the respondent claimed to have been victimized by a consumer fraud. After many such checks, it will be possible to identify characteristics of persons who are least or most likely to report consumer frauds to interviewers. Of course, there is no way to record an offense if it is not reported to the police or to the victim survey interviewer.

Sufficient enforcement agency records are needed from which to begin a reverse record check. The paucity of agency records with which to verify response error, coupled with other acute problems associated with response error in occupational crime victim surveys (particularly non-perception of victimization), suggests that compiling accurate victim-based records of occupational crime is not a promising idea. Despite such problems, however, increased consumer advocacy and consumer education in the future might serve to increase the visibility and reportability of occupational victimizations, thereby increasing the validity of victim-based data.

An Example of Victim-Based Occupational Crime Recording

Bearing in mind these problems, it is instructive to present the results of one of the very few occupational crime victim surveys. Although the first victimization study, conducted for the President's Commission on Law

Enforcement and Administration of Justice by Ennis (1967), contained mostly "street" offenses, respondents also were asked to answer questions related to three occupational crime victimizations: bribery solicitation by governmental officials, exposure of renters to unsafe living conditions, and consumer fraud.

For bribery, persons were asked to respond to the following question: "Within the last 12 months, have you or anyone in your household had to pay money to a public official, such as a policeman or an inspector, or some official like that, so he would not make trouble for you, even though you had not done anything wrong?" The estimated rate of bribery victimization was 9.1 per 100,000 persons (Ennis, 1967:11). Ennis (1967:10) noted, however, that bribery victimization is probably underreported because ". . . there is an aura of victim involvement in these situations, and this will tend to diminish forthrightness in the interview."

Unsafe living conditions among rental tenants were estimated by the question: "Within the last 12 months, has the landlord or manager of this building failed to take care of anything that needed repairing or cleaning up after he had been informed about it by some public official such as the Sanitation, Health, or Building Departments?" The estimated rate for building violations was much higher than for bribery, at 42.5 per 100,000 persons (Ennis, 1967:11). This rate underestimates such violations because it is derived from all persons in the sample rather than only renters. Because of the low numbers of respondents who claimed victimization for these two offenses, sampling error was so high as to render the results extremely unreliable; as a result, no specific information about bribery and living environment victimizations other than the estimated rates of occurrence were reported by Ennis.

In the third question regarding occupational crime victimization, persons were asked: "In the last 12 months, have you or anyone in the household bought anything from someone who cheated you by misrepresenting what he was selling or by charging a higher price than you were told?" The estimated incidence of consumer fraud as tapped by the question was 121.3 per 100,000 (Ennis, 1967:11). This estimated rate was high enough to allow the presentation of other information. Before that information is examined, however, it must be emphasized that, after evaluation by Ennis's interview staff, two-thirds of the claimed consumer fraud victimizations were deemed "doubtful." This represented the greatest proportion of "doubtful" responses among all crimes in the survey (Ennis, 1967:108). Such gross overreporting would represent a systematic response error.

Table 2.1 reflects the survey's estimated rate of consumer fraud victimization according to various victim characteristics (rates are per 100,000 persons). People in the West were clearly the most likely to claim consumer fraud victimization, with a rate of 247, more than double the next highest regional rate (Northeast), and almost triple the rates in the Southern and North Central states. Perceived victimization by consumer fraud seems to remain about the same according to degree of urbanization across central metropolitan, suburban metropolitan, and nonmetropolitan areas. Among whites, those in the highest annual income category (above $10,000) had the highest claimed rate of consumer fraud victimization, while among nonwhites, only the middle income group ($3000-$5999) claimed any victimization, with a rate of 60. White males were more than twice as likely to claim victimization than white females, and about four times as likely to claim it than nonwhite males. None of the nonwhite females claimed to be victimized by consumer fraud.

Age and gender variations are also substantial. Among males, the 20-29 age group claimed a rate of 515, the largest of any age or gender specific rate, followed closely by males 30-39 (449). The opposite was true for females, among whom the highest rate was in the 30-39 group followed by the 20-29 group. Hence, the ages of 20-39 seem to be the most likely ages in which one claims to be a victim of consumer fraud. Among older respondents, males forty years of age and over report a combined rate of about 120 per 100,000 and females of the same ages report a combined rate of about a third of that of their male counterparts (36 per 100,000). And, as might be expected, the youngest age group (10-19) reported relatively low consumer fraud victimization among males and females (31 and zero per 100,000, respectively).

The survey also included information about whether the alleged victims notified the police about consumer fraud. A quarter of the 40 persons who claimed this victimization said that they had notified the police (Ennis, 1967:42). Of the thirty who did not notify the police, fifteen (or half) of them did not do so because it was not considered to be a concern of the police, twelve (40 percent) failed to contact the police because of a belief that the police would not be effective in resolving the situation, and three (10 percent) simply refused to involve the police (Ennis, 1967:46). In terms of the costs of the alleged frauds, the average claimed net loss per fraud was about $79 (the average loss was about $99 and the average recovery was about $20) (Ennis, 1967:16).

Ennis's study demonstrates the many kinds of information obtainable from surveys of occupational crime victims. As such, his survey is exemplary. But there currently remain many questions about sampling, response, and measurement error, both systematic and random, that must be considered before drawing any firm inferences from citizens' claims about victimization by any occupational crime. We can now turn to information based on another type of respondent close to the scene of the crime—the criminal.

CRIMINAL-BASED RECORDS

Criminal-based records of occupational criminality are compiled from offenders about their illegal behavior. Because the criminal is at the scene of the crime, criminal-based records are extremely close to the offense itself and have the potential to be excellent sources of information. Unlike

Table 2.1 Perceived Victimization by Consumer Fraud According to Selected Characteristics of Victims *(Estimated Rates per 100,000 Persons)*

REGION			
Northeast	*North Central*	*South*	*West*
114	85	96	247

URBANIZATION		
Central Metropolitan	*Suburban Metro*	*Non-Metro*
135	133	93

RACE AND INCOME						
White				*Nonwhite*		
$0 – $2999	$3000 – $5000	$6000 – $9999	$10,000 +	$0 – $2999	$3000 – $5999	$6000 +
87	137	115	203	0	60	0

RACE AND GENDER			
White Male	*White Female*	*Nonwhite Male*	*Nonwhite Female*
178	86	44	0

AGE AND GENDER						
	10–19	*20–29*	*30–39*	*40–49*	*50–59*	*60 +*
Male	31	515	449	263	0	98
Female	0	190	313	48	60	0

NOTE: Sampling Errors were not available from the source.

SOURCE: *Criminal Victimization in the United States: A Report of a National Survey* by Philip Ennis; Washington, D.C.: U.S. Government Printing Office (May, 1967), Pp. 22, 24, 31, 33–35.

agency-based and victim-based records, which usually attempt to estimate the incidence of criminality for the population as a whole, criminal-based records have typically been used to estimate the prevalence of criminality among a particular group of persons (e.g., juveniles, college students). Criminal-based records are commonly referred to as "self-reported crime" data, and they may produce high dark figures, especially in the area of occupational criminality.

The first major study of self-reported crime was undertaken by Wallerstein and Wyle (1947). They asked persons to complete a questionnaire about their past criminal activities. They obtained information from 1,020 men and 678 women of differing ages and with a wide range of occupations. Respondents confessed their involvement in 49 different offenses. Because the questionnaires were obtained only from persons who chose to respond to them, the responses are not necessarily representative of the population as a whole. Regarding occupational crime, 57 percent of the males and 40 percent of the females admitted to tax evasion.

Since then, studies of self-reported criminal involvement have become more plentiful, focussing primarily on juveniles (e.g., Short and Nye, 1957; Hindelang, Hirschi, and Weis, 1981; Elliott, Ageton, Huizanga, Knoles, and Canter, 1983) and to a lesser extent adults (e.g., Tittle, 1980; Grasmick and Green, 1980). However, self-report surveys of occupational crime are rare.

Problems With Criminal-Based Data on Occupational Crime

Systematic sampling error can be a major problem in obtaining valid criminal-based records because it is difficult to get individuals to agree to confess to illegal behavior. For instance, in a juvenile self-reported delinquency study, Hindelang, et al. (1981) found that only about 50 percent of the original sample agreed to participate. There was a strong tendency for persons who had been officially identified as delinquent by the police and the courts to fail to cooperate with researchers. In addition, black and female respondents were underrepresented. This systematic sampling error was so great that Elliott (1982:528) has stated that ". . . participating subjects can no longer be considered a [representative] sample of . . . youth aged fifteen through eighteen." Failure to cooperate with recorders may be especially high among occupational criminals.

Self-report occupational crime surveys encounter particular problems when organizational occupational criminals are included. For instance, it may be difficult to draw adequate samples of organizational employees. Employee function, organization size and diversification, and industrial representation are some of the factors that must be considered when sampling employees of organizations. Further, only employees who commit organizational crimes by themselves or in small groups (in which co-offenders are known in terms of their role in the event) will be able to answer questions about their participation in organizational crime. As Biderman and Reiss (1980:xli) point out, "Where offending partners are more diffuse and the behavior involves complex organizational activity, the perpetrator survey seems less appropriate, particularly to estimate frequencies of violation events."

If persons agree to participate as subjects in a criminal-based survey, they may nevertheless give inaccurate responses which produce systematic response errors. Underreporting response error should probably be of greater concern to recorders of criminal-based data than overreporting response error, because criminals are probably more likely to fail to admit to a crime they did commit than to report a crime that they did not commit. Many juveniles admit to no previous delinquency when there is, in fact, an official record of their delinquency (O'Brien, 1985:74). Some researchers have claimed 80 to 90 percent accuracy in self-reported delinquency data through cross-checking methods such as peer responses (Gold, 1966) and polygraph questioning (Clark and Tifft, 1966), but there is still an understandable concern about self-report data containing systematic underreporting response bias.

The majority of occupational criminals may be even less likely than juveniles to admit wrongdoing. While younger persons may display "bravado" about illegal behavior and would therefore be likely to admit to it (or even invent it), the majority of occupational criminals are adults who have probably outgrown the need to see themselves in a bravado light (they might be more embarrassed about their illegal behavior). Second, unlike juveniles who know that drug use, fighting, shoplifting and vandalism are crimes, some occupational offenders may not see their actions as criminal though, in fact, they are. Politicians who are bribed with gifts and free vacations, employees who pilfer scrap materials, income tax evaders who "interpret" tax laws to their own advantage, or corporate officers who fix prices may not consider (or may not want to consider) their behaviors criminal. Failure to define one's own behavior as criminal when it constitutes a legal violation may introduce an important bias in self-reported occupational crime surveys. As Ross pointed out as early as 1907 (see Chapter 1), many occupational criminals hold respectable positions and have created a respectable self-image, making them less likely to see the criminal nature of their behavior.

Third, although self-reported criminality studies are supposed to be anonymous, persons may still fear that they have something to lose by admitting to criminal behavior. This fear may be much greater if the criminality is in regard to a career or livelihood that has taken years to cultivate than if it involves occupational crime by someone without such an investment. In sum, even if recorders can convince enough people to participate in an occupational crime self-report survey to the extent that systematic sampling error does not occur, there are still concerns about accuracy. There seem to have been no attempts to validate (e.g., through polygraph examination) the accuracy of data on self-reported occupational criminal behavior.

An Example of Criminal-Based Occupational Crime Recording

The most extensive study to estimate occupational criminality rates from self-report data was by Tittle (1980), who interviewed almost 2,000 persons aged 15 and over in three states (600 from Iowa, 537 from Oregon, and 856 from New Jersey) about their past behaviors, including both occupational and other criminality. Although Tittle did not attempt to validate responses, he assumes a high degree of accuracy in his data because (1980:29) ". . . data gatherers [were] trained to neutralize the social desirability of responses, minimize their own influences on responses as well as their expectations of answers (called interviewer effects), and express in face-to-face situations the importance of accuracy, usually through appeals to scientific usefulness and the anonymity of reporting."

Tittle used "income tax cheating" and "occupational specific deviance" as categories, but in terms of our definition of occupational crime, only the tax cheating responses apply. Tittle's category of "occupational specific deviance" includes both overcharging clients if the respondent was self-employed and making personal use of an employer's equipment if the respondent was a wage earner. However, the category also includes cheating on an examination (for students) and spending money on oneself that should have been spent for other purposes (for homemakers). There is no way from Tittle's data presentations to disaggregate the "occupational specific deviance" category to exclude students and homemakers.

Table 2.2 presents respondents' self-reported tax cheating rates for an aggregated five-year period prior to the survey. Males are more likely to admit to tax cheating than females and nonwhites more than whites. Admitted tax cheating is much higher for the two youngest age groups than for the two oldest groups. Regarding socioeconomic level, which was constructed by Tittle (1980:100-101) based on a composite of income, occupation (blue-collar or white-collar), and educational attainment, those in the lowest levels are more likely to admit to tax cheating than those in the highest levels. Those separated or divorced are most likely to admit to cheating. Tittle's overall findings about admitted tax cheating and gender, age, and income are generally supported by other research (Mason and Calvin, 1978), but there may be some sytematic biases present regarding sampling, measurement and response.

Randomized Response Self-Report Models

A strong obstacle to obtaining truthful responses in self-report studies centers on respondents' belief that what they say will not be held in confidence. If a respondent is embarrassed about past behavior or believes that admitting that behavior would somehow put him or her at risk (with authorities or employers, for instance), there would be a strong tendency to

Table 2.2 Self-Reported Tax Cheating During Past Five Years According to Selected Characteristics of Offenders *(in Percent)*

GENDER	
Male	*Female*
16	8

RACE	
White	*Nonwhite*
11	15

AGE			
15–24	*25–44*	*45–64*	*65 +*
14	16	8	2

SOCIOECONOMIC STATUS LEVEL (Includes a composite of income, occupation and education)				
Low 1	2	3	4	*High* 5
15	15	11	9	9

MARITAL STATUS			
Single	*Separated/Divorced*	*Married*	*Widowed*
11	19	12	2

NOTE: Sampling errors were not available from the source.

SOURCE: *Sanctions and Social Deviance: The Question of Deterrence,* by Charles R. Tittle, New York: Praeger (1980), pp. 83, 87, 90, 102, 120.

underreport the criminality. Recorders need a method to obtain information that allows the respondents to be assured that their answers are anonymous. This is not an easy task. Fortunately, researchers have developed a self-report method that attempts to persuade respondents of the anonymity of their answers—the "randomized response" model. It has been used for the past two decades to increase the truthfulness of responses about sensitive information such as drunk driving (Folsom, 1974), illegal killing of deer (Wright, 1980), and criminal behavior in general (Tracy and Fox, 1981a). According to Tracy and Fox (1981b:43) randomized response is:

"... a survey technique for reducing response bias arising from respondent concern over revealing sensitive information. The randomized response method utilizes an indeterminate question (i.e., the question answered by the respondent is unknown to the researcher) and thus maintains the anonymity of the responses. In other words, not even the interviewer knows what question the respondent is acutally answering; the interviewer merely records the response to a random question. Based on various [statistical] relations between the questions and the observed responses, it is possible to obtain estimates of [criminality] in the aggregate. Because only aggregate estimates are possible, not only are respondents protected, many ethical concerns surrounding the solicitation of sensitive information are nullified."

The most simplified randomized response model presents the respondent with two questions, a nonsensitive one (asking information that is trivial) and a sensitive one (asking sensitive information, such as the number of occupational crimes committed). The question (sensitive or nonsensitive) to be answered by the respondent depends on the outcome of a randomizing device (such as a coin flip, a roll of a die, a spinner, or some other device that generates random outcomes). The recorder needs to know two things prior to the survey. First, the recorder must know the probability of a "yes" answer to the nonsensitive question. Second, the recorder must know the probability of the outcome that designates the nonsensitive question. With prior knowledge of these two probabilities, the recorder can estimate the number of persons who answered "yes" to the sensitive question.

Here is a very simplified randomized response model for eliciting the incidence of occupational criminality (in this case, crime by physicians). Let us presume that there is a total (universe) of five hundred physicians in a given area. Each is sent the following letter to ask his or her participation in the study and to emphasize the anonymity associated with the survey's methodology:

We are trying to estimate the incidence of occupational crime by physicians. There is no way to trace any given answer to any particular individual, and therefore we ask that you be entirely frank in your responses. Please flip a coin. If the outcome is "heads," please answer the following question about your mother's or father's birthdate (choose one randomly by flipping the coin again): "Was he/she born between January 1st and June 30th?" If the outcome of the first coin flip is "tails," please answer the following question: "Have you ever submitted a fraudulent claim to a patient's medical insurance company that included services or tests that were never performed?" Please answer only the question designated by the coin flip by checking a "yes" or a "no" on the the the enclosed stamped postcard. DO NOT TELL US WHO YOU ARE OR WHICH QUESTION YOU HAVE ANSWERED. Remember, we cannot trace responses to any individual, nor can we ascertain which question was answered by you. Thank you for your cooperation.

Suppose that all 500 postcards are returned and they contain a total of 150 "yes" answers and 350 "no" answers. The recorder would then estimate that 10 percent of physicians in the survey had submitted at least one fraudulent medical insurance claim. The figure is calculated as 10 percent because the probability of a "yes" answer to the nonsensitive (birthday) question is approximately .5 (about half the population was born during the first six months of the year) and the probability of receiving the nonsensitive question is also about .5 (heads or tails). Thus, if half the physicians answered the nonsensitive question and half of that group should have answered "yes" to it, then one expects 125 "yes" answers to be to the nonsensitive question ($.5 \times .5 = .25$; $.25 \times 500 = 125$). Thus, the remaining twenty-five "yes" answers ($150-125 = 25$) must be to the sensitive question. There were about 250 physicians who were supposed to have answered the sensitive question, and 25 is 10 percent of 250. Had the physicians who answered the nonsensitive question received the sensitive question instead, then the assumption is that they, too, would have had a ten percent violation rate.

Of course, the success of the above example is predicated upon full cooperation by respondents. The extent to which the subjects failed to follow instructions or failed to send in postcards is the extent to which estimates might be in error. Such a model can also be used to estimate employee theft, tax evasion, price fixing, insider trading, or any other kind of occupationally related offending. Additionally, similar but more sophisticated models can estimate the numbers of offenses individuals commit rather than merely whether an individual has committed at least one offense (Moors, 1971; Greenberg, Kuebler, Abernathy, and Horvitz, 1971; Folsom, Greenberg, Horvitz and Abernathy, 1973).

Tracy and Fox (1981a), comparing randomized response results with simple self-report results, conclude that this technique more closely approximates the true number of offenses committed by the sample. Although Tracy and Fox did not include occupational criminality specifically, it can be assumed that because randomized response worked better than simple self-report in their study of criminality generally, it will be superior to simple self-report for occupational criminality as well.

Although randomized response has been shown to be superior to simple self-report in important respects, it is also more limited, because there is no way to determine particular characteristics of individuals in the survey. If you wanted to ascertain whether medical fraud is more likely to be committed by male physicians, or specialists, or graduates from less prestigious medical schools, randomized response is of no help unless these groups are sampled separately. And if there are only a few offenders in the sample, known as a low "base rate," then randomized response will not be able to produce a reliable estimate. There is also a question about the extent to which occupational offenders would even cooperate in a randomized response survey. One could argue that the logical basis of this particular survey method is so tricky that it might arouse even more suspicion about whether answers are anonymous. In any case, there is certainly no compelling reason why sophisticated adult offenders will tell the truth about discreditable behavior, independent of their perceived anonymity.

Criminal-based records of occupational criminality, then, are fraught with problems. However, if recorders can identify the biases and confront them methodologically, such as with the development of workable randomized response models (see Fox and Tracy, 1986), significant reductions in systematic response errors might be realized. Unfortunately, except for a paucity of unconnected and probably systematically biased data, the occupational criminal-based information barrel is currently empty.

DIRECT OBSERVATION OF OCCUPATIONAL CRIMES AND CRIMINALS

The fourth counting method is to observe directly the universes of offenses and offenders (or a representative sample of them). Direct observation would tend to have very low dark figures relative to the three methods discussed previously. Third person direct observation is certainly close to the offense itself. Its major drawback, however, is that it is extremely limited in application—only a few offenses lend themselves to direct observation.

It is impossible to observe most offenses directly. To see all robberies or burglaries, it would be necessary to watch everyone all of the time. To observe all price-fixing, all corporate executives would have to be monitored continuously. To observe all employee thefts, all employees would have to be watched unceasingly. Clearly, direct observation is possible for only a select few offenses.

Examples of offenses that have been directly observed include cable television signal theft (Green, 1985b) and traffic violations (Sigelman and Sigelman, 1976). In the area of occupational crime, income tax evasion has been estimated through direct observation by an audit of a representative sample of returns (Schwartz and Orleans, 1967). Income tax evasion has also been observed directly by comparing returns with independently determined income and expenses (Groves, 1958). Bribe-taking by elected officials, too, is a directly observable offense, as was shown by the FBI in the ABSCAM cases (see, e.g., Noonan, 1984:604-619 and discussion in Chapter 5). Braithwaite (1979) directly observed fraudulent used car dealers who rolled back odometer readings (he compared the mileage of cars on lots with the mileage claimed by the cars' previous owners). And Tracy and Fox (1989) directly observed consumer fraud in the auto body repair industry by noting differences in repair estimates as a function of whether repairs were to be paid for by an insurance company.

Another clever attempt to observe occupational crime directly was undertaken by Jesilow (1982) in his doctoral dissertation on auto repair fraud. Jesilow sought to determine the proportion of auto repair firms in a given area that engaged in fraud. Members of his research team took "dead" batteries (that had been certified to be chargeable by a professional mechanic) to a large sample of repair firms and instructed each firm to try to charge the battery. By performing this scenario with a representative sample of firms, Jesilow could count the number of auto repairers who claimed a battery was in need of replacement. Jesilow could not count the prevalence of auto repair defrauders by this method, however. There may have been firms in the sample that engaged in fraud on other occasions but not during the battery incident. These fraudulent firms would be undercounted as criminals. But Jesilow was able to identify a group of occupational criminals that may easily have gone undetected by other methods. Overall, Jesilow (1982:124) found 34 of 313 (or 10.9 percent) of the firms in the study to be dishonest on that occasion.

From a systematic bias standpoint, direct observation does not have response error because responses are not elicited as in victim-based and criminal-based records. But there is the possibility of systematic measurement and sampling error. Mistakes can be made in interpreting observed behavior as criminal or noncriminal. Further, as in any other counting method, editing and processing mistakes can occur.

Systematic sampling error would be caused by excluding certain persons or other entities from observation. For instance, in the Jesilow study (1982:80), the relative share of the automotive repair market possessed by new car dealers was about a third, but because there were so few dealers, all of whom had a high volume, Jesilow could not sample enough of them so that new car dealers represented a third of his sample. For these reasons, new car dealers were systematically undersampled. Additionally, some firms did not want to bother with such nonlucrative services as battery charging, which could have resulted in either random or systematic sampling error.

Direct observation of criminal behavior is the preferred method for counting crimes and criminals because it tends to produce the lowest dark figures. It may also allow the recorder to gather data in addition to the number of offenses committed (e.g., time-location, offender characteristics, victim characteristics, offense characteristics). However, it is so limited in application that it cannot be depended upon for regular use by researchers. When the few opportunities for counting occupational and other crimes through direct observation are realized, they should be exploited to their fullest.

Before moving on to a discussion of public attitudes toward the seriousness of occupational crime, a comment on a different type of direct observation is in order. Direct observation of samples of the universe of offenses may in principle be the best method for counting crimes and criminals. However, observational data may also act as an alternative to counting when attempting to learn about causal processes leading to (or inhibiting) occupational crime. Thus, one may learn much about developing effective programs to control organizational offending simply by studying the interactions within an offending organization (e.g., Geis, 1968b; Vaughan, 1979; 1983; Hopkins, 1980; Braithwaite, 1984; Kramer, 1988). Similarly, studying the socialization of medical students into the role of practicing doctor has yielded significant understanding about why doctors behave the way they do (Becker, Greer, Hughes, and Strauss, 1961). Similar observational research can be done during the training of business professionals. For instance, Clinard and Yeager (1980:67-68) report that a Harvard Business School professor, in his business decisionmaking course, trained students to misrepresent their positions in negotiations and other business dealings. Students found that hiding certain facts, bluffing, and even outright lying allowed them a better position and a better grade. The point is that careful observations during field research and case studies have the potential to teach more about the dynamics of occupational crime than counting methods which yield raw frequencies and incidences.

THE RELATIVE SERIOUSNESS OF OCCUPATIONAL CRIME

Some general public attitudes about occupational crime, such as how these offenders should be punished and the perceived financial and moral costs of their crimes, were presented at the end of Chapter 1. Criminologists have devoted a great deal of attention to another dimension along which perceptions about occupational crime can be measured—its relative "seriousness."

The only way to know whether the crime problem is getting better or worse is to know which offense and offender categories are "better" and which are "worse." Suppose that political bribery is viewed as more serious than armed robbery, and that there is an increase of twenty armed robberies and a decrease of twenty political briberies. It could be argued that the crime problem overall has been reduced because, although there is a net reduction of zero in the two categories combined, there are fewer crimes of a more serious nature.

To arrive at a comprehensive method for counting and analyzing the incidence of crimes and criminals, the quality of an offense must be taken into consideration along with the quantity of it. This final section of Chapter 2 reviews methods to determine the relative seriousness of different offenses.

Issues in Crime Seriousness Scaling

The "seriousness" of one's behavior is a relative phenomenon because there is no behavior that is inherently "serious," "criminal," or "harmful." As Donald Black (1979:20) notes:

> "What is a 'crime' to one person may not be to another, and for a given person, whether an incident is a 'crime' may depend upon the conditions under which it occurs. This is because, in commonsense, what is a 'crime' is not merely a matter of fact; it is also an evaluation."

The very existence of behavior deemed wrongful depends on the government or culture defining it as such. How a person perceives the acceptability of an imaginary other's social action varies according to characteristics of the perceiver, such as socioeconomic status, criminal victimization experience, age, race, education, and geographical region (Wolfgang, Figlio, Tracy and Singer, 1985; Rossi, Waite, Bose and Berk, 1974). Each individual invokes his or her own normative standard of seriousness in attaching to a particular act the label of "bad." When there is a discrepancy between personal ideas about what is acceptable behavior and a given social action, the individual will experience "cognitive dissonance" (Kidd, 1979; Festinger, 1957).

Crime seriousness studies not only aid in the determination of whether the overall crime picture is getting better or worse, they also have several other uses. They can guide legislatures in setting penalties and help judges to sentence appropriately (however, see Braithwaite, 1982a). Public perceptions of crime seriousness can also aid criminal justice managers in their allocation of resources to combat the kinds of crime the public most abhors. Some (Wolfgang, et al., 1985:11) also have argued that behavior seriousness ratings may be "in and of themselves worth undertaking because they tap a piece of the moral consensus, or lack of it, at a given time and place."

The first comprehensive effort to construct a behavior seriousness index was undertaken by Thorsten Sellin and Marvin Wolfgang (1964). Their study, *The Measurement of Delinquency*, utilizes the work of S. S. Stevens (1957) in the field of psychophysical scaling. Stevens shows that for a variety of physical stimuli (such as sound level, pleasantness of odors, occupational or political preference), equal stimulus ratios produce equal perceptual ratios. Sellin and Wolfgang similarly suggested that perceptions of the severity of various crimes would be a function of the differential force produced by stimuli which reflect degrees of offensive behavior. It is this stimulus-response that provides the rationale for eliciting perceptions about the relative gravity of different acts. Occupational crimes were not included in their initial study.

It is often very difficult to translate qualitative matters such as attitudes and feelings into numerical measurements. Such measurement can be based on untestable rationales and assumptions. A major assumption by researchers who ask for ratings of the seriousness of behavior is that those ratings can be scaled unidimensionally. Can one score acts against property, such as theft, and acts against persons, such as rape, along the same dimension of harm or seriousness?   Can behaviors violating the public trust, such as political bribery, be scaled along the same dimension as behaviors harmful to property and individuals? Can offenses which vary in the diffusiveness of their harm (e.g., theft of ten dollars from an individual or theft of ten dollars from a public museum) be scaled along the same dimension? Although there is no independent source of behavior seriousness with which to validate the assumption of unidimensionality, users of behavior seriousness indices implicitly assume that it exists (see Gottfredson, Young, and Laufer, 1980).

There is also the question about whether a response to a behavior stimulus actually reflects a perception of behavior seriousness. The conditions under which a behavior occurs or the intent of the actor may affect whether the behavior is perceived to be serious (Sebba, 1984). Invariably, behavior stimuli are constructed to be short and glib, offering virtually no information about the circumstances or the frame of mind of the actor. Consider the following stimulus: "Manufacturing and selling drugs known to be harmful to users" (Rossi, et al., 1974). In this case, it is not known whether the actor is a street dealer selling "crack cocaine" or another illicit substance or whether the drugs are legally distributed by a pharmaceutical company. Nor is there any indication of the degree of harmfulness associated with the drug. As a result, different respondents may interpret different conditions to be associated with this stimulus. Users of behavior seriousness ratings assume, without evidence, that respondents perceive the same intent and other offense conditions to exist for the same stimulus.

There are two basic methods for measuring perceptions of seriousness. *Category scaling* asks the respondent to rate the seriousness of a behavior along a fixed scale, such as between one and nine (with nine being attached to the acts perceived as most serious). *Magnitude estimation* asks the respondent to rate the seriousness of a behavior along a limitless scale between zero and infinity (with zero attached to the acts perceived as absolutely nonserious). In order to ground different persons' perceptions along the same kind of scale, magnitude estimates include a modulus, which is used as a common comparison point. An example of a modulus would be, "Compared to a shoplifting of goods worth $50 scored as 20, how serious is the following behavior? . . . " There is considerable debate about which scale, category or magnitude estimation, yields the best results. Each has its strengths and weaknesses.

The major strength of a category scale is that it typically involves a relatively small scale and is therefore easier for the respondent to comprehend. Further, a category scale is fixed and therefore the respondent knows its upper and lower limits, so that different raters may more readily work within the same conceptual bounds.

The major weakness of a category scale is that it may be too constrained. First, there may be more qualitative differences between two behaviors than can be reflected within a fixed and relatively small scale. For instance, a respondent may want to rate a certain behavior somewhere between three and four, but cannot because there are no fractions in a category scale. Second, ratings of behavior on a category scale may be "truncated" or lopped off at the upper end of the scale (Figlio, 1978). A respondent may rate a behavior as "nine" and then come across a behavior perceived as more serious but he or she cannot rate it higher than "nine." Further, because category scaling is ordinal (e.g., three on the scale may not reflect three times the seriousness of one on the scale), obtaining simple averages of offense ratings (or a ranking of them) may be misleading. On the other hand, with magnitude estimation, the distance between successive numbers is assumed equal and therefore overall averages are more meaningful (e.g., a rating of three is considered to be three times a rating of one).

A major strength of magnitude estimation is that there is no upper limit and therefore no lopping effect. If a rater considers a given behavior stimulus to be the most serious thus far presented, he or she can give it a higher rating. Additionally, unlike a category scale, magnitude estimation allows more finite distinctions among various stimuli. However, because the ratings can be from zero to infinity, some respondents often give atypically high ratings (e.g., one million) for certain stimuli. This presents problems when attempting to arrive at an average for the entire population, since such extreme values tend to exaggerate artificially the overall average. Researchers using magnitude estimation adjust scores to help to eliminate this bias. However, there is still a possibility for some exaggeration of central tendency. It is also argued that, even with a modulus, magnitude estimation causes raters to judge stimuli based on different ideas of the maximum and minimum rating values that are acceptable. For instance, although raters are told that they can give a stimulus any rating they choose, some raters may have in mind an upper limit of one hundred and others may have in mind an upper limit of one thousand. (For a thorough critique of the use of magnitude estimation for crime severity scoring, see Wolfgang, et al., 1985: Chapter 1.)

Overall, category scaling is less complicated and less difficult to analyze, but magnitude estimation allows more in-depth kinds of statistical analyses and more finite distinctions among different ratings. Both scaling methods seem to show perceptions by the public that: (1) occupationally related criminal behavior is serious; and (2) it is not as serious as traditional common crimes, especially common crimes against the person.

Magnitude Estimation: The National Survey of Crime Severity

The National Survey of Crime Severity (NSCS), based on magnitude estimation scaling, represents the most extensive effort to survey public opinions about about the seriousness of illegal acts. The NSCS was conducted during the last half of 1977 and includes interviews with approximately 60,000 persons 18 years of age or older (Wolfgang, et al., 1985). Each respondent's ratings in the survey were weighted according to his or her representative proportion of the population, so the final ratings are expected to be reflective of the entire United States population 18 years of age or older. Wolfgang and his colleagues at the University of Pennsylvania (with help from the federal Bureau of the Census) compiled the relative seriousness scores for each of 204 behavior stimuli. All of the stimuli represented behaviors that have generally been defined as criminal violations. The modulus used in the NSCS was: "Compared to [a] bicycle theft scored at 10, how serious is. . . ." (This modulus score of 10 should not be used to interpret the ratings presented below in Table 2.3 because they have been scaled differently.) The NSCS ratings, which have been adjusted to account for extreme values, ranged from a low of 0.2 ("A person under 16 years old plays hooky from school") to a high of 72.1 ("A person plants a bomb in a public building; the bomb explodes and 20 people are killed").

Table 2.3 presents selected NSCS ratings of occupational and nonoccupational criminal behavior. In Table 2.3, the nonoccupational offenses have been selected because they are close in magnitude to the occupational crimes.

There are some interesting comparisons that can be drawn from Table 2.3. Fraud by the grocer and a ten-dollar embezzlement are viewed as seriously as an obscene phone call (1.9). A civil rights violation by the realtor is viewed as seriously as a strongarm robbery (5.4). Cheating the government of $10,000 through income tax fraud is seen to be as serious as a running a prostitution racket (6.1). Assaulting a person with polluted water is considered to be as serious as assaulting a person with one's fists (6.9). A bribe acceptance by a city politician is perceived to be as serious as a $1,000 armed robbery (9.0). Intentionally causing a person's death through poisoning the public water supply (19.9) is almost as serious as a forcible rape with injury (20.1). And pollution of a water supply from which 20 people become slightly ill is perceived to be more serious (19.7) than a vehicular homicide (19.5).

Both occupational crime and "common crime" seem to be viewed as serious behavior. That some crimes are occupationally related does not seem to affect the public's perception of their seriousness. "Common" street crimes are regarded as the most serious by the national sample. Causing the death of a person through knowingly selling tainted cooking oil (17.8) or through knowingly adding poisonous material to the water supply (19.9) was regarded as about half as serious as causing the death of an individual through public bombing (39.1) or by a spousal stabbing (39.2). Similarly, causing the death of 20 persons through intentionally poisoning the public water supply received only slightly more than half the seriousness rating (39.1) as causing the same number of deaths by intentionally detonating a bomb in a public building (72.1). Although the "proximate causes" of the deaths clearly are attributable to the perpetrators, there nevertheless seems to be a public belief that intentional occupationally related

Table 2.3 *National Survey of Crime Severity* Ratings: Selected Offense Stimuli *(Occupational Crimes are in Boldface)*

Ratings	Offense Stimuli
1.9	An employee embezzles $10 from his employer.
1.9	A store owner knowingly puts "large" eggs into containers marked "extra large."
1.9	A person makes an obscene phone call.
3.1	A person breaks into a home and steals $100.
3.2	An employer illegally threatens to fire employees if they join a labor union.
3.6	A person knowingly passes a bad check.
3.7	A labor union official illegally threatens to organize a strike if an employer hires nonunion workers.
5.4	A real estate agent refuses to sell a house to a person because of that person's race.
5.4	A person threatens to harm a victim unless the victim gives him money. The victim gives him $10 and is not harmed.
5.7	A theater owner knowingly shows pornographic movies to a minor.
6.1	A person cheats on his Federal income tax return and avoids paying $10,000 in taxes.
6.1	A person runs a prostitution racket.
6.2	A person beats a victim with his fists. The victim requires treatment by a doctor but not hospitalization.
6.2	An employee embezzles $1,000 from his employer.
6.4	An employer refuses to hire a qualified person because of that person's race.
6.5	A person uses heroin.
6.9	A factory knowingly gets rid of its waste in a way that pollutes the water supply of a city. As a result, one person becomes ill but does not require medical treatment.
6.9	A person beats a victim with his fists. The victim requires hospitalization.
8.0	A person steals an unlocked car and sells it.
8.2	Knowing that a shipment of cooking oil is bad, a store owner decides to sell it anyway. Only one bottle is sold and the purchaser is treated by a doctor but not hospitalized.
8.6	A person performs an illegal abortion.
9.0	A city official takes a bribe from a company for his help in getting a city building contract for the company.
9.0	A person, armed with a lead pipe, robs a victim of $1,000.
9.2	Several large companies illegally fix the retail prices of their products.
9.4	A person robs a victim of $10 at gunpoint. No physical harm occurs.
9.4	A public official takes $1,000 of public money for his own use.
9.6	A police officer knowingly makes a false arrest.

Table 2.3 (Continued)

Ratings	Offense Stimuli
9.6	A person breaks into a home and steals $1,000.
10.0	A government official intentionally hinders the investigation of a criminal offense.
10.9	A person steals property worth $10,000 from outside a building.
11.2	A company pays a bribe to a legislator to vote for a law favoring the company.
11.8	A man beats a stranger with his fists. He requires hospitalization.
12.0	A police officer takes a bribe not to interfere with an illegal gambling operation.
12.0	A person gives the floor plans of a bank to a bank robber.
13.3	A person, armed with a lead pipe, robs a victim of $10. The victim is injured and requires hospitalization.
13.5	A doctor cheats on claims he makes to a Federal health insurance plan for patient services. He gains $10,000.
13.9	A legislator takes a bribe from a company to vote for a law favoring the company.
14.6	A person, using force, robs a victim of $10. The victim is hurt and requires hospitalization.
15.5	A person breaks into a bank at night and steals $100,000.
15.7	A county judge takes a bribe to give a light sentence in a criminal case.
16.6	A person, using force, robs a victim of $1,000. The victim is hurt and requires treatment by a doctor but not hospitalization.
17.8	Knowing that a shipment of cooking oil is bad, a store owner decides to sell it anyway. Only one bottle is sold and the purchaser dies.
19.5	A person kills a victim by recklessly driving an automobile.
19.7	A factory knowingly gets rid of its waste in a way that pollutes the water supply of a city. As a result 20 people become ill but none require medical treatment.
19.9	A factory knowingly gets rid of its waste in a way that pollutes the water supply of a city. As a result, one person dies.
20.1	A man forcibly rapes a woman. Her physical injuries require treatment by a doctor but not hospitalization.
33.8	A person runs a narcotics ring.
39.1	A factory knowingly gets rid of its waste in a way that pollutes the water supply of a city. As a result, 20 people die.
39.2	A man stabs his wife. As a result, she dies.
43.9	A person plants a bomb in a public building. The bomb explodes and one person is killed.
72.1	A person plants a bomb in a public building. The bomb explodes and 20 people are killed.

SOURCE: *The National Survey of Crime Severity* by Marvin Wolfgang, Robert Figlio, Paul Tracy, and Simon Singer (1985). Washington, D.C.: U.S. Government Printing Office. (Pp. vi-x).

behavior that causes injury or death is sometimes less serious than intentional injury or death inflicted nonoccupationally.

Category Scaling: The Baltimore Study

In a well known category scaling study undertaken five years prior to the *NSCS*, Peter Rossi and his colleagues (Rossi, et al., 1974) surveyed a representative sample of 200 Baltimore residents (125 whites and 75 blacks and equal gender counts within race categories). The sample tended to overrepresent older, nonworking, and less active members in the sampling area. Respondents, through a card sorting task, were asked to rate offenses on a category scale between a low seriousness of "1" and a high seriousness of "9." About 15 percent of the 140 offenses judged by the respondents were occupational offenses. All respondents rated the same twenty offenses, and two groups of 100 each rated 60 different offenses. Therefore, all respondents did not rate all occupational offenses because the two groups of 100 respondents each rated different sets of occupational crimes. The results for selected offenses from the Baltimore study are presented in Table 2.4.

It is not possible to compare directly the Rossi, et al. results with the those of the *NSCS* because of differences in the measurement (category and magnitude estimation) and the wording of stimuli. However, in terms of overall relative position, there seem to be some similarities in the two studies regarding occupational crimes. For instance, income tax cheating is ranked relatively low by both samples, as is price-fixing. Deaths caused knowingly through occupational decisions are ranked relatively high by both samples. As in the *NSCS*, in which a reckless vehicular homicide was rated as slightly less serious than a death from knowingly polluting the water supply, the Rossi, et al. sample rated a reckless vehicular homicide as less serious than a death caused by knowingly selling contaminated food. Acceptance of bribes by public officials were given moderately serious ratings in both samples. Overall, however, while occupationally related crimes against persons in both studies were often given relatively high rankings, street crimes against persons and drug distribution crimes received the highest rankings in both studies.

Additional Studies of Crime Severity

Following up on the Baltimore study, Cullen, Link and Polanzi (1982) attempted to determine whether perceptions about the severity of occupational crimes had increased. They presented a sample of residents in Macomb, Illinois with the same stimuli used in the Baltimore study. On the

Table 2.4 Average Seriousness Ratings Given to Selected Offenses in the Rossi, et al. Baltimore Study *(Occupational Crimes are in Boldface)*

Rank	Stimulus	Average Rating
1	Planned killing of a policeman	8.47
2	Planned killing of a person for a fee	8.41
3	Selling heroin	8.29
6	Planned killing of a spouse	8.11
9	Armed robbery of a bank	8.02
12	Kidnapping for ransom	7.93
18	Assault with a gun on a stranger	7.85
21	Forcible rape of a neighbor	7.78
25	**Manufacturing and selling drugs known to be harmful to users**	**7.65**
26	**Knowingly selling contaminated food which results in a death**	**7.60**
27	Armed robbery of a company payroll	7.58
30	Armed holdup of a taxi driver	7.51
36	Killing someone in a bar room free-for-all	7.39
39	Armed robbery of a supermarket	7.31
46	Killing a pedestrian while exceeding the speed limit	7.12
50	Father-daughter incest	6.96
51	**Causing the death of an employee by neglecting to repair machinery**	**6.92**
56	Mugging and stealing $200 cash	6.80
57	**Causing the death of a tenant by neglecting to repair heating plant**	**6.70**
58	Killing spouse's lover after catching them together	6.69
63	**Manufacturing and selling autos known to be dangerously defective**	**6.60**
64	Beating up a stranger	6.60
67	**Practicing medicine without a license**	**6.50**
68	Burglary of a home stealing a color TV	6.44
73	**A public official accepting bribes in return for favors**	**6.24**
74	**Employee embezzling company funds**	**6.21**
78	Theft of car for the purpose of resale	6.09
79	**Knowingly selling defective used cars as completely safe**	**6.09**
82	**Knowingly selling stolen goods**	**6.02**
84	Printing counterfeit $10 bills	5.95
91	Beating up a spouse	5.80
106	**Under-reporting income on income tax return**	**5.31**
110	**Overcharging on repairs to automobiles**	**5.13**
121	**Knowingly using inaccurate scales in weighing meat for sale**	**4.79**
126	**Fixing prices of a consumer product like gasoline**	**4.63**
132	**False advertising of a headache remedy**	**4.08**
140	Being drunk in a public place	2.85

SOURCE: Peter H. Rossi, Emily Waite, Christine Bose, and Richard Berk, "The Seriousness of Crimes: Normative Structure and Individual Differences," *American Sociological Review,* Vol. 39 (April): pp. 228–229.

basis of a 53 percent response, they concluded that ratings of the seriousness of occupationally related behavior have increased, particularly for
price-fixing and for offenses that can inflict injury and death. The average
rank for 24 crimes in the Macomb sample that might be considered occupationally related (79.71) was 12 places higher than for the original Baltimore sample (91.75). However, it is not certain whether these differences
reflect a change in attitude or whether the differences are artifacts caused
by comparing two very different samples of respondents.

Two other studies using the Baltimore stimuli deserve mention. First, a
1977-78 investigation by McCleary, O'Neil, Epperlein, Jones, and Gray
(1981) employed a sample of probation officers and attorneys working for
criminal justice agencies. Second, Pontell, Granite, Keenan, and Geis
(1985), used 105 police chiefs in a 1982 sample. For 20 of the 24 Baltimore stimuli that might be considered occupationally related, the average
seriousness rating among police chiefs was 5.68, which is lower than the
average for those offenses from the original Baltimore study (5.81) and the
Cullen, et al. Macomb study (6.93), but higher than the McCleary, et al.
study of probation officers and attorneys (5.32). It appears that criminal
justice system personnel, whose views are likely to influence the manner in
which the criminal law is enforced, rate occupational crimes as less serious
than the public does. However, this was not true for occupational offenses
across the board. For instance, Pontell, et al. (1985) report that the chiefs
ranked a public official who accepts a bribe 11 places higher than the
Rossi, et al. sample (23/34) and 16 places higher than the Cullen, et al.
sample (23/39). Some of the differences between these four samples could
be caused by the different methods employed (e.g., face-to-face interviews
or mailed questionnaires, card sorting, presentation order of stimuli, totality of offenses presented) rather than a true reflection of differences in
opinion. In all four samples, common crimes against the person and drug
distribution offenses are rated as most serious.

Common and occupational crime can also be compared along the dimension of their impact—whether economic, physical, or potentially
physical. Using the Rossi, et al. category data from Baltimore, Schrager
and Short (1980) sought to determine systematically whether crimes of
similar impact are rated similarly without regard for occupational relatedness. They found a significant statistical relationship between ratings
of occupational crimes with harmful physical conseqences (selling drugs
known to be harmful, selling contaminated food which results in death)
and ratings of common crimes with harmful physical consequences (im-
pulsive killing of an acquaintance, reckless vehicular homicide, killing
someone in a serious argument, and death from arson). Further, there
was a significant statistical relationship between ratings of economic oc-

cupational crimes (overcharging for credit, used car fraud, business machine price-fixing) and economic common crimes (shoplifting, check fraud, credit card fraud, and use of false identification to purchase goods). Type of impact dominates occupational relatedness in public ratings of offense seriousness. However, as noted in the discussions of Tables 2.3 and 2.4, common crimes that are a danger to the person are rated as more serious than occupational crimes with similar personal danger.

In sum, it has been shown consistently that previous assertions that the public does not consider occupational crime as harmful as common crime are false. The public rates occupationally related offenses as more serious than many common crimes. Recent media events surrounding occupational crime and criminals (e.g., Watergate, ABSCAM, Ford Pinto case, Ivan Boesky and insider stock trading) probably have sensitized the public to the harms of such behaviors. As hostile as public attitudes may be toward occupational crimes, there is nevertheless the belief that common crimes such as gun and knife murders, forcible rape, assault, robbery, and illegal drug distribution are more serious. When an occupational crime causes the death of 20 persons, it is rated no more serious than one stabbing death (Table 2.3). In short, the public is more concerned about being assaulted on the way to the grocery store (or having its home broken into while away) than about buying products that are tainted, fraudulently advertised, price-fixed, or overweighed. All told, though, occupational crime is considered to be serious offending behavior, and although it has not yet reached the level of seriousness attached to nonoccupational crime, it most certainly deserves to be included in any discussion of the "crime problem."

QUESTIONS FOR DISCUSSION

1. Why is it important to differentiate between the universe of offenses and the universe of offenders?
2. Discuss the problems associated with agency-based record keeping for the following four offenses: insurance fraud by physicians, illegal price-fixing, assault by a law enforcement officer, and sexual molestation of children in day care centers.
3. Discuss the problems associated with victim-based record keeping for the following four offenses: unnecessary surgery, illegal working conditions, bribery of a public official, and employee theft.
4. Discuss the problems associated with criminal-based record keeping for the following four offenses: sexual molestation of patients by physicians, trade secret theft, obstruction of justice, and insider trading.

5. How well do you believe the randomized response model example presented in the chapter (study of insurance fraud among physicians) would actually work? What are the strengths and weaknesses of it? How would you improve it?

6. Would randomized response models be applicable to the following offenses: illegal distribution of pharmaceuticals by pharmacists, falsification of product test results by a firm, criminal human rights violations such as physical torture, and illegal tax cheating? Why? Or why not?

7. Name three occupational crimes that can be counted by direct observation (bearing in mind the Bill of Rights).

8. Should category scaling or magnitude estimation scaling be used to estimate public perceptions about behavior seriousness? Why?

9. What are the benefits and uses of behavior seriousness indices? Are they sufficient for those uses? If not, why not and how can they be improved?

10. Whose perceptions about behavior seriousness are more important— persons in the criminal justice system or the public? Why?

11. Although much of the information presented in this chapter demonstrates that the public is aware of the dangers and harms associated with occupational crime, there is still a tendency for the criminal justice system to allocate its resources away from these kinds of offenses. Why?

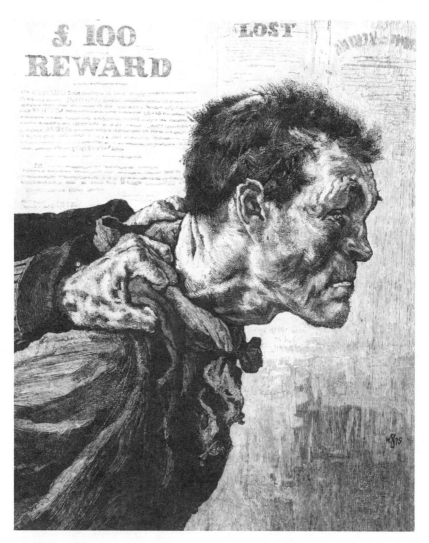

Conflict criminologists have pointed out how the criminal justice system has perpetuated the definition of certain persons as representing the foundation of the "crime problem." Politically powerful occupational offenders often help to contribute to such definitions by undercutting their own censure while at the same time spotlighting others as the "real criminals." (The Bettman Archive)

THREE

EXPLANATIONS OF OCCUPATIONAL CRIMINALITY

This chapter will present major approaches to crime causation and apply them to the explanation of occupational offending. The theoretical approaches in criminology run an intellectual gamut. On the far left is the Marxist idea that crime is a byproduct of the government's attempt to harness productive workers and help capitalism survive. At the other end are the rightist Lombrosians, who believe that criminality is genetically transmitted. Between these extremes lies a vast array of "theories" that have enjoyed prominence at one time or another during the past fifty years.

The term "theory" is used in this chapter rather loosely, because none of the approaches discussed completely meets the minimal requirements for the proper intellectual grounding required of a sound criminological theory (see Gibbs, 1985; 1987). Nor can any single theory about the causes of occupational crime account for all of it, or even a majority of it, because there are so many different causes. Although occupational crime is a class of crime that can be treated as unique because it is based on opportunities at the job, there is not a single theory that can explain why all occupational crimes occur or why all occupational criminals behave the way they do.

Further, as Binder, Geis, and Bruce (1988:185-86) caution, some explanations for criminal behavior are unique to certain situations, when one theory or even a set of theories may have no relevance. To illustrate this point, Binder, et al. describe findings from a juvenile delinquency study. Short and Strodtbeck (1965) found that boys dropped their association with their gang if the girl with whom they had been having sexual intercourse became pregnant. They married, and the new husbands used as an excuse for disaffiliation from the gangs that their wives did not want them to continue in gang activities. Conversely, if the girlfriend of a gang member did not become pregnant, then the gang member would continue to associate with the gang and probably end up in increasingly more difficulty with the law. Binder, et al. state:

"The enigma raised by this set of circumstances, of course, is that the key variable separating the first group from the second group of gang members is the chance that the girlfriend would conceive. This is hardly the kind of circumstance upon which a convincing causal explanation of [criminal] behavior can be built, and it illustrates that the theories that we have, given the nature of the behavior being examined, might have to be kept at a general level, rather than reduced to a level of explanation that can account for the [criminal] act of any particular individual."

Theories about criminal behavior, then, may not be able to explain why individual crimes are committed under certain circumstances.

Many theories have been developed in criminology. Fortunately, the field can be narrowed when attempting to explain occupational crime. First, biologically-based approaches to crime causation offer little help. In their earliest forms, late nineteenth century proponents such as Cesare Lombroso (1835-1909) believed that criminals were physically, mentally, and emotionally incapable of functioning properly in society (Lombroso, 1911). According to Lombroso's daughter two years after his death, such criminals should avoid "occupations which may pave the way for other crimes: lockmaking, brasswork, engraving, photography, and calligraphy . . . ." And such individuals should avoid occupations ". . . which require [the] dangerous tools [of] shoemaking, cabinet making, and carpentering . . . ." (Lombroso-Ferrero, 1972:197).

Ms. Lombroso-Ferrero's caveats aside, however, a biocriminological approach is not intuitively appealing as an explanation for occupational crime. It is hard to conceive of an embezzlement, illegal pollution, pricefix, unnecessary surgery, insider stock trade, employee theft, or virtually any other occupational offense being caused by pro-criminal genes or an extra chromosome. This should not imply that there is absolutely no place for biological approaches in the explanation of occupational crime. They may be applicable in extremely isolated instances. For example, a given act of aggression by a police officer may be exacerbated by a body chemical imbalance. However, on the whole, biological approaches add nothing to our understanding of occupational crime.

Second, there are several theories that have been advanced in the area of juvenile delinquency which also have very limited applicability to occupational crime. Several approaches that view delinquency primarily as a lower class phenomenon (e.g., Cohen, 1955; Miller, 1957) are not appropriate to the explanation of occupational crime because they generally assume a high unemployment rate among lower class youths. Additionally, the "labeling" idea—that official involvement in the criminal justice system has a negative criminogenic effect on a person's self-image, especially the young (e.g., Lemert, 1951)—also does not seem appropriate for the study of occupational crime. This approach would be extremely limited as an explanation for occupational crime, even by juveniles, because of its implication that those affected negatively by official labeling either drop out of the legitimate work force voluntarily or are institutionalized by the criminal justice system.

Third, other theories are only tangentially related to job crime. For instance, Sellin's (1938) ideas about conflict among sets of conduct rules can explain some occupational crime, but his approach is not as powerful as other theories that will be discussed. Sellin believes that crime will occur when the conduct rules of a dominant culture are in conflict with the conduct rules of any of the following groups: migrants, colonized peoples, and persons living at border areas between divergent cultures. Suppose that fee-splitting (that is, taking kickbacks for professional referrals) is common practice among physicians in a particular culture, and it is not treated as criminal in that culture. When physicians from this site split fees after moving elsewhere, where the behavior is unacceptable, then they may be committing a crime because of culture conflict. When there is a conflict among occupational conduct norms in any of Sellin's three situations, and crime results, it can be said that the lawbreaking was "external" to the offender, because he or she was only acting as one would normally in the original culture. The proportion of occupational crime that can be explained by Sellin's conflict with "external" conduct norms is probably quite small.

Another example of a theory tangentially related to occupational crime is David Greenberg's approach to explaining why juveniles commit a great deal of property crime. Greenberg (1981) believes that because juveniles are systematically excluded from the full-time labor force and other legitimate opportunities to create wealth, they often cannot support the major expenses associated with their social life. Even middle- and upper-class youths who may have wealthy parents can come up short on funds because they desire more than what is given. Property crime becomes a source of producing wealth. In terms of our focus, Greenberg's approach may help to explain some of the occupational crimes against property committed by juveniles (e.g., stealing money or goods while working at a part-time job).

The explanations that will be addressed in this chapter cover almost the full spectrum of the remaining approaches in criminology. They will be divided into two major sections. First, there are several theories that interpret criminality as a political phenomenon. These "legal conflict analyses" are presented first because of the inexorable link between the power associated with some occupations and the making of laws. Conflict analyses are based on the premise that the behavior of laws (that is, their establishment and application) is a reflection of the interests of persons with political power. Those who wield power can sometimes exert pressure on lawmakers and law enforcers to criminalize certain actions and individuals, and can pressure them to ignore other actions and individuals. Conflict analyses basically assert that there are no fundamental differences between criminals and noncriminals other than the fact that criminals' behaviors have been deemed illegal by persons who affect the making and enforcement of law.

On the contrary, the approaches discussed in the second part of this chapter try to identify and explain factors associated with the individual criminal that are assumed to set him or her apart from noncriminals. They include: (a) differences in learning about conduct rules; (b) differences in access to the legal opportunity to gain wealth; (c) differences in the willingness to neutralize (explain away) their criminality; and (d) differences in opportunities for crime and abilities to control selfish and compulsive behaviors. The focus of explanation in these approaches is on the behavior of the individual, whereas in conflict analyses it is on the behavior of the law.

EXPLANATIONS OF THE BEHAVIOR OF CRIMINAL LAW

Marxist Legal Conflict Analyses

One general group of conflict analyses, called "Marxist" or "radical," base their work on the writings of Karl Marx (1818-1883) and Friedrich Engels (1820-1895). The crux of the Marx-Engels theory revolves around the conflict between the material forces of production (that is, technological equipment and knowledge to use it) and the social relations of production (that is, relationships which determine the distribution of goods produced by the material forces of production). Marx and Engels predicted that capitalist systems will further develop the material forces of production, but the social relations of production will continue to favor only those who own the means of production. As a result, more property will be concentrated among fewer and fewer people, while at the same time more and more people will become wage earners instead of working for themselves. Even relatively "big fish" will be gobbled up by even bigger ones because of the "survival of the fittest" basis of capitalism. This, coupled with a decreased need for workers because of mechanization and automation, will result in many more workers than jobs. Because the supply of workers far exceeds the demand for them, persons desperate for jobs will be willing to work for extremely low wages. Eventually, then, capitalist societies will polarize into two conflicting groups—the very few rich and the many, many poor. It is this tendency toward polarization that Marx and Engels regarded as the inherent contradiction in capitalism. For these two theorists, only a revolutionary restructuring of the social relations of production will bring a balance back into society. The inevitable result of such a revolution would be socialism, in which the ownership of the means of production is distributed through the state to all workers collectively.

Marx and Engels did not use the concept of "crime" as a central aspect of their theories. However, "crime" and "law" are relevant to a Marxist criminology because they are manifestations of the components of Marx's and Engels's theories (O'Malley, 1986). Thus, the establishment or application of law, both civil and criminal, is relevant to a Marxist criminology only insofar as it represents state powers which are used to hinder or facilitate various material forces of production. Modern Marxist criminologists essentially view "crime" as an ideological and political category generated by state practices (Hirst, 1975:220).

Marxist analyses generally posit that laws are very often a reflection of the interests of the "ruling class" or "bourgeoisie" (owners of the means of production), rather than a reflection of worker class ("proletariat") interests. Early "instrumentalist" Marxists saw the state as a political tool easily manipulated by an organized ruling class. However, more recently, "structuralist" Marxists take the view that ruling class interests are not necessarily organized in their influence on the making and enforcing of laws. Rather, structuralists see owners' interests as being reflected naturally in the law, because the economic well-being of a society depends on the development of the material forces of production. As Vold and Bernard (1986:310-11) point out,

> "If the social relations of production include private ownership of the means by which goods are produced, then the economic well-being of the society depends on the economic well-being of a set of private citizens. The state, then, has no choice but to arrange things so that the economic interests of those people are served, regardless of what consequences that has for the economic interests of other groups."

Hence, "structural" Marxists view the primary function of the state as ensuring that the social relations of capitalism endure. This sometimes requires that different interests be served at various times in order to prevent the downfall of the economic system. Thus, at any given time, there may be interests other than those of the owners of production which have to be served. Even so, the owners may still be described as a "ruling class" because, first, the state will, in the long run, serve more of the owners' interests than the interests of other groups. Second, owners have more political power generally than other groups, and can therefore pressure the state to serve their immediate and long-term needs.

Much of Marxist criminological analysis has been aimed at explaining common crimes committed by the poor. The initial Marxist view that poor people commit crimes of theft and violence because of a "primitive rebellion" against capitalistic conditions of exploitation and domination has been generally abandoned by Marxist analysts. The current emphasis is on a more complex explanation of crime within a broader view of political-economic systems. Marxists, however, still hold the basic belief that behaviors defined as criminal are committed by rational individuals as logical reactions to a situation structured by the social relations of capitalism. Individuals are said to act and think in ways that are consistent with their economic interests. This view might be applicable to occupational crimes by all strata of society—such as the underpaid employee thief who steals money to buy food, the middle-class embezzler who steals to have a more affluent lifestyle, and the wealthy corporate decisionmaker who illegally fixes prices to survive in the capitalist market system (Vold and Bernard, 1986: Chapter 16).

A capitalistic mode of production encourages the passage and enforcement of laws that further its ends. Actions that promote unfair competition or otherwise adversely affect free enterprise (such as antitrust actions, trade secret theft, and insider stock trading) are harmful to the basic competitive foundations of capitalism, so they are outlawed. Price-fixing is outlawed in capitalistic systems not only because it restricts fair competition, but also because it contributes to inflation. In addition to criminalizing behaviors that discourage a healthy marketplace, capitalistic interests also tend to criminalize the various behaviors associated with a sluggish labor force (e.g., drug use, vagrancy, property crime). Owners of the means of production may be able to thwart, at least for the moment, the passage of laws that forbid, for example, exposing individuals to dangerous working conditions or unsafe consumer products. If such practices are considered as counterproductive to capitalism in the long run, however, laws forbidding such conditions and products will eventually be passed, independent of any immediate negative effects on owners' interests. A case in point is the Beef Inspection Act in 1906. Although compliance with that law cost meat packers considerable initial financial outlay, in the long run it increased the beef trade because the public was no longer in fear of eating tainted meat (see discussion in Chapter 4).

Some Marxist-oriented writers (Quinney, 1970; Reiman, 1979; Pearce, 1976) have argued that criminologists (and the criminal justice policies they help to create) also tend to support ruling class interests in the long run. Criminologists do this by fostering a self-perpetuating image of the "crime problem" that emphasizes common crimes committed by the poor and excludes "crimes of the powerful." The image is self-perpetuating because by concentrating on the prosecution and conviction of common criminals, the system reinforces such criminal conceptions as the foundation of the crime problem. This emphasis, coupled with middle- and upper-class offenders' benefits from flexible sentencing policies, favorable conditions of court processing, and alternatives to incarceration, results in Reiman's (1979) adage that "the rich get richer and the poor get prison."

Marxist analysis may help to explain why some occupational behaviors are legal and why some are illegal. It may also aid in discovering some individual motivations to commit occupational crimes when such offenses are "rational" responses to the capitalist ethos. The assumption that the legal system, in the long run, is responsive primarily to those who own the means of production constitutes the major difference between Marxist analysis and other legal conflict explanations. The other conflict approaches emphasize the relationship between group power on the one hand and law formation and administration on the other, but they do not relate power primarily to the means and relations of production. These nonpartisan conflict theories can be applied to any form of economically or politically organized society.

Nonpartisan Legal Conflict Analyses

George Vold—"Group Conflict."   One conflict approach that concentrates on group power as a generic force, rather than capitalist group power as the major force, is that of George Vold. Vold, one of the original conflict criminologists, states (1958:204-207) that

> "[M]an always is a group-involved being whose life is both a part of, and a product of his group associations. Implicit also is the view of society as a congerie of groups held together in a shifting but dynamic equilibrium of opposing group interests and efforts. . . . The end result is a more or less continuous struggle to maintain, or to defend, the place of one's own group in the interaction of groups, always with due attention to the possibility of improving its relative status and position. Conflict is viewed, therefore, as one of the principal and essential social processes upon which the continuing on-going of society depends. . . . Groups come into conflict with one another as the interests and purposes they serve tend to overlap, encroach on one another, and become competitive. . . . The logical outcome of group conflict should be, on

the one hand, conquest and victory for one side with utter defeat and destruction or subjugation for the other side; or, on the other hand, something less conclusive and decisive, a stalemate of compromise and withdrawal to terminate the conflict with no final settlement of the issues involved. . . . The group that will survive and avoid having to go down in defeat is the one strong enough to force some compromise settlement of the issues in conflict."

According to Vold, then, it is the struggle among group interests and the compromise of their conflicts that constitute the dynamics of the socio-political process. The groups which control the legislative process can influence which behaviors are defined as criminal. Accordingly, the group that has the greatest number of votes in the legislature will pass laws that promote its interests. Those who win a legislative majority win control of the police power of the state and can selectively apply criminal definitions.

Vold also maintained that some criminality is a symptom of group alliance rather than individual antisocial behavior. Some occupational crimes can be traced directly to group interests. For instance, professional labor group leaders sometimes commit crimes during strikes because of their quest for power for their group. Physicians who have a stronger attachment to a "medical business" group than to a "medical profession" group may commit insurance fraud or perform unnecessary surgery. Fixing prices in an industry may be caused by alliance to the group that cherishes corporate survival. Burglary, bribery, and obstruction of justice were committed by persons in the Watergate scandal to further the interests of their political group to reelect President Nixon—they believed that the ends justified the means.

Foremost, Vold's group conflict conception explains why meretricious actions of big business have not been censured by criminalization—big business groups control the legislative process more effectively than groups that oppose them. On the other hand, in cases in which actions by big business groups have been criminalized by consumer and employee protection laws, labor and consumer groups have more effectively won in the legislature. Vold also accounted for individuals' crimes committed because of an alliance to a greater group cause, although he did not discuss the dynamics of how group positions are created or reinforced.

Austin Turk—"Theory of Criminalization." Austin Turk's (1969) conflict analysis is also nonpartisan in its approach because the formulation can be applied to any organized society. Turk is not concerned with how a government originally came to power. Rather, he concentrates on what happens between a government and the people it governs after rule has been established and laws passed by specifying the relative probabilities that authorities will prosecute and convict law violators.

He maintains that the extent to which enforcement officials believe in the validity of a law is the most important factor promoting the prosecution and conviction of criminals. Turk makes a distinction between low-level enforcers (e.g., police and regulatory agency investigators) and high level enforcers (e.g., prosecutors and judges). If both levels of enforcers consider a law to be important, then deprivations to its violators (arrest, conviction, punishment) are extremely likely. However, if low-level enforcers consider legal violations worth citing but high-level enforcers do not, then arrest rates will be high and conviction and punishment rates will be low. The opposite (low arrest rates and high punishment rates) will occur if judges and prosecutors believe in the validity of the law and low-level enforcers do not. Turk was anticipated on this point in Sutherland's *White Collar Crime* (1949:257): "statutes . . . have little importance in the control of business behavior unless they are supported by an administration which is intent on stopping the illegal behavior."

To illustrate Turk's theory of criminalization in one area of occupational crime, suppose that high- and low-level enforcers of mine safety strongly believe in laws promoting proper working conditions. Here, there will be the highest probability of convicting companies for mine site violations, because authorities (from inspectors to prosecutors to judges) consider worker safety to be a priority. When mine inspectors consider occupational safety an important issue but prosecutors and judges do not, inspectors will file complaints, but the complaints will not be acted upon. And high-level enforcers who believe in the importance of maintaining safe mines will react negatively to all violators cited, regardless of the number of violators that come before them.

Given that authorities are aware of a violation, there are two major factors affecting the probability of prosecution in addition to the importance authorities attach to enforcement. First, as noted, conflict theory generally asserts that prosecution is more likely if violators have little power. If violators have sufficient power, then they can effectively avoid prosecution because they can influence changes in the law that will reflect the violators' position.

Second, "realism in the conflict moves" also affects the chances of prosecution—the more realism, the less prosecution. Realism refers to the extent to which one side's actions do not invite an increase in unwanted activity by the other side. For authorities, realistic moves will not provoke increased norm resistance. For subjects, realism will not provoke increased enforcement. In the mining industry example, it would be unrealistic for authorities to threaten to increase enforcement of mine safety laws dramatically, as this may provoke the industry into greater violation. Similarly, it would be unrealistic for the mining industry to ignore openly the safety laws, because such actions may cause authorities to assert their power by increasing enforcement.

The foregoing mining industry example represents a group of violators who may have the power and sophistication to avoid prosecution. That industry has considerable economic clout. However, there are also many occupational criminals who are relatively powerless and unsophisticated. Employee thieves, child molesters in day care centers, and other individual occupational criminals lack the prerequisites to undercut attempts to criminalize them. Therefore, given that the legal norms that these individuals violate are important to authorities, there is virtually no chance of avoiding criminalization if the violation is discovered.

The remaining approaches to be discussed are quite unlike legal conflict analyses because they shift the level of explanation from the behavior of law (its enactment and application) to the behavior of the individual. In the following nonconflict approaches, there is the assumption that there are fundamental differences between criminals and noncriminals.

EXPLANATIONS OF THE BEHAVIOR OF CRIMINAL INDIVIDUALS

Learning Conduct Norms: Differential Association, Operant Conditioning, and Normative Validation

Differential Association. As noted in Chapter 1, when Edwin Sutherland addressed the American Sociological Society in 1939, he introduced the concept of "white collar crime" and asseverated that his theory of "differential association" could explain why individuals in all strata of society commit crime. This was an important claim because most explanations that had been advanced at the time equated crime with poverty. Poverty-based theories were inadequate for Sutherland because they did not apply to criminality in the upper economic classes. Sutherland (1940:12) believed that the best explanations of criminal behavior are those that relate factors "to a general process characteristic of all criminality." Sutherland's theory of differential association attempts to identify that general process among all criminals, rich and poor alike. It also attempts to identify the general processes that are charactistic of persons who do not commit crimes. However, as noted earlier, it is unrealistic to hope for a single theory that can explain all crime.

Differential association has two levels. First, the approach attempts to explain the criminogenic and anticriminogenic processes that occur on an individual level. Second, the social conditions under which these processes are more or less likely to take place are specified by Sutherland. By so doing, he essentially predicts when more or less crime will take place. The basis of differential association is that persons are exposed to others' values that encourage or discourage the commission of certain crimes, thereby teaching definitions that are favorable or unfavorable toward the violation of law.

Sutherland's theory, which is based on the individual level of analysis, eventually comprised nine points (Sutherland and Cressey, 1974:75-76):

1. Criminal behavior is learned.
2. Criminal behavior is learned in interaction with other persons in a process of communication.
3. The principal part of the learning of criminal behavior occurs within intimate personal groups.
4. When criminal behavior is learned, the learning includes (a) techniques of committing the crime, which are sometimes very complicated, sometimes very simple; (b) the specific direction of motives, drives, rationalizations and attitudes.
5. The specific direction of motives and drives is learned from definitions of the legal codes as favorable or unfavorable.
6. A person becomes delinquent because of an excess of definitions favorable to violation of law over definitions unfavorable to violation of law.
7. Differential associations may vary in frequency, duration, priority and intensity.
8. The process of learning criminal behavior by association with criminal and anticriminal patterns involves all of the mechanisms that are involved in any other learning.
9. While criminal behavior is an expression of general needs and values, it is not explained by those general needs and values because noncriminal behavior is an expression of the same needs and values.

In short, criminal behavior and noncriminal behavior are the products of learning through individual associations with those whom we shall term "significant others." For our purposes, a "significant other" is a person who has great influence on one's self-evaluation and who has great impact on one's acceptance or rejection of social norms. In the socialization of a child, for instance, the significant others usually include parents, teachers, and playmates. If a person is exposed to significant others who transmit an excess of values that promote illegal behavior, then he or she will become a criminal. Similarly, if one is exposed to significant others who transmit an excess of values that do not promote illegal behavior, then criminality will not result. These differences in associations constitute the major difference between criminals and noncriminals for Sutherland. The term "differential association," then, refers to the difference among significant others with whom one associates in terms of whether they encourage or discourage law violations. Differential association does not attempt to explain why an individual has the associations he or she has, only the influence of those associations.

Associations with criminal and noncriminal significant others vary in frequency (how often), duration (length of time), priority (how early in life) and intensity (significance of the other). Associations that occur most often, for the greatest length of time, early in life, and with individuals of greatest importance are the ones that have the most influential effects on criminal or noncriminal behavior patterns. Associations with criminal or noncriminal influences *per se* are not the critical factors; rather, close personal associations have the most effect. Police and prison personnel who are constantly in the company of criminals rarely are going to become criminals themselves because such associations are not influential or significant on a close and personal level. Additionally, the same set of associations may transmit an excess of definitions unfavorable to the commission of some crimes (e.g., armed robbery and forcible rape) and an excess of definitions favorable to the commission of other crimes (e.g., insider stock trading, tax evasion). Although not explicitly stated in the theory, differential association implies that when an excess of definitions favorable to violation of law exists, then the offender is less likely to feel remorse or moral guilt about contemplating or committing such violations.

When criminal behavior is learned, the learning includes the specific techniques for crime commission. This point has been attacked by critics who claim that it is not necessary to learn from others how to commit certain crimes. For instance, learning occupational criminal techniques from others may not be necessary prior to stealing office supplies from employers, juggling books for embezzlement, or failing to provide legally safe working conditions. Learning criminal behavior only sometimes involves the specific techniques that are necessary. Additionally, Sutherland refers to the learning of criminal "motives, drives, rationalizations and attitudes" from significant others. Sutherland also emphasizes that noncriminal motives, drives, and attitudes are learned through association with significant others. Learned criminal and anticriminal patterns are counteracting forces, and the extent to which one is present in excess of the other will determine whether one becomes a criminal.

Sutherland tried to apply differential association as an explanation for essentially all criminal behavior. For him, differential association would explain, for instance, why some juveniles commit delinquency and others do not, why some turn to burglary and robbery to gain money and others do not, and why some corporate executives fix prices and others do not. From Sutherland's perspective, delinquents, burglars, robbers, and price-fixers have all been exposed to associations which have transmitted to them an excess of values favorable to their law violations.

Social Disorganization and Differential Association.   As noted, the social conditions under which differential association into crime is more or less likely to take place was specified by Sutherland. The criminogenic conditions are characterized by what has been termed "social disorganization," which refers to a failure within a social system to hold common rules for conduct. Sutherland identified two types of social disorganization: "anomie" and "differential social organization."

Anomie, or "normlessness," refers to an absence of conduct rules in a social system. The term "anomie" was first used to denote "normlessness" in the late sixteenth century (Merton, 1968:189n), and was later resurrected by Durkheim almost a century ago. A condition of normlessness can result from a variety of factors. Sutherland believed such a lack of conduct rules was likely when a person moves from one social system to a different social system. During such a transition, there is a breakdown of conduct rules from the former system, and a failure to form and diffuse conduct rules for the new system. The fact that the old has not yet been replaced by the new causes a lack of conduct rules altogether. Sutherland (1949:255-56) offers as an example of anomic social disorganization the American period of transition from governmental nonintervention ("lassez-faire") to governmental intervention in the marketplace, which occurred about thirty or forty years after the Civil War. Prior to governmental regulation of the marketplace, the business social system was based on essentially unencumbered and unmanipulated competition and free enterprise. During the transition to governmental regulation, "businssmen passed through a period of uncertainty. . . . They were dissatisfied with the system of free competition and free enterprise and had no substitute on which they could reach consensus" (Sutherland, 1949:256). Because of this lack of consensus, businessmen were more likely to be exposed to significant others who encouraged violation of the new social system's conduct rules than if those rules were already in place. Eventually, as the business world moved toward more concretely identified conduct rules, differential associations were less likely to occur, as was criminal business behavior.

The other form of social disorganization described by Sutherland (1949:285)—"differential social organization"—applies to a social system that is characterized by a conflict in rules for conduct. The conflict is between the system's law abiding conduct rules and the different procriminal conduct rules subcribed to by some organized entitities within that system. Members of some groups in a social system will be law abiding because their group is organized around unfavorable definitions toward violation of law. Other groups are organized around favorable definitions toward violation of law, promoting procriminal conduct rules. Hence, differential social organization refers to the extent of difference among groups in a social system in terms of their organization around prolegal conduct rules.

A strong example of occupational differential social organization was found by Geis in the heavy electrical equipment industry during the 1930s, '40s and '50s. The major manufacturers in that industry specifically encouraged illegal price-fixing among their employees as a normal response to market pressure. Specific rewards in the forms of promotions and bonuses were allocated by employers to those that participated in the offense. Price-fixing was an "established way of life" (Geis, 1968b:109), and new employees entered into it as they would any other aspect of their job. Motives, drives, rationalizations, and attitudes favorable toward violation of antitrust statutes were learned by the offenders, for, as one of those convicted stated, "We did not fix prices . . . all we did was recover costs" (Geis, 1968b:112). Another conspirator, responding to a United States Senate subcommittee, believed his actions were "Illegal . . . but not criminal" (Geis, 1968b:108).

Differential association may be a valid explanation for why some individuals participate in occupational crime and others do not, and the theory is drawn upon substantially in the following chapters. If Sutherland is correct, then prediction of greater levels of occupational crime within particular occupational social systems are inexorably tied to greater levels of social disorganization in those systems.

Problems in Applying Differential Association.   Differential association is intuitively very appealing as an explanation for criminality, but there are several pitfalls when the theory is applied. First, as emphasized at the outset of this chapter, no single explanation can account for all crime. Sutherland's idea that differential association is a "general process characteristic of all criminality" is overly optimistic. As noted, one need not learn the techniques for crime from others. Further, it has been shown that persons in order to commit crimes need not associate with others who transmit definitions favorable to the violation of law. Both Cressey (1953) in the case of embezzlement and Clinard (1946) in the case of price regulation violation during World War II found that association with criminal patterns and techniques are not necessary prerequisites for those offenses.

Second, it is impossible to test any effects of differential association on the commission of criminal behavior because of the theory's empirical specifications. The crux of differential association lies in an excess of certain definitions toward violation of law. To determine which definitions are in excess, one must determine which of an individual's lifelong definitions are favorable and unfavorable toward violation of law, and then tally them. This is an impossible research task (see Gibbs, 1985; 1987).

Third, there may be things that are learned about law breaking or law abiding behavior that are not learned from close associations with others. Specifically, "operant conditioning" and "normative validation" may also be integral parts of learning about proper conduct.

Operant Conditioning and Normative Validation. "Operant conditioning" is based upon the idea that by consistently rewarding persons for appropriate behavior and withholding rewards for inappropriate behavior, they learn to expect such responses. These expectations derive from personal experience and from watching the fates of others. Persons may avoid committing acts because they have learned that they will be punished for committing them. Punishments need not be in the form of conviction or incarceration formally meted out by the government. Informal (nongovernmental) punishments, such as being ostracized by close friends or the loss of a job, can also act as operant conditioners.

"Normative validation" refers to an educative effect of sanction threat apart from its operant conditioning impact (Gibbs, 1975:79-82; Andenaes, 1974:Chapter 2). When a formal or informal sanction is given for a behavior, one can infer from the fact that a sanction is meted out that the behavior is unacceptable. The negative consequences attached to an act deem it inappropriate while simultaneously validating opposite conduct rules. When conduct rules are morally validated in this way, an individual may come to believe that derogated behavior is inappropriate, and decide not to commit it. As in the case of operant conditioning, the concept of normative validation indicates that the learning of appropriate conduct rules may not only be the product of definitions about the legal code learned from significant others.

To understand fully the process of learning about conduct norms, it is necessary to determine the conceptual boundaries between differential association, operant conditioning, and normative validation. Suppose that a mother castigates her son for stealing from his workplace. Such a reaction presents the son with a significant other's value that is unfavorable toward stealing. This is very much what Sutherland referred to as learning definitions about law violation from intimate personal groups. The sanctions by the mother: (a) operantly condition her son to avoid behaviors that will be castigated by her in the future; and (b) affirm the moral validity of rules against stealing. Informal sanctions (or threatened ones) meted out by significant others for crime commission represent, for Sutherland, an associational transmission that is unfavorable toward that legal violation, and the transmission occurs *through* operant conditioning and normative validation. On the other hand, a lack of sanctions meted out by significant others for crime commission would also transmit, through Sutherland's associational influences, definitions favorable toward law violation (here, through the absence of operant conditioning and normative validation). Of course, there are other ways besides sanction and threatened sanction by which significant others transmit definitions toward law violation (e.g., through simply teaching the acceptability and unacceptability of various behaviors).

Suppose the employee thief was also subject to a negative informal sanction meted out by nonsignificant others, such as being fired from the job. For Sutherland, this sanction would not constitute an associational definition unfavorable toward law violation, because it is not transmitted from a significant other. However, being fired would still act as an operant conditioner and a normative validator against future employee theft for the employee and others. Similarly, when the thief is given formal punishment by nonsignificant others (e.g., a day in jail), such a sanction also acts as an operant conditioner and a normative validator against committing the offense in the future for both the offender and for others. However, these formal and informal sanctions from nonsignificant others would not be considered by Sutherland as an associational definition unfavorable toward violation of law.

Written and spoken ideas from nonsignificant others, such as those found in the media, can also act as operant conditioners and normative validators, but would not constitute differential association. Suppose an individual sees Al Capone as a person to be emulated. Then, that person realizes that Capone was convicted of tax evasion and served time in Alcatraz. Capone's prison sentence would act as an operant conditioner and normative validator against being a gangster. If, on the other hand, persons who openly commit crimes are shown as going unpunished, there would be a lack of operant conditioning and normative validation.

In a modern version of learning theory, Burgess and Akers (1968) noted the importance of operant conditioning as a reinforcer during the learning of conduct norms. Akers, Krohn, Lanza-Kaduce, and Radosevich (1979) later formulated a social learning theory that incorporates differential association and operant conditioning into a sequential process. First, an individual is exposed to an excess of definitions favorable to the violation of law by others who act as role models and who provide social reinforcement for such behavior (significant others). Second, after the individual begins to commit crimes, the consequences (from nonsignificant others) of those behaviors determine the extent to which he or she will continue to commit crimes. Operant conditioning, in the forms of rewards and punishments directly experienced by the offender or vicariously experienced through observation in others, will then determine whether any future criminality will take place.

Differentiating through research the effects of these three sources of learning conduct norms is extremely difficult. At this point, differential association can only be assumed to exist in an enhancement-counteraction relationship with operant conditioning and normative validation.

Social Structural "Strain" Theories

"Strain" approaches concentrate on the financial motivations to commit crime. These theories, based on the work of Robert Merton (1968:185-214), stress that individuals often become "strained" because they cannot reach their financial goals through the legal opportunities open to them. The strain approach is particularly relevant to social systems that place a strong emphasis on financial achievement. As a result of the lack of integration between financial goals and legal means to achieve them, some persons elect to employ illegal means to reach their goals. Strain approaches account for the reasons why some people believe they need to commit crimes. According to the Marxist analysts, this social structural strain (between financial goals and the lack of legal means to achieve them) is a major force associated with capitalism to which persons "rationally respond" by committing crimes.

Strain theories do not account for the reasons why, among those whose access to legal opportunity to reach their financial goals is blocked, some choose crime to reach goals and others refrain from crime and drop their financial goals. Sutherland's ninth point of differential association succinctly illustrates this shortcoming of strain theories: "While criminal behavior is an expression of general needs and values, it is not explained by those general needs and values, since noncriminal behavior is an expression of the same needs and values" (Sutherland and Cressey, 1974:76). For Sutherland, persons who are faced with a lack of legal opportunity to gain desired wealth have two choices. They can either retain the desire and turn to crime or drop the desire and maintain their legal behavior. Strain accounts for the motivation behind the criminal behavior, but not the choice to commit it. Strain itself is not an explanation for criminal behavior because there are noncriminals who are similarly strained. There must be additional factors explaining why some similarly strained individuals choose crime and others do not.

Strain is a very strong motivation, particularly for occupational criminals. Because of the extreme importance of financial success in America and similar societies, there is constant pressure to produce wealth. Financial goals need only be relative to individuals. Making $25,000 a year is a goal for persons in the lower economic sphere, while making $100,000 is a goal for those in the middle economic sphere, and making millions of dollars is a goal for executives of large corporations. Strain, therefore, can account for the motivations of blue-collar employee thieves, middle-class embezzlers, and corporate crimes by the wealthy.

Lack of legal opportunity to reach a financial goal can be a motivation for occupational crime among individuals in organizations and among individuals by themselves. Financial success is the major criterion by which profit-seeking organizations are judged in the larger marketplace. Success is equated with profit and relative market position, and persons in the business world are in constant competition to attain these goals. Diane Vaughan (1982:1380) points out that business managers not only compete for economic ends, but also for the resources that promote achievement of economic ends (e.g., personnel recruitment, product development, land acquisition, advertising space, sales territory). Such resources, she continues,

"may be constrained by the source, nature and abundance of the resource, by the behavior of other organizations in the environment in the roles of consumers, suppliers, competitors, and controllers, by individuals in the role of consumers, and by the resources already possessed by the organization and preexisting demands on those resources." (Vaughan, 1982:1381)

Optimally, a company's managers want to shift to the highest social and economic position within the overall marketplace. If that is not possible, business managers will strive to achieve at least a higher status among the same competition. Minimally, a company manager wants to maintain the firm's existing economic and social position. Even when an economic goal is reached, it is soon replaced with a higher one, and there is no necessary limit to profit maximization. A scarcity of resources and an emphasis on constantly enhancing a competitive position can create a strain on managers of businesses. Such strain may force them into the choice of having to manipulate or secure resources illegally, or lose market position or go bankrupt.

Individuals, too, generally desire to reach the highest economic strata and the high social positions usually attached to those strata. If this is not possible either because they have already reached them or are unable to do so, then they might well attempt to attain the highest possible position within their current stratum of competition. Minimally, individuals do not want to decrease their economic and social positions. And once a goal is reached, it is often replaced with higher goals. A lack of legal economic opportunity and an emphasis on enhancing social and economic positions may cause individuals to carry out illegal acts to fulfill those desires.

Individual financial success goals go well beyond the necessities of life. While it is true that some in the lowest economic strata must resort to crime for basic necessities (e.g., food, clothing, transportation, shelter), most persons who commit occupational crime have, by virtue of their employment, sufficient resources to pay for life's necessities. However, constant pressure may be felt to go beyond the basics (e.g., gourmet food, designer clothing, expensive cars and homes, costly leisure activities). Persons are seldom satisfied with only the necessities. Such a strain can cause someone who has a modest home and a used car to desire more prestigious living quarters and transportation. Resorting to crime at the job may be seen as a viable way to purchase such amenities.

However, as noted, those who feel similar strains respond to them differently. Some managers of organizations choose for their firm to lose market position or go bankrupt rather than commit occupational crimes. Some individuals choose to be satisfied with what they have rather than to steal to acquire more.

Crime is most likely to be chosen when social processes supporting legal conduct norms are lacking and it is least likely to be chosen when social processes supporting such norms are present. Hence, the enhancement-counteraction relationship between differential association, operant conditioning, and normative validation, discussed in the previous section, may account for the difference between similarly strained criminals and noncriminals. For instance, the reason why one executive in the electrical antitrust case refused to participate in the conspiracy, even though he was pressured by his "strained" company, seems traceable simply to his learned belief that such conduct was inappropriate (Geis, 1968b: 110). In short, strain is a powerful motivator for criminal behavior, but individual attitudes about conduct rules affect whether strained individuals choose to retain their goal and pursue illegal means to achieve it or choose to drop their goal and remain noncriminal.

Neutralization of Criminality

Another major explanation for occupational crime is "neutralization" theory. This approach attempts to explain why persons who are otherwise law abiding occasionally drift into and out of criminality. Whereas differential association implies that law violators do not feel guilt for their illegal behavior (because they have been exposed to an excess of definitions favorable to crime), neutralization theory assumes many criminals do feel guilty about their illegal behavior. For such persons, neutralization of the behavior's wrongfulness is necessary in order to commit the offense and to deal with their self-image afterward.

The theory's originators, Gresham Sykes and David Matza (1957), studied juveniles who were uncommitted to criminal values. This seemed odd to Sykes and Matza, because most juvenile delinquency theories of their day (mid-1950s), including differential association, tended to assume that delinquents were committed to an antilegal value system and had little or no remorse for their group-supported actions. Sykes and Matza identified a repertoire of "techniques of neutralization" employed by delinquents to counteract the criminal definition of their behavior and ease their moral guilt.

Sykes and Matza (1957) defined five neutralization techniques: (a) denial of victim (no crime was committed); (b) denial of injury (a crime was committed but nobody was hurt); (c) denial of responsibility (it was not my fault); (d) condemnation of condemners (penalizers are hypocrites); and (e) appeals to higher loyalties (I did it because of an allegiance to some higher abstraction, like loyalty to the gang). William Minor (1981) later added two more neutralizations: necessity (I have to have the gains of the crime) and metaphor of the ledger (I am not a "real" full-time criminal, just an occasional one). The concept of neutralization has the potential to make a major contribution to the explanation of many kinds of occupational crime, because most occupational criminals are generally law abiding and not committed to a criminal self-image.

The term "neutralization" should not be confused with the term "rationalization," although the two have been used interchangeably (e.g., Coleman, 1989: 211-217; Binder, et al., 1988:168). Strictly speaking, criminal actions are neutralized by perpetrators *prior* to their commission in order to mitigate criminal perceptions of self. The concept of rationalization, on the other hand, is most commonly associated with Sigmund Freud's (1856-1939) ideas about repression. Repression is a defense mechanism by which the perceived wrongfulness of one's action, idea, or impulse is excluded or banished from consciousness *after* it occurs. Repression is a form of "motivated forgetting," but is automatic and unconscious. Rationalizations are in the form of excuses, and are manifestations of repression. In short, if the excuses described by Sykes and Matza (1957) and Minor (1981) are invoked before the offense to avoid feelings of guilt, they are neutralizations. If the excuses are used after the offense to repress feelings of guilt, then they constitute rationalizations. Of the two concepts, only neutralization is relevant to an explanation of occupational crime because it occurs prior to the offense.

Sutherland's differential association discussed the learning of specific "motives, drives, rationalizations, and attitudes" favorable toward violation of law. He was referring to the internalization of reasons which legitimize criminal behavior. Neutralization theory, on the other hand, generally holds that procriminal values have not been internalized, and that excuses are only invoked momentarily during the contemplation and commission of an occasional crime. To illustrate the difference between these two apporoaches, recall the conspirators in the electrical equipment antitrust case (Geis, 1968b). Offenders claimed that the actions were "illegal but not criminal," that they were only "recovering costs," that no one was "damaged," that they did not "know that the consumer was injured," and that the actions fell into a "grey area." These excuses are products of an internalization (through differential association) of values that promote price-fixing. They are not the products of neutralization; rather, the conspirators actually believed that price-fixing was not inappropriate. When reasons which legitimize criminal conduct are learned from significant others and become internalized values, they then reflect Sutherland's differential association. When reasons which legitimize criminal conduct are not internalized, and are only used sporadically to ease moral conflict, then they are relevant to neutralization theory.

Research has shown that techniques of neutralization are often used by occupational criminals. The neutralization process, according to Cressey, is an integral part of the psychology of embezzlement. Cressey (1953) found that embezzlers must: (a) define a financial problem that confronts them as "unsharable" (i.e., they refuse to or are unable to seek funds elsewhere); (b) realize that they have the ability and opportunity to solve the unsharable financial problem by embezzling; and (c) define embezzlement in terms which enable them to look upon it as essentially noncriminal, as justified, or as irresponsibility for which they are not completely accountable. The third criterion explicitly implies neutralization of the embezzlement, although Cressey's work appeared prior to that of Sykes and Matza. Specifically, Cressey reported that embezzlers invariably used some form of the concept of "borrowing" in defining their behavior. They could not steal the money, only "borrow" it (denials of injury/victim/responsibility). Cressey (1953) found only five of over one-hundred thirty embezzlers who did not use this neutralization. Some examples are: "Maybe it was phony reasoning, but I was going to put [the money] back"; ". . . in my way of thinking, it wasn't embezzlement because I was borrowing it"; and "I did not plan to keep the money permanently, though I never thought much about just how I was going to get it back" (Cressey, 1953:102-36).

Other researchers, too, have explicitly documented neutralizations invoked by occupational criminals. Donald Horning (1970) studied eighty-eight male employees of a large midwestern electronics assembly plant. Well over a third (38/88) did not consider the pilferage of company property as theft. One subject stated, "People have a different attitude toward the company than they do toward each other or you. . . . They wouldn't come into your home and take thirty cents, but they will take from the company. They figure it's got plenty of money and a few cents don't [sic] mean nothing to them. . . ." Another replied, "They've got plenty . . . they're not losing anything on what I take." Among those who did steal, two-thirds did not feel guilty after the thefts because of their neutralizing attitudes (Horning, 1970:48-64). In another study, by Zeitlin (1971), there were similar denials of injury and victim expressed by workers discharged for stealing: "It's not really hurting anybody—the store can afford it."

Parallel denials of injury or victim were claimed by Erwin Smigel's (1970) respondents. He investigated the attitudes of 212 Indiana residents toward stealing as related to victim size. His data indicate that most respondents disapprove of stealing, regardless of victim size. Despite this consensus of disapproval, there were important differences in its degree. More disapproval was found in regard to stealing from small business than large business or the government. In the terms of Sellin and Wolfgang (1964:156), Smigel's respondents were much less likely to condone "primary" theft victimization (victimizing discernible individuals or small groups) than either "secondary" victimization (diffusively large company) or "tertiary" victimization (includes the community at large).

Smigel's respondents overwhelmingly said they would prefer to steal from larger business (102) and from government (53) than from small business (10). The popularity of denying the existence of injury or victim can be illustrated by the following reasons given by some of the 102 respondents who preferred theft from large businesses: "business can afford it most" (69); "business is insured against theft" (13); and "business allows for theft by raising prices" (8). The 53 respondents' reasons for preferring to invoke tertiary victimization by stealing from the government are similar. Seventeen stated that "government can afford it." An appeal to higher loyalties was made by fifteen of Smigel's respondents who stated that the "government is supposed to take care of the needy" (7) and "the thief is taking back his own money" (8). Based on data from Horning, Zeitlin, and Smigel, the inference is that theft is more likely to occur when victim diffusiveness enhances abilities to neutralize.

"Condemnation of condemners" may also be used by occupational criminals when they feel a sense of injustice. For instance, employees may justify their stealing because they believe that they are underpaid or because their employer also commits crime (e.g., unsafe working conditions or consumer products, tax cheating). Two of Zeitlin's (1970:22) employee thieves, for example, condemned their employer for not paying them enough: "the store owed it to me" and "I felt I deserved to get something additional for my work since I wasn't getting paid enough." Similarly, in his study of pilferage among dock workers, Mars (1974:224) found that thieves defined their thefts as a "morally justified addition to wages" or an "entitlement due from exploiting employers." Cressey (1953:57-66), too, found some similar condemnations of employers among his embezzlers.

"Necessity" may be invoked by persons who are "strained" because they perceive pressure to acquire wealth yet have no legal means to meet that pressure. "Metaphor of the ledger" denotes that the individual admits to being a criminal, but in the total scheme of things, such criminality is said to be only fleeting and therefore does not effectively tarnish a noncriminal self-image.

In a later work, Matza (1964) asserted that delinquents consider their behavior morally wrong, but believe that extenuating circumstances render their behavior guiltless. A "sense of irresponsibility" develops around perceptions of delinquent behavior, particularly because the ideology of the juvenile court does not consider juveniles responsible for their actions. When a person's moral ties with the legal norms are loosened because of a sense of irresponsibility (denials of responsibility, injury, and victim, appeals to higher loyalties), sense of injustice (condemnation of condemners), or a sense that the behavior is acceptable (necessity, metaphor of the ledger), then the occupational criminal would be in a state of "drift" and would then be free to choose among a variety of actions, some illegal, some lawful. After illegal actions are committed, the occupational criminal would be "motivated to continue committing them because he has learned the moral [neutralizations] necessary to consider himself guiltless, and because he has learned the technical means to carry out the offenses" (Vold and Bernard, 1986:241).

Although persons may have have been exposed, through differential association, to an excess of definitions unfavorable to violation of law, they may or may not commit crimes, depending upon their abilities to invoke techniques of neutralization. Neutralization theory would then explain why law abiding individuals sometimes commit crimes. Anticriminal definitions learned from significant others (through differential association) may be mitigated by the development of a sense of irresponsibility and injustice. Further, an absence of normative validation against occupational crime from nonsignificant others may encourage development of the senses of irresponsibility and injustice. If people are not censured through formal and informal sanctions for their illegal behavior, it becomes easier for them to justify their crimes. However, if formal or informal sanctions are imposed or threatened by nonsignificant others against occupational criminals, then the latter's ability to feel senses of irresponsibility and injustice will be diminished, as will their ability to invoke many of the techniques of neutralization. They should be less able to commit crime because the criminal nature of their behavior becomes a point of emphasis.

"Control" Theories

The final approach to be discussed generally has been referred to as "control" or "containment" theory. This explanation assumes that the motivation for crime is part of human nature and that persons would naturally commit crimes if they were not otherwise restrained. Control theorists try to identify the reasons people do *not* commit crimes, and have postulated several factors that they believe refrain individuals from criminal and other "uncontrolled" behaviors. Unlike the other individual-based theories we have discussed, control theory believes "individuals . . . commit crime because of the weakness of forces restraining them from doing so, not because of the strength of forces driving them to do so" (Vold and Bernard, 1986:232).

Travis Hirschi (1969) has advanced a control theory of juvenile delinquency in which the absence of certain social "bonding" is declared to be criminogenic. Hirschi maintains that persons who are tightly bonded to social groups, particularly those in the family and school, are less likely to be involved in delinquency. He identified four kinds of anticriminogenic bonding. First, the most important element of the social bond is "attachment," which refers to caring about the interests and feelings of others. Attachment is necessary for the internalization of values. Second, "commitment" refers to the rational investment one has in conventional society. The extent of commitment is the extent to which risks of deprivation increase for committing illegal behavior, so that crime is avoided by persons with the most commitment. Third, "belief" refers to the extent to which persons are convinced that they should obey the rules of society. If persons do not believe that the rules of society are legitimate or otherwise deserve to be adhered to, then they will be more likely to break them. The fourth element, "involvement" in conventional activities (e.g., organized athletics, extracurricular activities, school homework), is based on the idea that keeping busy restricts opportunities for illegal behavior. Hirschi found strong empirical support for all of these bonding mechanisms except involvement.

In an extension of Hirschi's control theory of delinquency, Hirschi and Gottfredson (1987) have proposed a "Propensity-Event" theory that, like

Sutherland's differential association, attempts to identify processes characteristic of all criminality (see also Gottfredson and Hirschi, 1989; in press). They assert the need for "a general theory of crime capable of organizing the facts about [any] crime at the same time it is capable of organizing the facts about all forms of crime" (Hirschi and Gottfredson, 1987: 949).

This "Propensity-Event" approach discards previous emphases on the type of criminal (e.g., "white collar") and concentrates on characteristics allegedly common to all forms of crime. Hirschi and Gottfredson (1987: 959) state,

> "A concept of crime that will reveal attractive properties common to diverse acts presupposes a concept of human nature . . . . [that is] motivated by the self-interested pursuit of pleasure and the avoidance of pain . . . . To be maximally pleasurable, events should take place immediately; pleasure is therefore enhanced by the rapidity with which it is obtained . . . . To be maximally pleasurable, events should be *certain* in outcome . . . . and require *minimal effort*." (emphasis original)

This conception about the commonalities of criminal acts provides the basis for their theory. For Hirschi and Gottfredson, criminality "is the tendency of individuals to pursue short-term gratification in the most direct way with little consideration for the long-term consequences of their acts" (1987:959). Hirschi and Gottfredson (1989:360n) later refer to this tendency as "low self control" (see Gottfredson and Hirschi, in press). Indicators of such a tendency include impulsivity, aggression, and a lack of concern for the opinion of others. People who have such tendencies are "relatively unable or unwilling to delay gratification; they are relatively indifferent to punishment and to the interests of others" (Hirschi and Gottfredson, 1987:959-60). It is also assumed that such a personality pattern is present over a substantial period of time.

The tendency to pursue short-term gratification does not always lead to crime, however. All crimes require physical opportunity and can result in punishment of the offender if he or she is caught. For a crime to occur, then, the unchecked tendency for short-term gratification must be coupled with both physical opportunity to commit crime and a perception on the part of the offender that he or she is immune from at least immediate formal and informal sanctions.

Our definition of occupational crime is consistent with that used in the theory by Hirschi and Gottfredson—the offenses are treated as events that take place in an occupational setting rather than as characteristics (such as "white collar") of people employed in those settings. Hirschi and Gottfredson maintain that occupational criminals are not different from other criminals because all offenders share common characteristics. Similarly, they maintain that persons who do not commit crimes in the course of their occupation are not different from other noncriminals. Differences in criminality rates (e.g., between occupational criminals and occupational noncriminals, between some occupational criminals and other occupational criminals, and between occupational criminals and nonoccupational criminals) are explained primarily by the differential forces of control (or bonding) over self-gratification tendencies, opportunity differences, and perceptions about the immediacy of punishment.

Hirschi and Gottfredson's theory would predict lower rates of criminality among those who have greater "attachment" to the feelings of others, greater "commitment" to an investment in the social order, and greater "belief" in the legitimacy of society's rules. Regarding commitment, for instance, Hirschi and Gottfredson (1987) explicitly predict that the overall rate of occupational offending among corporate executives should be lower than that among laborers, because selection processes inherent to the high end of the occupational structure tend to recruit people with relatively low propensity to crime, such as educational persistence ("commitment") and willingness and ability to defer to the interests of others ("attachment").

An *absence* of "attachment" to the interests of others, however, can account for corporate decisions that allow the pollution of the environment, unsafe working conditions, and the marketing of unsafe products. An absence of attachment would also account for embezzlement and armed robbery. An absence of "belief" in the legitimacy of social rules can account for decisions to become involved in antitrust activities, employee theft, and burglary. Occupational offenders who have a long term "commitment" to a rational investment in society (e.g., corporate executives, physicians) will be less likely to commit crimes than those who do not have such an investment because they have more to lose if caught.

The propensity-event theory may have some unresolved conceptual inconsistencies (see Steffensmeier, 1989 and rebuttal in Hirschi and Gottfredson, 1989). The theory states that some persons, more than others, have a "tendency" to commit crime. This seems contradictory to the basic tenet of control theory, which asserts everyone is inclined to commit offenses. Moreover, as emphasized in earlier discussions, any theory that attempts to explain all criminality is probably overly optimistic. In this instance, first, the propensity-event theory fails to account for crimes which are not motivated by self-gratification, such as illegal mercy killings by physicians. Second, the theory cannot account for crimes which are not influenced by perceptions about punishment threat, such as political terrorist crime. Third, the theory may not explain why persons who are willing to commit one kind of crime (e.g., price-fixing, toxic pollution) are not likely to commit other kinds of crime (e.g., armed robbery), holding self-gratification, opportunity and perceptions about punishability constant. Based upon the theory's specifications, it may be necessary to measure accurately individuals' self-gratification levels during the time they make choices about behavior patterns, and this is not an easy task.

The propensity-event theory needs substantial refinement in terms of explicitly delineating which individuals and which behaviors are most affected by social bonding. The theory should also try to determine the points in the life cycle at which bonding is most likely to occur and the personal experiences and associations that are most likely to affect bonding. Nevertheless, Hirschi and Gottfredson have advanced a unique approach to the explanation of crime that seems to incorporate many other theories about the behavior of criminal individuals (see following discussion of Figure 3.1). The theory is relatively new, and future research will determine its longevity. Unlike most other theories in criminology, control theory can be expressed through various "if-then" statements (e.g., if there is more tendency toward self-gratification or less belief in punishability, then there will be a greater likelihood of criminality). Control theory therefore offers a considerable number of propositions that can be tested more easily than those found in other theories. As Binder, et al. (1988:189) note, "Testable propositions are indeed what genuine science is all about, and in this regard control theory clearly has moved the study of [crime] several giant steps forward."

Interrelationships Among Theories About the Behavior of Occupational Criminal Individuals

Figure 3.1 was constructed to help the reader appreciate the commonalities and differences among the various theories discussed in the second part of this chapter (differential association, operant conditioning, normative validation, strain, neutralization, and control theory). Control theory states that attachment to the feelings of others is necessary before one can internalize and believe in conventional values not to violate the law. Attachment also tends to force one to repress self-gratification tendencies. An inability or unwillingness to repress self-gratification tendencies increases propensity to commit crime.

Perceived ramifications of formal and informal sanctions act as operant conditioners (i.e., deterrents) against occupational crime. Included in these perceptions and conditioning is control theory's proposition about "commitment"—the extent to which one has a stake in conventional soci-

Figure 3.1 Interrelationships Among Theories About the Behavior of Occupational Criminal Individuals

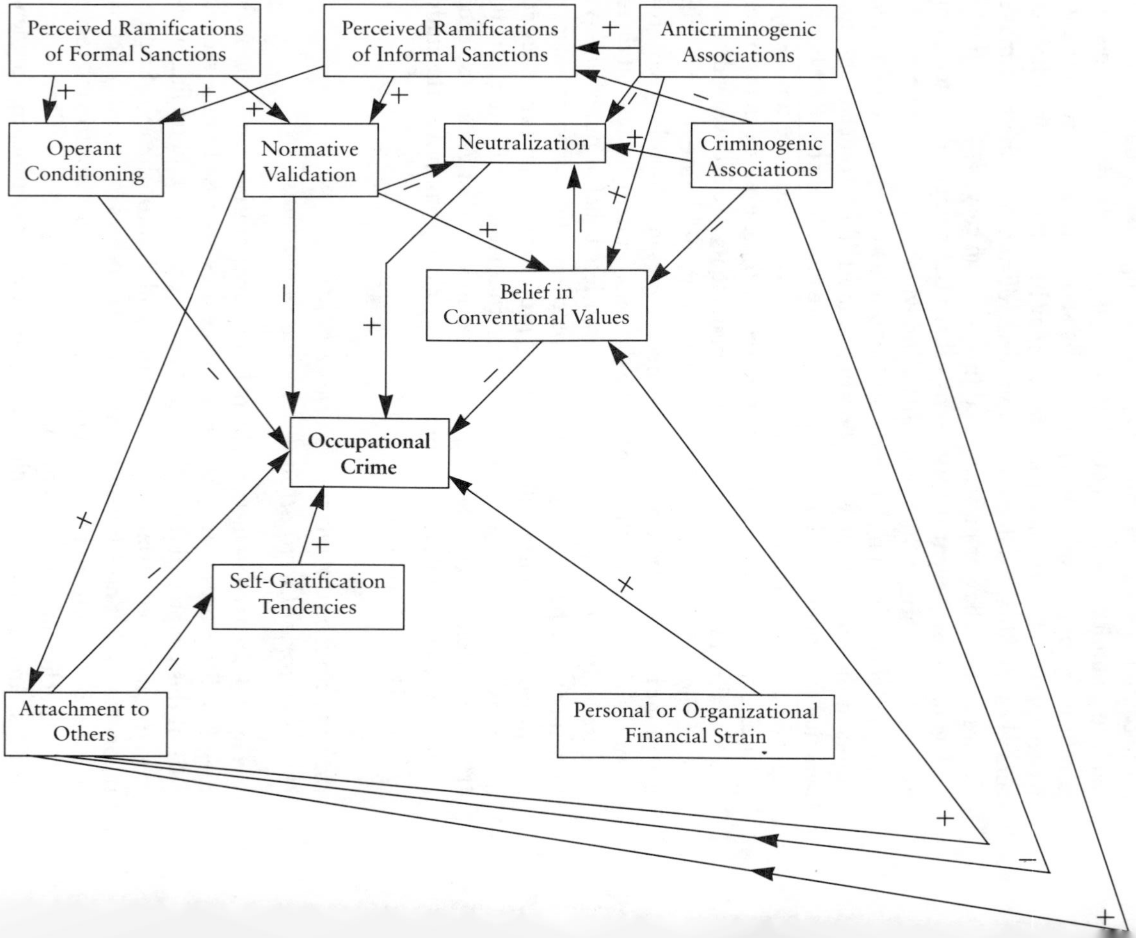

ety is the extent to which one will have more to lose if caught for occupational crime.

Perceptions about formal and informal sanctions for committing occupational crime may not only act as operant conditioners, but also may act independently as normative validators against occupational crime. Normative validation increases beliefs in conventional values by reemphasizing that occupational crime is unacceptable. Normative validation also increases attachment to the feelings of others by demonstrating the wrongfulness of victimizing others. And, normative validation helps to counter neutralizations (which increase propensity to commit crime) because it validates the wrongfulness of the behavior. Similarly, the extent to which one has a belief in conventional values is the extent to which techniques of neutralization are also less likely to be invoked, since the techniques will be seen as an attempt to negate the legitimacy of rules.

Differential association states that significant others have the most influence in moulding beliefs about conventional (i.e., law-abiding) values. A person is exposed *ab incunabulis* (since infancy) to a unique variety of significant others, which affect beliefs about the legitimacy of rules and levels of "attachment" to the feelings of others. Thus, a person brings to any given job a pre-existing set of beliefs which may or may not support certain conventional values to abide by the law and may or may not support feelings of attachment to others. Hence, it is only the extent to which post-employment associations *alter* pre-employment value systems (about belief and attachment) that post-employment associations affect propensity toward occupational crime at a given job (such associations need not be job-related). For instance, organizational associates may mitigate a person's pre-employment belief in conventional values and attachment to others, such as by causing him or her to believe that marketing unsafe consumer products is acceptable because it helps the organization make a profit. Marketing unsafe consumer products shows both an absence of belief in the legitimacy of rules (it is illegal) and a lack of attachment to the feelings of others (consumers can be maimed or killed). In short, belief in the legitimacy of rules and levels of attachment to others are increased through anticriminogenic associations with significant others before and after employment. On the other hand, belief and attachment are mitigated by criminogenic associations with significant others before and after employment. A person may or may not view post-employment associates (at the job or elsewhere) as "significant others," but the extent to which they are so regarded is the extent to which a person will be influenced by them through differential association.

Any lengthy social interaction, independent of whether it involves "significant others," is bound to have at least some effect on an individual. Anticriminogenic associations are likely to relay the message that informal sanctions will be meted out for occupational criminal behavior. The opposite is true for criminogenic associations. Anticriminogenic associations also help to negate the propensity to neutralize the wrongfulness of occupational crime, because that group is not likely to accept the validity of neutralization. On the other hand, criminogenic associations may teach specific neutralization techniques.

Last, personal or organizational financial strain may be motivations to commit occupational crime.

This is not a formal model; it was constructed only to show the various interactions among some of the approaches discussed in this chapter. Testable theoretical specifications have not been given (see Gibbs, 1985; 1987). It would be quite difficult to test this model, because many of the individual components have simultaneous effects on other components, and isolating these simultaneous effects would be extremely difficult. Moreover, all of the relationships in the model are unidirectional; there may be some additional unspecified relationships that reflect interactive directionality (see, e.g., Thornberry, 1987). For instance, normative validation may increase belief in conventional values and the greater one's belief in conventional values, the more likely that person is to be affected by normative validation. Despite its informality, the model should nevertheless add greater understanding to the unique and interdependent relationships among the various components.

The first three chapters of the book have defined occupational crime, and discussed its measurement and causes. We shall now turn to in-depth discussions of the four types of occupational crime: Organizational Occupational Crime, State Authority Occupational Crime, Professional Occupational Crime, and Individual Occupational Crime.

QUESTIONS FOR DISCUSSION

1. What are the differences between theories about the behavior of criminal law and theories about the behavior of criminal individuals? Why is it important to distinguish between the two?
2. How do the legal conflict theorists Marx, Vold, and Turk differ in their approach to the explanation of the behavior of law?
3. What part does the threat of formal punishment play in the following kinds of theories: learning, strain, neutralization, and control?
4. What is the difference between operant conditioning and normative validation? Can they be mutually exclusive? If so, give examples.
5. How might neutralization theory be applied to noncriminal deviant behavior? Give five examples and the specific neutralization technique(s) associated with them.

6. In the discussion of the Hirschi-Gottfredson control theory, mercy killing by physicians was given as an example of a crime that does not typically involve self-gratification. Find five other crimes that also lack this element (excluding strict liability offenses).
7. How did Akers and his colleagues integrate differential association and operant conditioning?
8. How did Sutherland's differential association theory influence the work of Sykes and Matza?
9. How do the theories about the behavior of criminal individuals (learning, strain, neutralization, control) vary in their recognition of individual free will?
10. To what extent do the theories of Marx, Vold, and Turk account for individual free will?
11. Sutherland's differential association and the Gottfredson-Hirschi control theory both attempt to advance a theory that will explain all crime. How do these theorists differ in their approach to this task?

Seven died aboard the Challenger when it exploded in January of 1986. The errors on the part of NASA which led to the disaster are an example of organizational wrongdoing, though no actual crime was committed. (AP/Wide World Photos)

F O U R

ORGANIZATIONAL OCCUPATIONAL CRIME

There have been many approaches to the concept of "organizational crime." Some (e.g., Schrager and Short, 1980; Gross, 1980; Ermann and Lundman, 1978; Vaughan, 1979) consider the term to refer primarily to offenses committed for the benefit of large, complex organizations. More encompassing is Albanese's (1987:7) conception, which includes planned acts of deceit for personal or group gain. For our purposes, such crime was defined in Chapter 1 as a legal violation committed to further the goals of an employing organization. The term "organization" as used here refers to anything that has been "established for the explicit purpose of achieving certain goals" (Blau and Scott, 1962:1). Thus, an organization does not necessarily have to be huge or complex for its employees to commit "organizational crime," though most of the discussion in this chapter refers to larger organizations.

Although organizational occupational crimes can further the personal goals of the perpetrator-employee indirectly through organizational reward systems (e.g., salary raises, bonuses, promotions), its benefits accrue most directly to the owners of the organization. The extent to which a person owns an organization is the extent to which his or her crime for the benefit of their organization is individual rather than organizational. The rationale for this differentiation is that if a person owns an organization, then he or she is the organization, and crimes that benefit organizational goals are crimes which directly (rather than indirectly) benefit that individual.

There are some knotty problems with this conceptualization, however. First, stockholders (who technically are owners of an organization) often do not play a role in the organization's day-to-day operations, and it is therefore difficult to conceive of them as "individual occupational criminals" when offenses are committed by others for the benefit of the organization. Second, as noted in Chapter 1, employees often own stock in their employing firm, and therefore would accrue benefits both indirectly (as employee) and directly (as owner). The best way to express the concept of "organizational occupational crime" is offenses committed by managers and employees for the direct benefit of organizational owners, *rather than themselves*.

CRIMINAL LIABILITY AND ORGANIZATIONAL CRIME

The fact that organizational crime involves both natural persons and organizations gives it a unique dimension that makes the assignment of criminal responsibility more difficult than in the other occupational crimes discussed in this book. There is considerable legal debate (Parisi, 1984) and policy debate (Fisse, 1984) about whether individuals or organizations should be held criminally responsible for crimes committed for the benefit of the organization, although either or both can be liable under certain circumstances. However, independent of whether the person who commits the crime or the organization for which he or she works is seen as the "offender" under the law, organizational crime is in all cases reducible to some human action or inaction. Parisi (1984:41) makes a similar point in reminding us of the adage that "guns don't kill people, people kill people." Weapons, like organizations, are subject to the control of human beings. Hence, Parisi continues, "If [an organization] is like a gun, then there must be someone comparable to a triggerman." From a structural perspective, however, an organization as such may be seen as a criminal actor in the sense that organizational crime is the outcome of a pattern of activities by interdependent parts, which together constitute the form of the organization.

Numerous legal statutes outlaw certain acts committed by individuals for the benefit of their employing organization, including criminal homicide, assault, and fraud. Because organizations are usually legally treated as "persons," they, along with human actors, fall within statutory language that includes phrases such as "any person," "whoever," or "anyone." Several precedents have affirmed the personage of organizations for the purposes of statutory criminal liability. One of the earliest judicial decisions to rule in this manner was *State vs. Lehigh Valley Railroad Co.* (90 N.J.L. 372, 103 A. 685, 1917). The question before the court was whether corporations can be held liable for criminal homicide, which is the "killing of one person by another." In its refusal to limit offenders to biological beings, the *Lehigh* court saw organizations as "persons" capable of committing crime. Courts also have been sensitive to the intentions of those who drafted the statutes. In *People vs. Ebasco Services, Inc.* (354 N.Y.S. 2d 807, 1974), two employees were killed after superiors had made the decisions leading to their deaths. A New York court upheld a negligent homicide charge against the corporate defendant because it believed that the legislators wanted corporations to be included as "persons" under criminal statutes (the case was dismissed on other grounds) (Parisi, 1984: 57-58; Cullen, Maakestad and Cavender, 1987:133-135).

In the 1980 Ford Pinto trial, attorneys for Ford argued that the automaking organization was not a "person" because the statute in question (Indiana Code Sec. 35-42-1-5) read "A *person* who recklessly kills *another human being* commits reckless homicide" (emphasis added). The defendant's lawyers argued that "another" means one of the same kind, and therefore "person" refers only to another human being. Although this line of reasoning may represent some interesting logic, the court rejected it outright because the Code had explicit provisions for the prosecution of corporations, and had explicitly defined "person" to include corporations and other organizations (Cullen, et al., 1987: 209-212).

In addition to violating statutes which outlaw "common" crimes such as assault and fraud, both organizations and individuals can violate regulatory administrative criminal statutes. These laws forbid organizational criminal acts such as restraints of trade, falsification of product research reports, food and drug adulteration, environmental pollution, unsafe working conditions, and unsafe consumer products. These violations result in various consequences in addition to or besides criminal indictment, including stipulations, injunctions, and cease and desist orders.

The rationale noted in Chapter 1 for including nonindictment violations under the concept of "crime" is that they involve a legal violation carrying an official punishment. As Sutherland (1945:135-36) put it: "This is evident both in that they result in some suffering on the part of the [organization or individual] . . . and also in that they are designed by legislators and administrators to produce suffering." Although there are basic differences between these sanctions and a criminal indictment in several important respects (e.g., rules of evidence and proof, assumption of innocence), Sutherland continues, such differences do "not make . . . [them] categorically different from the violations of law by other criminals."

As an example of an administrative statute, violation of federal antitrust laws carries a maximum individual penalty of three years imprisonment and a $100,000 fine and a maximum organizational penalty of divestiture and a $1 million fine. Violation of the regulations of the Packers and Stockyards Administration (Department of Agriculture) can carry punishments of five years imprisonment, a $10,000 fine, and license revocation for individuals, and the same fine and delicensure for organizations.

Most criminal statutes require that the perpetrator (individual or organization) have a *mens rea* ("guilty mind" or intent) to commit the offense. On the other hand, many administrative criminal statutes impose no requirement of intent on organizations or individuals, and are based on the notion of "strict liability." Offenders are viewed as criminally responsible, even though they may not have intended their illegal actions. For instance, a company that distributes a portion of its promotional literature that unintentionally reads "two-year warranty" when in fact the product is backed by a one-year warranty would be guilty of fraudulent advertising under a strict liability holding, even though the error was completely accidental.

Organizations are liable for crimes committed by their employees through the modern legal theories of "identification" and "imputation." These concepts consider the organization responsible for the intent and action of its employees when such intent and action is to further organizational goals (see, e.g., Parisi, 1984; Gross, 1980). "Identification" directly assumes organizational liability from employees' actions when the employees and organization are seen as one and the same. Identification is invoked particularly when the criminal employees are also the owners.

"Imputation" assumes organizational liability vicariously rather than directly—the organization is assumed to be responsible for the intent and action of its employees. Imputation is based on the common law tort doctrine of *respondeat superior*, or "let the superior respond." The *respondeat superior* doctrine originated in the seventeenth century from civil suits, and was meant to deter employers from denying financial responsibility for the actions of their employees. Modern theories based on *respondeat superior* impose both civil and criminal liabilities on organizations, and are also very much based on the idea of deterrence. *People vs. Rochester Railway and Light Co.* (195 N.Y. 102, 1909), a manslaughter case involving the negligent installation of a gas device by an employee of the defendant corporation, was one of the first criminal cases to apply the doctrine of *respondeat superior*, imputing the liability of the agent to the organization. However, unlike in *Lehigh* and in the Pinto trial, the indictment was dismissed in *Rochester* because, in the definition of homicide ("the killing of one person by another"), "another [human being]" was not considered to encompass a corporation. A similar result occurred in *Commonwealth vs. Illinois Central Railroad Co.* (132 KY. 320, 153 S.W. 459, 1913) (Parisi, 1984:57; Cullen, et al., 1987: 133-134).

One variation of the imputation theory allows the organization, and not its employees, to be held criminally liable. In the relatively few situations in which employees' collective actions constitute a crime but each person's individual actions do not, it is possible for only the organization to be held criminally responsible under the legal concept of "collective knowledge" (Parisi, 1984). To use the previous analogy, the gun is prosecuted but not the triggermen. The concept of "collective knowledge" is particularly novel, because it imputes an intent to an organization that never existed among its human actors.

Organizations and individuals that are civilly and criminally charged with statutory or other violations often plead *nolo contendre* ("I neither admit nor deny the charges"). Although this plea is essentially equivalent to a "guilty" plea in the eyes of observers, *nolo contendre* cannot be used to prove completely an admission of tort liability in civil litigations related to the violations. Fear of future civil litigation, then, is a major impetus behind entering a plea of *nolo contendre*.

Cressey (1989) noted that "accidental" organizational crimes or any other organizational crimes which do not involve human intent (e.g., some "strict liability" and *respondeat superior* offenses and all "collective knowledge" crimes) cannot be explained by any theory about the behavior of criminal individuals. He argued that such offenses arise only because of a legal doctrine, and not because of any purposeful actions on the part of those charged—the "cause" is completely independent of the individual. From a "behavior of law" perspective, on the other hand, the creation and application of the statutes and legal doctrines would be a major focus of attention in the study of organizational occupational crime, because these provisions and ideas come to define which acts and entities are criminal.

CRIMINOGENIC ORGANIZATIONAL STRUCTURES AND PROCESSES

Edward Gross has asserted that all organizations are inherently criminogenic (1979:199), but not inevitably criminal (1980:63). Their inherent criminality arises from the emphases on performance that are both internal and external to the organization. Satisfactory performance by members of an organization is important, of course, because organizations almost invariably operate in environments that are competitive in some way, particulary a financial one.

Perrow (1961:855) sees two types of goals operating within organizations. "Official" organizational goals are ". . . the general purpose of the organization as put forth in the charter, annual reports, public statements and other authoritative pronouncements." "Operative" goals, on the other hand, "designate the ends sought through the actual operating policies of the organization; they tell us what the organizations actually is trying to do regardless of what the official goals say are the aims." When organizations believe they will not be able to attain their operative goals, they often resort to illegal practices to reach them. Gross (1979:200) even believes that "given a situation of uncertainty in attaining goals . . . one can predict that the organization *will*, if it must, engage in criminal behavior to attain those goals" (emphasis added). It is the stress on operative goal attainment, then, that generates the organizational pressures to violate the law.

There are many aspects of internal organizational structures and processes which in some way or another encourage illegal behavior as a means for reaching otherwise unobtainable operative goals. The specialized structure that accompanies departmentalization in larger organizations often creates operative goals for subunits that are different from the overall profitability goals of the organization. For instance, a manufacturing organization will have an overall concern for profitability, while the subunit responsible for shipping goods may have a concern only for timely and proper transportation. To attain its subgoal, the shipping department must compete with other organizations and other units within its own organization. As Williamson (1970:143) noted, because a subunit's concern with reaching overall organizational goals may be subordinate to its concern with reaching its own goals, lower-level managers may tend to maximize their department's interests rather than those of their organization.

In addition to promoting at times an emphasis on departmental rather than organizational goals, specialized organizational structures also produce what Gordon Tullock (1965) called "authority leakage." This refers to the idea that, as organizations become larger, there is less control and authority over middle-level managers. Anthony Downs (1967:143) formalized this notion into a "Law of Diminishing Control," which states "The larger any organization becomes, the weaker is the control over its actions exercised by those at the top." Moreover, specialization isolates subunits from scrutiny by persons both within and outside the organization. Because specialization emphasizes subunit self-interest and diminishes external control and scrutiny, we can expect more crime in organizations that have more departmentalized structures.

Organizational processes also can be criminogenic, because they encourage organizational loyalty. Vaughan (1982) has considered the several ways in which loyalty is encouraged by organizational processes, especially among employees of larger organizations. First, the organization tends to recruit individuals who are similar to the ones already there; it wants only those who possess the motivations, values, and skills that are consistent with organizational goals. Second, there are formal rewards such as salary raises, bonuses, and promotions for those who most exhibit the persona of the "company individual"—one who puts the organization as the first priority. There are also informal perquisites organizational individuals can earn, such as swankier offices and automobiles, more assistants, and exclusive parking spaces. Third, long-term commitment to the organization is encouraged by retirement benefits, profit-sharing, and other forms of delayed remuneration. In fact, profit-sharing allows the employee to have a direct piece of the pie. Fourth, in some cases, many of the employee's social and recreational activities are based on organizational membership and involve interaction primarily with other members of the organization. Fifth, isolation from communities outside the organization can be further encouraged by frequent transfers and long working hours. Sixth, employee positions and knowledge may be so idiosyncratic to the organization that employees are hindered from seeking commensurate jobs elsewhere. In short, the organization creates an environment that is conducive to loyalty by fostering a "dependence . . . that is social, as well as financial" (Vaughan, 1982:1390). Moreover, one's status in the community is inexorably linked to the status and success of the organization for which he or she works. Thus,

> Organizational processes . . . create an internal moral and intellectual world in which the individual identifies with the organization and the organization's goals. The survival of one becomes linked to the survival of the other, and a normative environment evolves that, given difficulty in attaining organizational goals, encourages illegal behavior to obtain those goals. (Vaughan, 1982: 1391).

Criminogenic organizational structures and processes tend to create and transmit criminogenic attitudes. Stone (1975) described these attitudes as constituting the "culture of a corporation:"

> a desire for profits, expansion, power; a desire for security (at corporate as well as individual levels); a fear of failure (particularly in connection with shortcomings in corporate innovativeness); group loyalty and identification (particularly in connection with citizenship violations and the various failures to "come forward" with internal information); feelings of [extensive knowledge] (in connection with adequate [product] testing); organizational diffusion of responsibility (in connection with the buffering of public criticism); corporate ethnocentrism (in connection with limits in concern for the public's wants and desires). (Stone, 1975:236)

Managers and executives seem to be the major sources of ethical attitudes within organizations. For instance, about half of the sample surveyed by Brenner and Molander (1977:60) believed that there was pressure from superiors to commit unethical behavior. Specifically, superiors pressured subordinates to "support incorrect viewpoints, sign false documents, overlook superiors' wrongdoing, and do business with superiors' friends" (Clinard and Yeager, 1980:59). Similarly, after conducting confidential interviews with board chairmen and chief executive officers of major corporations, Clinard and Yeager (1980:60) conclude that the top management, particularly the chief executive officer, sets the ethical tone of his or her organization. Corporate personnel told Clinard and Yeager the following: "some corporations, like those in politics, tolerate corruption," "by example and holding a tight rein a chief executive officer . . . can set the level of ethical or unethical practices in his organization," and "[organizational crime must be] congenial to the climate of the corporation." Thus, although more departmentalized organizations are structurally more criminogenic because of a lack of top control over middle-level managers (authority leakage), in many cases the process of an organization entails top-level executives exerting pressure on middle managers to violate the law.

Indeed, the influence of executives' ethics on the attitudes of organizational employees is cogently illustrated in Geis's (1968b) study of the heavy electrical equipment price-fixing case. It will be remembered from the previous chapter that price-fixing was seen as an organizational "way of life." Similarly, an executive in the folding carton manufacturing price-fixing conspiracy that occurred during 1960-1974 (in which 50 persons and 23 firms were indicted) stated: "Meetings of competitors were a *way of life* in the folding carton industry" (emphasis added) (Clinard and Yeager, 1980:62). In another similarity with the electrical equipment case, carton executives stated that "Each [involved executive] was introduced to price-fixing practices by his superiors as he came to that point in his career when he had price-fixing responsibilities" and "[persons] just picked it up from working along with [their superior]" (Clinard and Yeager, 1980: 64-65).

A particularly compelling example of the effect of top-management ethics on employees appears in the Equity Funding case, which involved one of the most colossal frauds in history (to be discussed further in Chapter 7). An especially shocking aspect of Equity's blatant crimes was the fact that they were kept secret by 50 to 75 employees of the firm, some of whom remained silent for almost a decade. Thus, much of the organization was collusive in the offenses, including the allegedly "independent" auditors (later convicted of fraud), who concealed the firm's crimes from, among others, the Securities and Exchange Commission, the National Association of Securities Dealers, and the New York Stock Exchange. Robert Loeffler (1974:140-141), the trustee appointed by a federal court to sort out the massive amounts of phony paper in the scandal, emphasized the company's collusion and criminal socialization into secrecy in his 239-page report when he stated, "Of almost equal importance [to the lies, audacity and luck of the ringleaders] was the surprising ability of the originators of the fraud to recruit new participants over the years. Closely related was the moral blindness of those participants, including several who helped execute the scheme and then left the Company, but remained silent."

The various price-fixing conspiracies indicate that criminogenic attitudes may permeate several organizations within a given industry. Using aggregated counts of organizational violations, both Sutherland (1949; 1983) and Clinard and Yeager (1980) found many industries in which certain crimes were repeatedly committed by certain organizations (these works will be discussed in detail shortly). Industry-wide propensity to violate the law is an indication of Sutherland's concept of differential social organization (see Chapter 3). One telling instance of the diffusion of illegal practices within an industry can be found in statements before a U.S. Senate subcommittee investigating illegal foreign payoffs in the aircraft manufacturing industry. According to one member of that subcommittee, Northrop Corporation "learned how to do it from Lockheed" (Clinard and Yeager, 1980:61).

Lane (1953), however, found that certain labor violations in the shoe industry were more concentrated in certain locales, even though all organizations in the industry were subject to the same laws. He concludes that differences in local attitudes toward law and morality most likely explain regional variations in offending rates. Shoe executives in areas with higher violation rates probably "lunched" with each other and were isolated from executives in areas with lower violation rates, and vice versa. The point is that differential social organization may be localized in an industry as well as universal.

Yet, the fact that organizational structures and processes, and the attitudes that they produce, are criminogenic does not necessarily mean that crime is inevitable within a particular organization or industry. First, normative structures that discourage legal violations may be generated by immediate work groups, occupational associations, individual organizations, or entire industries. Second, individual employees will weigh the personal benefits and detriments of committing crime on behalf of their organization. It is possible that, after rational consideration, the route to goal attainment may be directed away from illegal alternatives. Third, individuals may be morally opposed to the commission of violations of the law under any circumstances. Fourth, pressures to commit violations are not constant because they vary over time for each organization and each subunit within an organization. Fifth, because organizations function within interorganizational settings, organizational crime may be reduced by the multiple organizations which can contribute to its control (e.g., regulatory agencies, other organizations within the same industry, consumer and labor advocate groups). Hence, individuals' choices and the contextual variations in which those choices occur affect the extent to which organizational structures and processes will be criminogenic.

THE PREVALENCE OF ORGANIZATIONAL CRIME

There have been several attempts to compile statistics on the number of organizational violations. Unfortunately, there have been no studies which include regulatory violations against all firms, so that no statements can be made about the overall rates of organizational crimes and criminals in the general population. The counts that are available tabulate the number of regulatory violations against firms in a predefined group. Three such studies will be discussed—Sutherland (1949; 1983); Clinard and Yeager (1980); and Ross (1980). Before we approach these studies in detail, it should be remembered that agency-generated information includes only those violations which authorities have uncovered and recorded. Agency records would not include the large numbers of violations not known to authorities, nor those known yet not censured. Criminal violations by organizations and their employees may also be obscured because civil rather than criminal actions were sought by administrative agencies. Moreover, as the discussion in Chapter 2 emphasized, administrative agency violations, which constitute the bulk of organizational crime counts, probably reflect selective enforcement policies more than they reflect the occurrence of violations.

Edwin Sutherland

In researching his book *White Collar Crime*, Sutherland compiled the frequencies and types of certain crimes committed by seventy of the larger American corporations (and their subsidiaries) of his day. He excluded public utilities, transportation and communication companies, financial institutions, and petroleum companies. Sutherland tabulated all officially recorded violations against those organizations he researched from their beginning through the time of his writing. Organizational ages ranged from 18 to 150 years; the average was 45 years.

Sutherland was keenly aware of the shortcomings in his method. He knew that organizations with more violations should not necessarily be viewed as more criminal. He also knew that organizations with more of a given type of violation are not necessarily more likely to commit that type of violation than another kind. At various points throughout the book (e.g., 1949:18-19, 257-66), Sutherland emphasized the following problems. First, there may have been violations about which he was unaware. Second, opportunities to commit crime vary with organizational size and age. Third, single adverse decisions sometimes involved large numbers of separate violations. And fourth, the kinds of violations committed by organizations are closely related to their location in the economic system. System location affects both direct opportunity to commit crime and profit motivations to commit certain types of crime. For example, organizations in labor-intensive industries have more opportunity to commit violations of labor laws and derive proportionately more profit from them than they would other offenses. Similarly, retail industries have more opportunity to violate truth-in-advertising laws and have greater potential to derive profit from that type of violation than organizations in other, nonadvertising industries.

In the original version of *White Collar Crime*, the names of the organizations were deleted allegedly because, as Sutherland (1949:xiii) noted in the Preface, "First, the identity of criminals is frequently concealed in scientific writings about living offenders. Second, . . . [a] theory of criminal behavior . . . can be better attained without directing attention in an invidious manner to the behavior of particular corporations." However, Donald Cressey, a graduate student of Sutherland's who worked on the later phases of the research for *White Collar Crime*, had a different story behind the anonymity of the material. According to an interview with Cressey more than three decades after *White Collar Crime* first appeared, Sutherland and his publisher were sensitive to libel suits because "in those days, at least, people could sue you if you called them criminals and then could not prove your allegation. . . . There was no pressure from the corporations themselves [to delete names]. It was all from the publisher's lawyers" (Laub, 1983:137-38). Sutherland was probably correct when he noted that knowledge of the identitites of the seventy criminal organizations was not instrinsically important. Nevertheless, thirty-four years after its original distribution, Sutherland's (1983) work reappeared in an expanded "uncut" version that finally included the identities of the seventy corporations he had studied.

Fourteen firms had at least twenty violations: Swift & Co. (50); Armour & Co. (50); General Motors (40); Montgomery Ward (39); Sears Roebuck (39); Loew's (31); Ford (28); U.S. Steel (26); American Tobacco (25); General Electric (25); Paramount (25); Warner Brothers (25); Gimbel (25); and American Sugar Refining (25) (Sutherland, 1983:16-18). These violations involved restraints of trade; misrepresentations in advertising; patent, trademark, and copyright infringements; unfair labor practices; illegal rebates and other types of violations. Indeed, almost all the companies reviewed were "recidivists" and many were serious repeaters— only two organizations (Pittsburgh Coal and Reynolds Tobacco) had only one official censure found by Sutherland during their existence. The average number of violations was fourteen.

Sutherland (1983:64-65) found 307 restraint of trade violations (including 47 private suits) among sixty (86 percent) of the seventy companies, with a range from 1 to 22. The average was 5.1 per offending organization, and almost three-fourths of these violators (73 percent) committed more than one offense. The motion picture industry was the most visible, ranking first through third (Loew's—22; Paramount—21; Warner Brothers—21). American Tobacco had 19 adverse decisions, followed by General Electric (13), Armour (12), Swift (12), International Harvester (11), Westinghouse (10), and U.S. Steel (9). Sutherland (1983:73; 1949:61) concludes, ". . . practically all large corporations engage in illegal restraint of trade, and . . . from half to three-fourths of them engage in such practices so continuously that they may properly be called 'habitual criminals'."

"Rebating" is a special kind of restraint of trade. It is a form of discriminatory pricing which involves charging some customers less than others. Organizations securing rebates, of course, can compete in the marketplace with an unfair advantage. Rebating was especially practiced by petroleum companies, railroads, and meatpackers. Sutherland only studied rebating violations of the Interstate Commerce Act committed by railroads, although illegal rebates can also be exchanged between nontransportation organizations. Sutherland (1949:92; 1983:96) found fifty-nine decisions against twenty-six of the seventy companies—twenty-eight resulted in fines, twenty-five involved desist orders, one involved damages, and five had no known disposition. American Sugar Refining had ten adverse rebating decisions, and was probably responsible for approximately half of all the fines assessed for rebating during the period 1905-07 (Sutherland, 1949:91 and 1983:16). Although Bethlehem Steel was convicted and fined only twice during 1910, one decision was based on ninety-seven counts and the other was based on sixty-three counts (Sutherland, 1983:95). Sutherland (1949:94; 1983:98) notes, however, that the fact that almost two-thirds (63 percent) of the seventy companies (mostly mercantile firms and light manufacturers) do not have any recorded adverse railroad rebating decisions does not mean that they would not rebate if they could; rather, their noninvolvement in this offense is probably explained by the fact that shipping cost is a relatively trivial part of their total production expenses.

Regarding infringements of patents, trademarks, and copyrights, Sutherland (1949:97-98; 1983:100) documented 132 violations among forty-four (63 percent) of the seventy companies, or an average of exactly three per violator. General Motors had considerably more infringements than other organizations with 22; followed by General Electric (8) and Ford (7) (Sutherland, 1983:100). Patent infringements were especially common in the mercantile industry. Seven of the eight retail organizations included among the seventy companies had at least one patent infringement decision, stipulation or consent decree (Sutherland, 1949:100; 1983:104). There was a total of 72 such violations in the mercantile industry, ranging from 2 to 19, and averaging more than ten per violator. In one series of infringements studied by Sutherland, the Maiden Form Brassiere Company and the Snug-Fit Foundations Company litigated for many years regarding their patented designs. In another series, the Good Humor Corporation engaged in patent litigation for more than a decade with the Popsicle Company and other ice cream manufacturers (Sutherland, 1949:109). Trademark infringements were less numerous, involving only seven of the seventy companies in ten decisions (Sutherland, 1949:101; 1983:105). Copyright infringements were even more infrequent, involving only five of the seventy companies in eight decisions (Sutherland, 1949:101-2; 1983:107). Of these five, Sutherland (1983:107) claims that only one of the offending organizations (Loew's) appears to have been deliberate in its plagiarism when it used copyrighted novels as bases for motion pictures.

Misrepresentations in advertising resulted in a total of eighty-five decisions against twenty-six of the seventy companies for violation of the Federal Trade Commission Act (Sutherland, 1949:113; 1983:124). This translates into an organizational offender rate of 37 percent for FTC advertising violations and an average of 3.3 decisons per violator. However, if the twenty-seven "nonadvertising" organizations are excluded, this offender rate jumps to 60 percent. As one might expect, leaders in the mercantile industry were well represented among FTC advertising violators— Sears Roebuck, Montgomery Ward, and Gimbel led the list with eighteen, twelve, and eleven adverse decisions, respectively. Other advertising violations included misrepresentation under the Pure Food Laws, which involved four organizations in eleven decisions: Armour (5); Great A & P (3); Corn Products (2); and Swift (1). For instance, Armour was fined in New York State in 1938 for selling butter with the label "Made in USA," when the butter in fact was imported from Siberia (Sutherland, 1983:125). Among the articles found in the ordinary middle class home, the following had been advertised falsely by 1949, according to decisions of the Federal Trade Commission: Quaker Oats, Wheaties, Cream of Wheat, Fleischmann's Yeast, Knox Gelatine, Carnation Milk, Morton Salt, Welch's Grape Juice, Ivory Soap, Scott's Tissue toilet paper, Schick Dry Shaver, Bayers' Aspirin, Phillips Milk of Magnesia, Absorbine Jr., Murine Eye Wash, Elizabeth Arden Cosmetics, Hart Schaffner & Marx men's suits, Life Savers candy, Wurlitzer pianos, radios (Philco, Zenith, Magnavox), Hoover Sweepers, Encyclopedia Britannica, Buick automobiles, Goodyear tires, and Quaker State motor oil (Sutherland, 1949:116; 1983:125-126).

Sutherland (1949:132-3; 1983:138) also documented a total of 149 decisions against forty-three of the seventy firms by the National Labor Relations Board for unfair labor practices. More than half (58 percent), however, were not referred to court. The automobile manufacturing industry led the list—General Motors had fifteen decisions against it, and Ford had nine (Sutherland, 1983:138). NLRB violations by these two companies, then, constituted about one in six of all such violations in the sample. Regarding the types of labor violations, complaints involving interference, coercion, and restraint were each levied against thirty-nine organizations. Thirty-four firms were charged with forming illegal company unions, thirty-three were charged with discrimination, and twenty-five organizations were charged with refusal to bargain collectively (Sutherland, 1949:136; 1983:140).

As noted, inferences about organizational criminality from Sutherland's statistical analysis have limitations. Moreover, Cressey (1989) pointed out that Sutherland's biggest theoretical problem was that there was a strong tendency in *White Collar Crime* to anthropomorphize organizations into criminal actors, rather than treating the organizations' employees as the criminals. Although Sutherland defined "white collar crime" in terms of illegal actions committed by respectable persons in the course of their occupation, he actually studied the crime rates of corporations, not live persons. He frequently treated corporations as persons without specifying how those organizations could take on human capabilities (e.g., 1949:241). Similarly, Sutherland casually assumed that an organization can commit crime without acting through its employees (e.g, 1949:262, 264). Despite the flaws in *White Collar Crime*, however, Sutherland still succeeded convincingly in his main task—to "reform the theory of criminal behavior" (1949:v) through demonstrating that crime is abundant in the upper strata of society.

In the tradition of Sutherland's analysis, we shall now turn to more recent efforts to document the overall prevalence of organizational crime through the use of agency-based information.

Marshall Clinard and Peter Yeager

Marshall Clinard and Peter Yeager and their colleagues (Clinard, Yeager, Brissette, Petrashek, and Harris, 1979; Clinard and Yeager, 1980), in a project funded by the U.S. Department of Justice, studied federal administrative, civil, and criminal actions either initiated or completed during 1975 and 1976 by twenty-five federal agencies against 582 of America's largest corporations. Most of their analysis concerned the 477 largest manufacturing firms; the remainder included 105 of the largest wholesale, retail, and service corporations. Banking, insurance, transportation, communication, and utilities organizations were excluded because, as Clinard and Yeager (1980:111) state, "These types of businesses are subject to special regulations and/or licensing because of the particular nature of their enterprises."

The researchers were aware, as was Sutherland, of the limitations of agency-based information sources—"official actions taken against corporations are probably only the tip of the iceberg of total violations" (Clinard and Yeager, 1980:111). They also note (pp. 115-16), as did Sutherland, that an organization's location in the economic system will affect the kinds of crime it is both eligible and motivated to commit. However, unlike Sutherland, the Clinard and Yeager research employed cross-sectional information for the same two-year period (rather than including the varying life-spans of the organizations), so that it holds constant the time available in which to commit offenses. It also attempted to keep organizational size constant by differentiating companies according to their annual sales (small—$300-$499 million; medium—$500-$999 million; large—$1 billion or more).

As many as three-fifths of both groups of corporations studied by Clinard and Yeager had violations charged against them during the two-year period. This indicates that organizational occupational crime commonly occurs. It is probably even more common than this because the two-fifths which had no recorded violations may have been adroit at avoiding detection and citation or were not monitored adequately by the regulatory agencies. Of the three-fifths of the manufacturing corporations which had at least one violation during the time period, 200 of them (42 percent of the total and 66 percent of the violators) had more than one violation. Moreover, a small percentage was responsible for a highly disproportionate share of all infractions. Of the 300 manufacturing corporations that had at least one violation, thirty-eight (13 percent) accounted for over half (52 percent) of all violations attributable to the 300; these chronic offenders averaged 23.5 violations each during the two-year period. In terms of size, small corporations accounted for only a tenth of all violations, medium-sized firms for a fifth, but large corporations accounted for almost three-fourths of them (nearly twice their proportionate percentage).

Clinard and Yeager (1980) divided violations into six categories: administrative (noncomplaince with agency requirements or court orders), environmental (pollution), financial (e.g., illegal payments, overcharging customers, false financial reports, tax violations), labor (discrimination in employment, unsafe working conditions, unfair labor practices, and wage and hour violations), manufacturing (distribution of unsafe consumer products or failure to recall them, misrepresentations in labeling) and unfair trade (e.g., price-fixing, bid-rigging, illegal mergers, false advertising). About 22 percent of the corporations involved in environmental violations committed 60 percent of all such infractions; one in five manufacturing violators accounted for two in three such violations; a fifth of administrative violators were responsible for two-fifths of those violations; and 18 percent of the labor law violators were responsible for 26 percent of labor violations. Thus, although some of the violators may have committed relatively trivial infractions, it is clear that many firms are much more criminal than others and tend to commit the same kinds of violations repeatedly.

It has already been noted that a certain industry may be characterized by differential social organization when many organizations within it are likely to commit violations. Sutherland (1949; 1983) found this to be true in the motion picture, mercantile, and railroad industries, for instance. Clinard and Yeager have also found that certain kinds of violations were concentrated in certain industries. In particular, the oil, pharmaceutical, and motor vehicle industries were the most likely to violate the law.

The oil refining industry was charged in one in every five legal cases during the two-year period. That industry was also responsible for almost three-fifths of all serious and moderately serious financial violations, almost half of all environmental violations, almost one in six moderate and serious trade violations, and one in seven administrative violations. In the oil refining industry, twenty-two (of twenty-eight) companies violated the law at least once; only two of these violations were not rated as serious or moderate. Oil refining firms had 3.2 times their proportionate share of all violations.

The motor vehicle industry (which includes automobile manufacturers, parts manufacturers, and non-auto motor vehicle manufacturers) was responsible for one in six total violations, and a fifth of all serious and moderately serious violations. That industry was involved with a third of the manufacturing violations, a ninth of serious and moderately serious labor violations, and one in eight trade infractions. All but one of the nineteen firms in this industry had at least one violation, all but two had at least one serious or moderately serious infraction, and four firms accounted for at least twenty-one violations each. All told, the motor vehicle industry had about four times its proportionate share of violations generally, and five times its share of serious and moderately serious infractions.

The pharmaceutical manufacturing industry accounted for a tenth of all violations, or 2.5 times its proportionate share. It was responsible for an eighth of the serious and moderate violations, or 3.2 times its share. All seventeen pharmaceutical companies violated the law at least once during the two-year period, and fifteen (88 percent) committed at least one serious or moderate infraction. Two of the drug firms had more than twenty violations.

Based on the foregoing figures, these industries would also have had greater involvement in the various kinds of violations than would be expected by their size. The petroleum refining industry accounted for almost ten times its share of serious and moderate financial violations and more than five times its share of serious and moderate environmental infractions. The motor vehicle industry was responsible for 7.7 times its share of the total of serious and moderate manufacturing violations, and 3.8 times its share of administrative violations. And the pharmaceutical industry was responsible for 5.8 times its share of serious and moderate manufacturing violations.

Clinard et al. (1979: Chapter 8; Clinard and Yeager, 1980: Chapter 5) employed their tabulations in an attempt to predict organizational violation. First, they tried to ascertain whether violation rates were inversely affected by organizational financial perfomance (i.e., as financial performance decreases violations increase and vice versa), as strain theory would predict. Second, they constructed several variables associated with each organization's financial structure to determine how these might affect individual violation rates: size, growth rate, diversification, market power, and resource concentration (labor or capital). Both financial performance and economic structure variables were establshed based on the five-year period between 1971-1975.

Financial performance was measured by three factors. "Profitability" was defined as net income divided by total assets, which reflects the proportionate return on what the organization owns. "Efficiency" was defined as total sales divided by total assets, which reflects the sales generating ability of the assets. And "liquidity" was defined as working capital (the difference between current assets and current liabilities) divided by total assets, which reflects how easily an organization can raise money if needed. Each of these factors was determined for each violating organization for the five-year period. In regard to both overall violation counts and specific environmental, labor, and manufacturing violations, financial performance was, as expected, inversely related to illegal behavior (except in a few cases). However, although firms in depressed industries and poorly performing firms in all industries tended to have more violations, there was only a moderate relationship between financial performance and organizational violation generally. Unexpectedly, Clinard and Yeager found that in the case of environmental violations, firms that were relatively more prosporous tended more often to pollute illegally. Although it was not investigated by the researchers, they nevertheless note that in some cases violations affect financial performance (i.e., more violations cause more expenses) rather than vice versa (see Asch and Seneca, 1976; Clinard, et al., 1979:151).

Regarding the economic structure of the firms, one of the more interesting findings by Clinard and Yeager was that, after controlling for relative size (i.e., number of violations per $100 million in sales), larger corporations in general commit no more violations per unit size than do smaller corporations. In some cases, larger corporations had more infractions generally, but smaller corporations had more violations per unit size. Thus, policing ten large organizations may yield greater numbers of violations than policing ten small ones, but it will not necessarily yield greater proportions of violations according to market share. Firms with lower growth rates were more likely to commit violations generally, as well as more environmental and labor violations. However, firms with higher growth rates tended to commit more manufacturing violations.

Clinard, et al. (1979:153-54) also hypothesized that more diversified firms will violate more often. Diversified organizations would seem to have more opportunity to violate because they are exposed to greater numbers of regulations. They are also more departmentalized, which, as noted, often causes authority leakage, lack of scrutiny, and intrafirm subunit pressures. Clinard and Yeager discovered that violating firms as a group tend to be more diversified than nonviolating firms. Additionally, more diversified firms seem more likely to violate labor and manufacturing laws than those less diversified.

The research of Clinard, et al. also found that firms with more market power had slightly fewer violations per unit size than less dominant firms, which suggests that market power may diminish pressures to violate the law. Last, Clinard, et al. tested whether labor-intensive firms are more likely to violate labor laws, because those firms derive the greatest proportionate benefit from those kinds of violations. Standardizing for labor-intensiveness (total assets divided by number of employees), they found that firms and industries with greater labor concentration tend to have more official censures for labor violations.

Despite the various relationships found by Clinard, et al., however, none of their variables convincingly predicted corporate violation:

"compared to nonviolating corporations, the violating firms are on average larger, less financially successful, experience relatively poorer growth rates and are more diversified. . . . [However], knowledge of a firm's growth, diversification, and market power added virtually no predictive power when combined with size and financial measures, which were themselves not strong predictors of corporate involvement in criminal activity" (Clinard and Yeager, 1980:132).

Irwin Ross's "Roster"

It is important to have an idea about the kinds of offenses organizational executives actually commit, even if they are difficult to predict. Irwin Ross (1980), writing for *Fortune* magazine, compiled vignettes of the major successful federal cases during the 1970s against large corporations. His research staff canvassed the 1,043 companies that appeared at some point during that period on the magazine's lists of the 800 largest industrial and nonindustrial corporations. Included were five kinds of offenses, all of which were committed for the benefit of the organization rather than for personal profit: bribetaking or bribegiving by high-level corporate officials (including kickbacks and illegal rebates), criminal fraud, illegal campaign contributions, tax evasion, and criminal antitrust violations. Crimes against the person (unsafe consumer products and working conditions, pollution) were excluded. Eleven percent (117) of the companies were offenders.

Table 4.1 presents Ross's results. All of the cases resulted in either conviction on criminal charges or consent decrees (or similar administrative settlements), in which the individuals neither confirm nor deny past offenses (*nolo contendre*) and agree not to commit them in the future. Fifty executives from fifteen companies went to jail in various cases. Fines were levied against most of the convicted companies, but are not listed in Table 4.1 unless they came to $500,000 or more. In Table 4.1, the dates refer to the year that the indictments or complaints were filed.

ORGANIZATIONAL CRIMES AGAINST CONSUMERS

Misrepresentations in Advertising

Consumers are constantly bombarded with highly competitive advertising. There are usually several brands of a particular product to choose from, and manufacturers must convince consumers both that there is a need for their product and that their product does the best job for the price. False advertising involves claims which are simply not true (e.g., about the presence of an ingredient or the effectiveness of a product). Misleading ad-

Table 4.1 A Roster of Wrongdoing

Company	Offense
Allied Chemical	1974—Fixing prices of dyes. Pleaded nolo contendere. 1979—Tax fraud related to paying kickbacks. Nolo plea on some charges.
Amerada Hess	1976—Fixing prices of gasoline. Convicted after trial. Executive acquitted. Conviction being appealed.
American Airlines	1973—Illegal campaign contributions of $55,000. Guilty plea. 1975—CAB charges related to slush fund used for contributions. Settlement. 1977—SEC charges related to same. Consent decree.
American Bakeries	1972—Fixing prices of bread. Nolo plea.
Amer. Beef Packers	1975—Company and president charged with defrauding a creditor. Both found guilty on some counts. 1976—SEC charges related to same matter. Injunction against president.
American Brands	1978—James B. Beam subsidiary and two executives charged with bribery of state liquor official. All pleaded guilty.
American Can	1976—Company and executive charged with fixing prices of folding cartons. Nolo pleas by both.
American Cyanamid	1974—Fixing prices of dyes. Nolo plea.
American Export Ind.	1979—American Export Lines subsidiary[1] charged with fixing prices of ocean shipping. Nolo plea.
Anheuser-Busch	1977—SEC charges concerning $2.7 million in payments to customers. Consent decree. 1978—Treasury Dept. charges about same matter. Settlement and $750,000 fine.
Archer-Daniels-Midland	1976—Defrauding grain buyers by short-weighting. Nolo plea.
Arden-Mayfair	1971—Company and executive charged with fixing prices of dairy products. Nolo pleas. 1977—SEC charges related to $4.4 million in rebates and off-book accounts. Consent decree. 1978—Price fixing of dairy products. Nolo plea.
Armco	1973–77—Three cases of fixing prices of steel reinforcing bars. Nolo pleas by company and three executives.
Ashland Oil	1973—Illegal political contribution of $100,000. Guilty plea. 1975—SEC charges about allegedly illegal payments. Consent decree. 1977—Fixing prices of resins used to make paint. Nolo plea. 1980—Ashland—Warren subsidiary pleaded guilty in three cases involving bid rigging in highway construction. Fined a total of $1.5 million.
Associated Milk Prod.	1974—Illegal political contributions. Guilty plea.
Beatrice Foods	1974—Fixing prices of toilet seats. Company and president of Beneke division pleaded nolo. 1978—SEC charges about improper accounting for $11.7 million in rebates. Consent decree.

Table 4.1 (Continued)

Company	Offense
Bethlehem Steel	1973–74—Two cases of fixing prices of steel reinforcing bars. Company and one employee pleaded nolo; another convicted after trial. 1980—Mail fraud related to bribes paid for ship-repair business. Guilty plea.
Boise Cascade	1978—Fixing prices of corrugated containers. Nolo pleas by company and two plant managers.
Borden	1974 & 1977—Two cases of fixing prices of dairy products. Company and three executives pleaded nolo.
Borg-Warner	1971—Fixing prices of plastic pipe fittings. Nolo plea.
Braniff International	1973—Illegal political contribution of $40,000. Guilty pleas by company and chairman. 1975—CAB allegations about contribution. Settlement. 1976—SEC charges related to $900,000 slush fund and contributions. Consent decree. 1977—Criminal restraint of trade. Nolo plea.
CPC International	1977—Fixing prices of industrial sugar. Nolo plea.
Carnation	1971—Fixing prices of dairy products. Company and executive pleaded nolo. 1973—Illegal political contributions of $9,000. Company and chairman pleaded guilty. 1974—Fixing prices of dairy products. Nolo pleas by company and general manager.
Carter Hawley Hale	1974—Bergdorf Goodman subsidiary charged with fixing prices of women's clothing. Company and executive pleaded nolo.
Ceco	1973–77—Three cases involving fixing prices of steel reinforcing bars. Company and one executive pleaded nolo; another executive convicted after trial.
Celanese	1971—Fixing prices of plastic pipe fittings. Company pleaded nolo; executive acquitted.
Cenco	1976—SEC charge related to falsifying inventory. Seven of eight former executives signed consent decrees. 1979—Seven executives indicted on criminal charges of mail fraud related to the same scheme. Three pleaded guilty, three convicted after trial, and one acquitted of fraud charges. Convictions are being appealed.
Champion Intl.	1974—Bid rigging in purchase of timber from public lands. Company found guilty after trial. Executive acquitted. 1976—Fixing prices of folding cartons. Nolo plea.
Chemical New York	1977—Chemical Bank charged with violations of Bank Secrecy Act in scheme by two branch officials to launder money for alleged narcotics dealer. Officials pleaded guilty to tax charges and company to reduced charges.
Chicago Milwaukee	1976—SEC allegations of improper use of assets and political contributions. Consent decree.

Table 4.1 (Continued)

Company	Offense
Combustion Engin.	1973—Fixing prices of chromite sand. Company and executive pleaded nolo.
Consolidated Foods	1974—Fixing prices of refined sugar. Nolo plea.
Continental Group	1976—Fixing prices of paper bags. Company and one executive convicted after trial; two others acquitted. Company fined $750,000.
Cook Industries	1976—Defrauding grain customers by short-weighting. Company pleaded nolo and five executives pleaded guilty.
Dean Foods	1977—Price fixing of dairy products. Nolo pleas by company and executive.
Diamond International	1974—Illegal campaign contributions of $6,000. Company and executive pleaded guilty. 1974—Fixing prices of paper labels. Nolo pleas by company and two executives. 1976—Fixing prices of folding cartons. Company and seven executives pleaded nolo.
Diversified Industries	1976—SEC charges related to alleged short-weighting of customers in metal-recovery processes. Consent decree.
DuPont	1974—Fixing prices of dyes. Nolo plea.
Equity Funding	1973—SEC charges relating to $2 billion in fictitious insurance policies. Consent decree. 1973—Former chairman and 21 other former executives charged with fraud. All pleaded guilty to some counts.
FMC	1976—Fixing prices of persulfates. Company and executive pleaded nolo.
Federal Paper Board	1976—Fixing prices of folding cartons. Company and two exeuctives pleaded nolo.
Federated Dept. Stores	1976—I. Magnin subsidiary charged with fixing prices of women's clothing. Nolo plea.
Fibreboard[2]	1976—Fixing prices of folding cartons. Company and executive pleaded nolo.
Firestone	1976—SEC charges about slush fund and allegedly illegal political contributions of $330,000. Consent decree. 1979—False tax-return charges related to $13 million in set-aside income. Guilty plea on some counts.
Flavorland Industries	1979—Fixing prices of meat. Nolo plea.
Flintkote	1973—Fixing prices of gypsum board. Company, chairman, and president pleaded nolo.
Franklin New York	1974—SEC charges against nine executives relating to the bankruptcy of Franklin National Bank. Company and eight executives signed consent decree. 1975—Eight former executives and employees of bank charged with fraud. All pleaded guilty. 1978—Three other former executives charged with fraud. All convicted after trial.

Table 4.1 (Continued)

Company	Offense
Fruehauf	1975—Company, chairman, and vice president charged with criminal tax evasion. All convicted after trial.
GAF	1974—Fixing prices of dyes. Nolo plea.
GTE	1977—SEC charges relating to political contributions and payments to local officials. Consent decree.
General Dynamics	1977—SEC allegations of improper accounting to disguise political contributions. Consent decree.
General Host	1972—Fixing prices of bread. Nolo plea.
General Tire & Rubber	1976—SEC charges concerning slush fund and allegedly illegal political contributions. Consent decree.
Genesco	1974—Fixing prices of women's clothing. Nolo plea.
Gimbel Bros.[3]	1974 & 1976—Saks & Co. subsidiary charged with two cases of fixing prices of women's clothing. Company and executive pleaded nolo.
B. F. Goodrich	1978—Tax evasion related to slush fund used for illegal political contributions. Nolo plea by company; charges against an executive dropped.
Goodyear	1973—Illegal political contribution of $40,000. Company and chairman pleaded guilty. 1977—SEC charges concerning slush fund of $500,000 for contributions. Consent decree.
Great Western United[4]	1974—Great Western Sugar subsidiary charged with fixing prices of refined sugar. Nolo plea.
Greyhound	1974—Illegal campaign contributions of $16,000. Guilty plea.
Gulf Oil	1973—Illegal political contributions of $100,000. Company and executive pleaded guilty. 1975—SEC charges about $10-million slush fund used for political contributions. Consent decree. 1977—Company and two employees charged with giving illegal gifts to an IRS agent. Company pleaded guilty, one employee pleaded nolo, the other convicted after trial. 1978—Fixing prices of uranium. Pleaded guilty.
Gulf & Western	1976—Brown Co. subsidiary charged with fixing prices of folding cartons. Company and two executives pleaded nolo.
Hammermill Paper	1978—Palmer Paper Co. unit charged with fixing prices of paper products. Company and executive pleaded nolo.
Heublein	1978—Bribery of state liquor official. Guilty plea.
Hoerner Waldorf[5]	1976—Fixing prices of folding cartons. Company and four executives pleaded nolo. 1978—Fixing prices of corrugated containers. Nolo plea.
ITT	1972—ITT Continental Baking subsidiary charged with fixing prices of bread. Nolo plea.

Table 4.1 (Continued)

Company	Offense
Inland Container[6]	1978—Fixing prices of corrugated containers. Nolo plea by company and executive.
International Paper	1974—Fixing prices of paper labels. Company and two executives pleaded nolo. 1976—Fixing prices of folding cartons. Company and four executives pleaded nolo. 1978—Fixing prices of corrugated containers. Nolo plea. Fined $617,000.
Walter Kidde	1977—SEC charges against U.S. Lines subsidiary[7] related to $2.5 million in alledgedly illegal rebates. Consent decree. 1978—Federal Maritime Commission charges related to same. Settlement. 1979—U.S. Lines charged with fixing prices of ocean shipping. Nolo plea. Fined $1 million.
Koppers	1979—Bid rigging in connection with sale of road tar to State of Connecticut. Nolo plea.
LTV	1978—Agriculture Dept. charges against Wilson Foods subsidiary related to alleged illegal payoffs to customers. Settlement.
Liggett Group	1978—Paddington Corp. subsidiary charged with bribery of state liquor official. Guilty plea.
Litton Industries	1974—Fixing prices of paper labels. Convicted after trial.
3M	1973—Illegal campaign contribution of $30,000. Company and chairman pleaded guilty. 1975—SEC charges related to $634,000 slush fund for contributions. Consent decree.
Marcor[8]	1976—Container Corp. subsidiary charged with fixing prices of folding cartons. Company and eight executives pleaded nolo. 1978—Subsidiary charged with fixing prices of corrugated boxes. Company and two executives pleaded nolo.
Martin Marietta	1978—Martin Marietta Aluminum subsidiary charged with fixing prices of titanium products. Company and executive pleaded nolo.
Mattel	1974—SEC charges related to false disclosures to influence stock prices. Consent decree. 1978—Former president indicted on criminal charges related to same matter. Nolo plea.
J. Ray McDermott	1976—SEC charges related to slush fund of more than $800,000 used for commercial bribes and illegal political contributions. Consent decree. 1978—Wire fraud and racketeering charges relating to the bribes and contributions. Guilty plea. 1978—Bid rigging and allocation of contracts relating to pipeline and offshore-oil-rig construction. Company, president, and three other executives pleaded nolo. Company fined $1 million.
Mead	1976—Fixing prices of folding cartons. Company and executive pleaded nolo.

Table 4.1 (Continued)

Company	Offense
National Distillers	1978—Bribery of state liquor official. Pleaded guilty. 1980—Treasury Dept. allegations of illegal payments to customers. Settlement and $750,000 fine.
Northern Natural Gas	1972—Mail fraud related to bribery of local officials to obtain right-of-way permits for pipeline construction. Company and one executive pleaded nolo to some counts; charges against another executive dropped.
Northrop	1974—Illegal campaign contributions of $150,000. Company and two executives pleaded guilty. 1975—SEC charges related to slush fund for $500,000 in domestic contributions. Consent decree.
Occidental Petroleum	1974—Illegal campaign contribution of $54,000. Executive and later the chairman pleaded guilty. 1977—SEC charges related to $200,000 slush fund for contributions in the U.S. and abroad. Consent decree.
Olinkraft[9]	1978—Fixing prices of corrugated containers. Company and one executive pleaded nolo; another executive acquitted.
Owens-Illinois	1978—Fixing prices of corrugated containers. Company and one executive pleaded nolo; two others acquitted.
Pan American	1975—Illegal fare cutting. Nolo plea. 1977—Fixing prices of military fares. Nolo plea.
Peavey	1977—Defrauding grain customers by short-weighting. Nolo plea.
Penn Central	1974—SEC charges of fraud relating to the bankruptcy of the railroad. Consent decree.
PepsiCo	1970—Frito-Lay subsidiary charged with fixing prices of snack food. Nolo plea. 1977—Parent company charged with fixing prices of industrial sugar. Nolo plea. 1979—Parent company and two executives of Monsieur Henri subsidiary charged with bribing a union official. All pleaded guilty.
Pet[10]	1970—Fixing prices of snack foods. Nolo plea.
Phillips Petroleum	1973—Illegal campaign contribution of $100,000. Company and chairman pleaded guilty. 1975—SEC charges related to $2.8-million slush fund, a portion of which was allegedly used for domestic illegal political contributions. Consent decree. 1975—Fixing prices of gasoline. Nolo plea. 1976—Tax evasion related to the slush fund. Guilty plea.
Pittston	1977—Brink's Inc. subsidiary charged with bid rigging and fixing prices of security services. Company and five executives pleaded nolo. Company fined $625,000.
H. K. Porter	1974—Fixing prices of steel reinforcing bars. Nolo plea.
Potlatch	1976—Fixing prices of folding cartons. Company and one executive pleaded nolo; another executive acquitted.

Table 4.1 (Continued)

Company	Offense
Purolator	1978—Bid rigging and allocation of markets for security services. Nolo plea.
Rapid-American	1978—Schenley subsidiary and three executives charged with bribery of a state liquor official. All pleaded guilty. 1979—SEC charges against Schenley related to $6 million in allegedly illegal payments to customers. Consent decree.
Reichhold Chemicals	1977—Fixing prices of resins used to make paints. Company and executive pleaded nolo.
R. J. Reynolds Ind.	1977—Federal Maritime Commission charges against Sea-Land Services subsidiary relating to illegal payments to customers. Settlement and $4 million fine. 1978—SEC suit against Sea-Land related to $25 million in allegedly illegal rebates and political contributions. Consent decree. 1979—Fixing prices of ocean shipping. Nolo plea. Fined $1 million.
Rockwell International	1978—Fixing prices of gas meters. Pleaded guilty.
St. Regis Paper	1976—Fixing prices of folding cartons. Company and executive pleaded nolo.
F.&M. Schaefer	1978—Treasury Dept. allegations of $600,000 in illegal rebates to customers. Settlement.
Jos. Schlitz Brewing	1977—SEC charges related to $3 million in illegal rebates to customers. Consent decree. 1977—Fixing prices of beer. Company and executive pleaded nolo. 1978—Treasury Dept. allegations of illegal marketing practices and rebates. Consent decree and $750,000 fine.
Joseph E. Seagram	1977—SEC charges related to over $1 million in allegedly illegal rebates to customers and political contributions. Consent decree. 1978—Seagram Distillers, three other subsidiaries, and four executives charged with bribery of a state liquor official. All pleaded guity. 1979—Illegal payments to members of a state liquor-control board. Guilty plea. Fined $1.5 million.
Seatrain Lines	1978—Payment of illegal rebates and violation of currency regulations. Guilty plea in criminal case and $2.5 million fine paid in Federal Maritime Commission case. 1979—Fixing prices of ocean shipping. Nolo plea. 1980—SEC suit related to $14 million in rebates to customers. Consent decree.
Singer	1975—Illegal campaign contribution of $10,000. Guilty plea.
SuCrest[11]	1977—Fixing prices of industrial sugar. Nolo plea.
Tenneco	1976—Packaging Corp. subsidiary charged with fixing prices of folding cartons. Company and four executives pleaded nolo. 1978—Mail fraud in connection with bribery of a local official. Guilty plea.
Textron	1978—Fixing prices of gas meters. Pleaded guilty.

Table 4.1 (Continued)

Company	Offense
Time Inc.[12]	1976—Eastex Packaging subsidiary charged with fixing prices of folding cartons. Nolo plea.
Trans World Corp.	1975—TWA charged with illegal fare cutting. Nolo plea. 1977—Fixing prices of military fares. Nolo plea.
Uniroyal	1977—SEC charges related to allegedly illegal political contributions. Consent decree.
United Brands	1975—SEC charges related to improper use of funds to pay a $1.2 million bribe to a Honduran official. Consent decree. 1978—Wire fraud charges related to the same matter. Guilty plea.
U.S. Steel	1973—Fixing prices of steel reinforcing bars. Company and an executive pleaded nolo.
Jim Walter	1978—Knight Paper subsidiary charged with fixing prices of paper products. Company and executive pleaded nolo.
Ward Foods	1972—Fixing prices of bread. Nolo plea. 1978—Fixing prices of meat. Nolo plea.
Weyerhaeuser	1976—Fixing prices of folding cartons. Company and three executives pleaded nolo. 1978—Fixing prices of corrugated boxes. Company pleaded nolo, fined $632,000. Two executives acquitted.
Wheelabrator-Frye	1976—A. L. Garber subsidiary[13] charged with fixing prices of folding cartons. Nolo plea.
Zale	1977—SEC charges related to slush fund to reimburse executives for political contributions. Consent decree.

1. Acquired by Farrell Lines in 1978.
2. Acquired by Louisiana-Pacific in 1978.
3. Acquired by BAT Industries in 1973.
4. Merged into Hunt Intl. Resources in 1978.
5. Merged into Champion Intl. in 1977.
6. Acquired by Time Inc. later in 1978.
7. Acquired by McLean Securities in 1978.
8. Acquired by Mobil in 1978.
9. Acquired by Johns-Manville in 1979.
10. Merged into IC Industries in 1978.
11. Now named Ingredient Technology.
12. Publisher of *Fortune*.
13. Now an independent company.

SOURCE: "How Lawless are Big Companies?" by Irwin Ross; *Fortune*, December 1, 1980, pp.58–61. © Time, Inc. All rights reserved. Reprinted by permission.

vertisements, on the other hand, contain true statements that are considered to lead the prospective user of the product to believe erroneously that some desirable condition will result. Misrepresentations in advertising affecting interstate commerce come under the jurisdiction of the Federal Trade Commission Act of 1914 (Title 15 U.S.C., Chapter 2). Whether a firm's advertising represents "unfair or deceptive acts or practices" (Section 45 (a)1) is usually determined by the Federal Trade Commission and subsequent court interpretations of the Commission's actions. In cases not involving blatant falsities, the decision about whether a particular advertisement is in fact "unfair or deceptive" is the result of a subjective determination by the federal government.

There is sometimes a fine line between legitimate and illegitimate claims. It is acceptable to claim that your product is the "best" or the "finest," because this would be a matter of opinion. It is not acceptable, however, to assert falsely that one product "works better" than other products, because such claims are a matter of fact. For instance, several analgesic manufacturing firms (makers of Anacin, Bufferin, Excedrin, and Bayer) were accused in 1972 of making incorrect statements about the relative superiority of their product's performance (Clinard and Yeager, 1980: 218). Similarly, it is not acceptable to assert that "Everybody needs milk," but it can be claimed that "Milk has something for everybody."

The FTC combats false and misleading advertising in regard to product performance and warranties. The following are some selected examples from the recent files of the FTC (1986):

- Biopractic Group, Inc., manufacturers of "Therapeutic Mineral Ice" arthritis pain remedy, agreed not to make unsubstantiated claims about the product's effectiveness and acceptance by the scientific community or the news media.
- Commodore Business Machines, Inc. agreed not to advertise that its computers have or will have in the future particular equipment or software capabilities unless the claim is true or there is a reasonable basis for the claim.
- Young, Rubicam/Zemp, Inc., an advertising agency, agreed not to misrepresent the ability of the "Ecologizer CA/90 Series 2000 Air Treatment System" or any other indoor air cleaner made to remove formaldehyde gas or tobacco smoke from household air, without competent and reliable substantiation.
- Sentronic Controls Corporation agreed not to claim its "Pest Sentry" ultrasonic pest control device eliminates insects and rodents, or make any other efficacy or performance claims, unless it has competent and reliable scientific evidence which substantiates the claims.

- Wein Products, Inc. agreed not to claim that its "Decimate" ultrasonic pest control product will eliminate rodents or insects from a home or business, or will work within a specified time period.
- Removatron International Corp., the maker of the Removatron brand hair removal device, was charged with deceptively advertising that the product can permanently remove hair and falsely claiming the device had been approved by the Federal Communications Commission.
- Buckingham Productions, Inc. was charged with making false, misleading, and unsubstantiated advertising claims for its "Rotation Diet" and several other related weight reduction plans.
- Sun Refining and Marketing Company agreed to honor lifetime warranty obligations for automobile batteries it sold with such a warranty and to notify eligible consumers.
- Craftmatic Comfort Mfg. Corp. and Craftmatic/Contour Organization, Inc., two sellers of electric adjustable beds, failed to inform consumers in advance that in order to obtain warranty service they will have to return the bed or any of its parts at their own expense. Shipping of beds or parts sold prior to the order are at the expense of the sellers.

Antitrust Violations

Price-fixing, bid-rigging, discriminatory pricing, rebating, trusts, and related agreements that threaten fair competition in interstate commerce (including foreign commerce) are illegal primarily under Title 15 of the United States Code, Chapter 1. This chapter includes the Sherman Act of 1890 (restraint of trade, price-fixing), the Wilson Act of 1894 (restraint of import trade), the Clayton Act of 1914 (stock acquisitions in restraint of trade, agreement not to use goods of competitors), the Robinson-Patman Act of 1936 (discriminatory pricing to buyers), and the Celler-Kefauver Act of 1950 (stock and asset acquisition which "may" be anticompetitive). The Federal Trade Commission Act of 1914, discussed in the previous section, also has provisions about unfair competitive practices. Restraint of trade violations can hurt both consumers (e.g., retail price-fixing) and competitors (e.g., discriminatory pricing favoring large buyers).

In the United States, federal antitrust prosecution is handled by the Antitrust Division of the Department of Justice. The major federal antitrust law is the Sherman Act, which outlaws any business behavior or conspiracy that is "in restraint of trade or commerce among the several States or with foreign nations" (Title 15, Section 1). Currently under Sherman (based on increased penalties passed by Congress in 1974), corporations are punishable by a fine of $1 million and divestiture; individuals face fines of as much as $100,000 and three years imprisonment. Violators are also subject to civil liabilities for damages, including triple damages. Additionally, individual states have laws against unfair competition affecting intrastate commerce.

Restraint of trade violations can be serious offenses. For instance, Congress exposed a pharmaceutical manufacturers' price-fixing conspiracy on the antibiotic tetracycline in the early 1970s (involving Pfizer, Cyanamid, Bristol, Squibb, and Upjohn). The price per hundred (250 mg) tablets dropped by about 90 percent, from as high as $30.60 in 1955 to as low as $2.47 in 1974 (Braithwaite, 1984: 177). Civil damages awarded in the tetracycline cases have exceeded $250 million (Braithwaite, 1984:187). A price-fixing conspiracy in Seattle, Washington during the period 1955-1964, involving loaves of bread, resulted in overcharges to consumers of approximately $35 million for the decade. Were that conspiracy to have operated nationwide during the period, Americans would have paid in excess of $2 billion more for bread. Restraints of trade also increase inflation, encourage a lack of industrial innovation, and force financial hardships on firms not participating in the restraint, especially small businesses (Clinard and Yeager, 1980:140).

Before the 1970s, Sherman Act violators were subject to relatively lenient sentencing. Although many individual and organizational violators prior to 1970 received fines, the fines were small compared to the gravity of the offense and the wealth of the offenders. For instance, the maximum fine for a firm or an individual under the Sherman Act was raised in 1955 to $50,000 in order to promote a greater deterrent (a tenfold increase over the original provisions). Yet, the average corporate fine for the period 1955-1965 was $13,420 and the average fine per individual was $3,365 (Nader and Green, 1972). Imprisonment was also rarely given as a Sherman sanction prior to 1970. Between 1890 and 1969, there were only 536 criminal cases in which individual offenders were subject to incarceration. Jail sentences were imposed in only 26 of these cases, or less than 5 percent. Of the 26 cases, 22 involved other federal charges such as racketeering. Thus, during the first seventy-nine years of the Sherman Act, federal judges imposed jail sentences in only four cases reflecting pure antitrust violation (Eckert, 1980: 244-45). One of the four cases involved jailing some of the executives implicated in the famous electrical equipment conspiracy discussed in Chapter 3.

Since 1970, sanctions for Sherman Act violations have increased, most notably during President Carter's administration. According to Eckert (1980), for the four-year period 1976-1979, there were 227 Sherman Act violators not indicted for other kinds of offenses (e.g., racketeering, perjury, mail fraud) who were subject to sentence (i.e., they either pleaded guilty or *nolo contendre*, or were convicted after trial). Fifty-nine were charged with felony Sherman infractions and 168 were charged with misdemeanor violations. All felons received some sort of a sentence: 48 (81 percent) were fined an average of $17,500 apiece; 22 were jailed for an average of 59 days apiece. A total of fifty-three felons were either jailed or fined, or both: 17 (32 percent) were jailed and fined, 5 (9 percent) were only jailed, and 31 (58 percent) were only fined. Six (10 percent) received only community service. Among the 168 misdemeanants, all but one (99 percent) received some sort of sanction: 153 (91 percent) were fined an average of $11,900 apiece and 35 (21 percent) were incarcerated for an average of 22 days apiece. Of the 167 receiving a sanction, 14 (8 percent) received only jail, 132 (79 percent) were only fined, and 21 (12 percent) were both fined and jailed. In corporate penalties for the four-year period, 175 firms were subject to misdemeanor fines (which averaged $30,400) and 134 firms were subject to felony fines (which averaged $174,300) (Eckert, 1980).

Although recent sentencing rates under Sherman have increased, there are still some glaring disparities. For instance, in 1976, the federal government brought action against twenty-three firms and fifty executives involved in the folding carton conspiracy that took place during 1960-1974 (mentioned in Chapter 3). The duration of the violations, the national diffusiveness of the harm, and the blatant and constant price-fixing behavior of the defendants were emphasized by the Department of Justice. However, only eighteen executives received sentences, all of which seem relatively light—ranging from only probation to fifteen days in jail and a $15,000 fine. Most jail sentences were a week or less, and the largest fine was $25,000 (given to one individual in addition to a day in jail, six months probation, and eight hours of weekly community service) (Clinard and Yeager, 1980:281). In another case, in 1979, a federal judge imposed huge financial penalties, fining thirteen executives a total of $650,000 and seven international shipping firms a total of $5.45 million after they pleaded *nolo contendre* to price-fixing charges (Clinard and Yeager, 1980:153).

By the mid-1980s, under the Reagan administration, the Antitrust Division seemed to continue its battle against trade restraint, although it is impossible to assess the Division's true effectiveness because the actual number of trade restraints are unknown. Further, what constitutes a restraint is sometimes a matter of interpretation by the Justice Department and the courts. However, one can derive some idea about trade restraint enforcement levels from the numbers of Antitrust Division actions listed in its annual report. The following are enforcement totals from the Justice Department for fiscal year 1986. The Division filed fifty-nine antitrust cases against a total of seventy-nine corporations and sixty-one individuals, and opened 274 formal investigations of possible antitrust violation. During fiscal year 1986, a total of 3,820 days of incarceration and almost $11 million in fines were imposed on Sherman Act violators (U.S. Attorney General, 1987:109). Under the Hart-Scott-Rodino Antitrust Improvements Act, the Antitrust Division reviews premerger factors to decide whether such mergers will affect fair market competition. During fiscal year 1986, the Division reviewed 1,949 potential transactions under the Hart-Scott-Rodino Act, and under applicable banking laws, the Division reviewed an additional 1,750 mergers and acquisitions involving banks. During that year, a $450,000 civil penalty was levied for failure to notify the Division of factors related to a proposed merger, and at least eight proposed mergers or acquisitions were abandoned or restructured because the Division deemed them anticompetitive (U.S. Attorney General, 1987:111).

Some have argued that the provisions of the Sherman Act and similar legislation are vague, and therefore both businessmen and the government have difficulty in deciding whether a particular act constitutes a restraint of trade. However, a century of Sherman Act case law interpretations have rather strictly defined various key terms, and objections about vagueness were rejected by the Supreme Court as early as 1913 (*Nash v. U.S.*, 229 U.S. 373). Although antitrust enforcement is discretionary, the Department of Justice claims that it seeks indictments only when there is a clear intent to price-fix, monopolize, or knowingly engage in other illegal predatory market practices (U.S. Attorney General, 1955: 349-50).

Unsafe Consumer Products

The federal government's first major efforts to regulate consumer product safety were the passages of the Pure Food and Drug Act and the Beef Inspection Act, both in 1906. Muckraking reformers at the turn of the century provided much of the impetus behind the passage of these and many other laws. Probably the most influential of these reformers was novelist Upton Sinclair.

Sinclair's *The Jungle* (1906), which was dedicated to the "workingmen of America," educated the public about the horrors of the meat packing industry in Chicago. Downs (1964:345) tells us that "for seven weeks Sinclair lived with the underprivileged, wretched aliens of the Chicago stockyards, and then returned to his home in New Jersey to write about what he had seen, heard, and smelled." Sinclair's work vividly depicted the unhealthy labor and sanitary conditions of slaughter houses in "Packingtown" (as Sinclair called the stockyards) through the eyes of a young

Lithuanian immigrant, Jurgis Rudkus. The gruesome details included, for instance, using ground poisoned rats in meat products, hogs dead of cholera used for lard, the sale of steer carcasses condemned as tubercular, and, most dramatic of all, the humans who occasionally fell into boiling vats became part of "beef" products sold to the public.

Although only a dozen of the more than three hundred pages in Sinclair's novel were devoted to the horrors of the meatpacking industry, it had a profound effect on public opinion. The country was engulfed by indignation as it realized that the canned goods and other meats it was ingesting were prepared amidst filthy conditions. Downs (1964:348) notes a familiar rhyme that was parodied in the press after the publication of *The Jungle*: "Mary had a little lamb, and when she saw it sicken, she shipped it off to Packingtown, and now it's labeled chicken!"

Sinclair, an early Socialist, tried to use *The Jungle* primarily to publicize the undesirable effects of unchecked capitalism. The novel depicted unsafe labor conditions and consumer products, prejudice, graft, and price-gouging. In this vein, fellow Socialist Jack London wrote, "What *Uncle Tom's Cabin* did for the black slaves *The Jungle* has a large chance to do for the white slaves of today" (Downs, 1964:349). However, the novel did more to inform the public about unsafe consumer products than rally the public against the oppressions of places like Packingtown. Sinclair later wrote, "I aimed at the public's heart and by accident I hit it in the stomach" (Downs, 1964:349). Despite Sinclair's disappointment, *The Jungle* is considered to be one of the more important forces behind public and political movements to rectify the consumer hazards of big industry through federal legislation. President Theodore Roosevelt was particularly moved by *The Jungle*, and personally ordered federal investigations of the meatpacking industry.

Packing executives at first vigorously denied the allegations in the novel, but after meat sales dropped by more than half at home and abroad soon after the release of the book, the packing industry realized that it must give way for the consumer legislation. Less than six months from the appearance of Sinclair's work, the Pure Food and Drug Act and the Beef Inspection Act were passed by Congress. These laws not only increased public confidence in the purity of meat products (which increased sales), their passage also forced smaller firms out of business because they could not meet the new federal sanitation standards.

The American "consumer movement," however, did not begin until twenty years after the passage of the 1906 laws. Coleman (1989) traced the first identifiable "consumer movement" in America back to the publication of Chase and Schlink's *Your Money's Worth* (1927), which appeared about twenty years after Congress passed the initial pure food legislation. The book attacked deceptive advertising and dubious sales techniques, and called for scientific testing of consumer goods. In 1929, Schlink established Consumer Research, Inc., which began publishing *Consumer's Bulletin* in order to disseminate research on consumer products. A few years later, Kallett and Schlink's (1933) *100,000,000 Guinea Pigs*, which detailed the pharmaceutical industry's lack of drug testing, won popular acclaim (Coleman, 1989:139-40). However, it was not until 1938, after more than one hundred people died from an untested sore throat remedy called Elixir Sulfanilamide (contaminated with di-ethylene glycol, which is usually used in antifreeze), that governmental regulation of the drug industry was strengthened (Clinard and Yeager, 1980:78-79; Braithwaite, 1984:113-114). Federal legislation then allowed the Food and Drug Administration to insure that products were safe *prior* to marketing.

Over a half century after Sinclair's muckraking novel, Congress pased another Pure Food and Drug Act in 1962, which allowed the FDA to determine the *effectiveness* of drugs (rather than only their safety) prior to marketing. In 1966, Congress enacted the Motor Vehicle Safety Act, which, among other things, established the National Highway Traffic Safety Commission which is charged with setting standards for the automobile industry and ordering recalls of defective vehicles. Ralph Nader, whose book *Unsafe at Any Speed: The Designed-in Dangers of the American Automobile* (1965) had just been published, was a major influence in the passage of this automobile safety legislation. You may recall that General Motors admitted to an attempt to prevent Nader from testifying before Congress about the inherent safety problems with GM's Corvair automobile by harassing him. GM also admitted to trying to discredit Nader by portraying him as anti-Semitic. Nader received a $425,000 court settlement over the matter, which he used to establish a program to monitor GM's activities concerning automobile safety, pollution, and consumer relations.

The most important piece of recent legislation for the health of the consumer is the Consumer Product Safety Act of 1972, which established the Consumer Product Safety Commission. Prior to the creation of this Commission, there was no federal agency that could identify and remove unsafe products from the market (other than products regulated by the FDA and the National Highway Traffic Safety Commission). The purpose of the CPSC was to reduce the estimated 20 million injuries caused each year by 10,000 consumer products (Clinard and Yeager, 1980:80). A quarter of the accidents may have been preventable by better product design (Weaver, 1975:133). This Commission is charged with setting safety standards on products marketed in the United States (except autos, tires, food, and few other products regulated by other agenices), recalling or banning products it deems harmful, and prosecuting those who do not heed its orders. Penalties inflicted on individuals for violations can be hefty—as much as a year in jail, a $50,000 fine, and up to $500,000 in civil penalties. Corporate penalties can total $50,000 in fines, a half-million dollars in civil penalties, and seizure of corporate assets.

There have been several well-known cases involving the willful distribution of consumer products which were known to cause injury and death. Some of the most infamous involve pharmaceutical and transportation products—the sedative drug Thalidomide (which caused thousands of prenatal deaths and birth defects) (Braithwaite, 1984:65-75); the Dalkon Shield intrauterine device (which caused thousands of spontaneous abortions and other health hazards) (Mintz, 1988); Beech Aircraft planes (with allegedly known crash-causing defective fuel systems) (Geis, 1974); the cholesterol reduction drug MER/29 manufactured by Richardson-Merrell (whose executives pleaded "no contest" to charges of fraudulently hiding debilitating side effects such as cataracts and sterility) (Braithwaite, 1984: 60-65); and Ford Motor Company's Pinto automobile (known to be susceptible to rear end fiery crashes) (Dowie, 1977;1988; Cullen, et al., 1987). Three of these cases will be discussed in detail here—Thalidomide, Dalkon Shield, and Ford Pinto.

Thalidomide.   Thalidomide was first manufactured in the 1950s by the German company Chemie Grunenthal. Silverman and Lee (1974:96) estimate that ten thousand babies in twenty countries were deformed (born with no appendages, or blind) by their mother's ingestion of Thalidomide during pregnancy. Braithwaite (1984:65) estimates a greater negative effect from the drug—eight thousand deformed babies in forty-six countries and perhaps as many as sixteen thousand deaths at birth. Thalidomide was never approved for marketing in the United States. FDA scientist Dr. Frances Kelsey refused to approve the drug, an action for which she was honored by President Kennedy. However, 2.5 million tablets were distributed to 1,267 doctors in the United States by Richardson-Merrell (of MER/29 infamy). The doctors gave the drug to twenty thousand patients, to whom at least ten "Thalidomide children" were born. Grunenthal, which had ignored complaints about the drug and had lied for several years about the extent of its adverse effects, was charged with intent to commit bodily harm in September, 1965 by prosecutors in Aachen, Germany. After a six-year court battle, Grunenthal bargained with prosecutors to drop the criminal charges in exchange for $31 million in compensation to German Thalidomide children. Many other settlements were also reached, including a $550,000 jury award against Richardson-Merrell

(Braithwaite, 1984:71-74). The lack of international communication about the problems of Thalidomide and the name variations under which the drug was marketed prolonged its infliction on unsuspecting patients for additional years.

Dalkon Shield. The "Dalkon Shield" was an intrauterine birth control device sold by the A.H. Robins company beginning in January, 1971. The Shield was touted as safe and effective. According to Mintz (1988), however, the seriously injured victims of the Dalkon Shield worldwide could number in the tens of thousands. Nearly all suffered some form of the infections known as pelvic inflamatory disease (PID), killing at least eighteen women in the United States; most of those who suffered the infections have lost the ability to bear children. The Shield was also ineffective, causing a pregancy rate of 5 percent (almost five times the rate claimed by promotional advertising). An estimated 60 percent of women in the United States who conceived with a Dalkon lost their unborn children, or about ten thousand more than would have done so had they been wearing other IUD's. Some of these women elected to have abortions, some suffered spontaneous abortions, and others suffered infection related septic spontaneous abortions. According to the FDA, 248 women in the United States alone endured this latter form of abortion, fifteen of whom died from them. In addition, hundreds of women who conceived while the Shield was in place gave birth prematurely during the third trimester to babies with severe birth defects, including cerebral palsy, mental retardation, and blindness. Robins distributed almost 4.5 million Shields worldwide, 2.2 million of which were implanted into women in the United States and 800,000 of which were implanted into women outside the country. Although the Dalkon Shield was officially taken off the market in the United States in June of 1974, it was continually used as late as 1980 in parts of Latin America (where there are fewer medical resources to treat the complications related to the device). Many PID victims of the Shield continue to suffer chronic pain and illness, often requiring prolonged hospitalization. By 1983, almost a decade after Dalkon was removed from the market, estimates of the number of women who still used the device ranged from a few hundred to as many as a half million. After a recall program was instituted by Robins, through which Robins would bear the expense for the removal of the Dalkons, almost 5,000 women had filed claims. In August of 1985, the A.H. Robins company filed for reorganization under Chapter 11 of the Bankruptcy Code (Mintz, 1988:30-33). In June of 1989, a federal court approved the bankruptcy reorganization, and set aside $2.5 billion for distribution to Dalkon victims (AP, 6/17/89a).

Ford Pinto. The Ford Pinto is a particularly noteworthy example of un-safe consumer product distribution, because it is associated with one of the first times that an organization was criminally indicted for its role in a homicide. According to Dowie (1977), in his well known piece "Pinto Madness," at the time of his writing Pinto crashes had caused at least 500 burn deaths to people who would not have been seriously injured if their car had not burst into flames. Prior to releasing the Pinto on the market, Ford allegedly knew that a crash into the rear end of the vehicle would easily rupture the fuel system. Assembly line machinery was already tooled when this defect was found. To avoid the increased production costs asso-ciated with retooling, top Ford officials decided to manufacture the car with its exploding gas tank, even though Ford owned a patent on a safer tank (Dowie, 1988:14). Ford's infamous memorandum about the benefits associated with a refusal to redesign the Pinto's fuel system projected a net savings of about $90 million—$11 improvement costs per vehicle for 12.5 million vehicles ($137 million) versus $49.5 million in damage suits in-volving 180 deaths, 180 serious burn injuries, and 2100 burned vehicles (Dowie, 1988:21; Cullen, et al., 1987:162). This cold calculation demon-strated Ford's lack of concern for anything but profit to several civil juries, one of which awarded a Pinto crash victim over $125 million in 1978 (most of this award, which was reduced to $6.6 million in 1981, was based on punitive damages equal to the savings Ford would have accumu-lated for their decision to market the unsafe vehicle) (Cullen, et al., 1987:164). In the criminal trial, Ford Motor Company was indicted on three counts of reckless homicide by a grand jury in Elkhart County, Indi-ana on September 13, 1978. The victims—Judy Ulrich (age eighteen), Lyn Ulrich (age sixteen), and Donna Ulrich (age sixteen)—died in a fiery rear end collision on August 10, 1978 while they were driving in a Ford Pinto down Highway 33 in northern Indiana. Although Dowie's (1977) exposé on Ford's "Pinto Madness" had unleashed a national consumer crusade against the large automaker, Ford was acquitted on March 13, 1980 of the three criminal charges after a ten-week trial and twenty-five hours of delib-eration (for the details of the trial, see Cullen, et al., 1987:189-308).

ORGANIZATIONAL CRIMES AGAINST WORKERS

Unfair Labor Practices

The United States Department of Labor is the major enforcer against unfair labor practice violations, including those involving minimum and prevailing wages and overtime, worker discrimination, labor-management disputes, child labor, and migrant or immigrant workers.

Criminal and civil charges are usually brought through the Labor Department's Office of the Solicitor for the alleged violation of many different federal labor laws (e.g., Fair Labor Standards Act, Labor-Management Reporting and Disclosure Act, Vietnam Era Veterans' Readjustment Assistance Act, Urban Mass Transit Act, Immigration Reform and Control Act, Comprehensive Employment and Training Act). The following are some examples of recent Department of Labor actions during fiscal year 1987.

- Five complaints were filed against companies with government contracts which refused to develop and submit affirmative action programs: Bruce Church, Inc.; Marathon Cheese; USAA Federal Savings; Electronic Data Systems; and Southwest Gas Co.
- Five complaints were filed against companies with government contracts for discriminating against the handicapped: Stencel Aero and Engineering (alcoholism); GTE Communications Systems, Inc. (back injury); Tyson Foods (mental handicap); and Consolidated Edison and PPG Industries (epilepsy) (U.S. Department of Labor, 1987:91). Harris Bank and Trust was found to have practiced a major pattern of sex and race discrimination against women and minorities in their initial job placements and starting salaries (U.S. Department of Labor, 1987:93).
- The Wage and Hour Division of the DOL found 19,077 minors employed in violation of the child labor provisions of the Fair Labor Standards Act. The Division assessed $1.5 million in child labor civil money penalties against 811 employers who were found to be illegally employing 10,160 minors (U.S. Department of Labor, 1987:42). In one such case, a distributor of Global Home Products, Inc. was found liable for extensive child labor violations in door-to-door candy sales (U.S. Department of Labor, 1987:105).
- The Wage and Hour Division conducted 72,028 complaint actions under the Fair Labor Standards Act, of which 55,203 were initiated as a result of complaints from workers or citizens. Employers agreed to pay a total of $99.7 million in back minimum and overtime wages ($20.2 million to 136,000 workers in unpaid minimum wages and $79.5 million to 293,000 workers in unpaid overtime). In one case alone, some 28,000 former service station employees of Hudson Oil and Affiliated Companies were to receive as much as $6.8 million in settlement of a lawsuit brought by the DOL, representing the largest Fair Labor Standards Act minimum wage and overtime pay recovery every obtained from a private employer by the DOL (U.S. Department of Labor, 1987:41).

- Employers agreed to pay $28 million in back wages to 44,300 employees for violation of prevailing wage laws.
- Wage and Hour Division conducted 4,880 Migrant and Seasonal Agricultural Worker Protection Act compliance actions, resulting in civil money penalties totaling $873,430 assessed against violators (U.S. Department of Labor, 1987:43).
- Several suits were filed by the Division of Labor-Management Laws. Not all of these cases involved union employers as offenders; union members and unions are also subject to suit by this Division. The following are some examples of organizational employer labor-management violations: a union member's job was reinstated because the court found that he was still "working at the trade" even though he was in the process of legally challenging his discharge; a National Guard member had been unlawfully discharged because of her military obligations; a veteran was entitled to adjustment in his seniority date for the time spent in military service because it was "reasonably certain" that he would have successfully completed police officer training if the training had not been interrupted by military service and because he did in fact complete the training after his release from active duty (U.S. Department of Labor, 1987:112–113).

Unsafe Working Conditions

The other major area of organizational crimes against workers involves unsafe working conditions, which, like unsafe consumer products and pollution, cause physical harm or have the potential to do so. Many industries are known to be inherently dangerous. For instance, conditions at some coal (Caudill, 1988), asbestos (Green, 1973), and textile plants (Guarasci, 1988) have been found to cause lung disease (pneumoconiosis and silicosis) from dust inhalation. Mines are known to explode (Braithwaite, 1985) and steel mills cause injuries and death (Reutter, 1988). The Film Recovery Systems case, first discussed in Chapter 1, involved exposing employees to cyanide fumes without any protection (Frank, 1988).

The primary federal agency that is responsible for enforcing safe job site law is the Department of Labor's Occupational Safety and Health Administration (OSHA), which began in 1970. In the mining industry, site standards are regulated by the Mine Safety and Health Administration (MSHA).

During fiscal year 1987, OSHA imposed several substantial penalties on organizational violators, including the largest ($2.6 million) in its sixteen-year history against IBP, Inc., for extensive violations of occupational safety and health recordkeeping requirements. In another case, a $1.57 million penalty was imposed against the Chrysler Corporation for 811 alleged instances of job safety and health violations, including overexposure of employees to lead and arsenic and failure to notify employees about the presence of toxic chemicals (U.S. Department of Labor, 1987:31). Hefty fines were also levied that year against several corporations for their failure to keep adequate records related to occupational health and safety incidents—General Motors ($500,000), Union Carbide ($408,000), Chrysler Corporation $295,000, and USX ($65,000) (U.S. Department of Labor, 1987:125).

During the calendar years 1985–86 (OSHA, 1988:116), highway vehicles were the major cause of death among workers in seven of eight industry groups (private sector, eleven or more employees, excluding railroads and non-gas/oil mining), accounting for a third of all work related deaths. Industrial vehicles and equipment caused another 11 percent of all job deaths, almost a quarter (23 percent) of mining deaths during oil and gas extraction and about one in six construction (17 percent) and manufacturing (15 percent) deaths. Almost one in twelve (8 percent) workers who died on the job suffered heart attacks. About the same proportion fell to their deaths (8 percent) or were electrocuted (7 percent) (these two causes were each responsible for 16 percent of the fatalities in the construction industry).

During calendar years 1986 and 1987 (OSHA, 1988:47), OSHA conducted about 61,000 inspections of work sites annually. There was a noticeable increase in all types of infractions during 1987 compared to the previous year: 39,965 serious violations (15 percent more than in 1986); 95,424 other-than-serious violations (an increase of 8 percent over 1986); 4,553 willful or repeated violations (35 percent more than in 1986); and 1,771 fail-to-abate infractions (130 percent more than in 1986). The overall citations-per-inspection ratio increased steadily between 1984 (1.55) and 1987 (2.31), by almost half. These figures do not necessarily imply that there were more violations in 1987 than in previous years; the increase could be due solely to an increase in OSHA activities, such as engaging in more comprehensive inspections or using lower thresholds for violation.

Despite this increase in citations, OSHA's critics have charged that the agency has failed to enforce laws protecting the nation's workers. In a 1988 report, the National Safe Workplace Institute charged that OSHA's ineffectiveness had resulted in more than nine thousand avoidable workplace fatalities since 1981. The basis of this claim is that the rate of high risk deaths declined by an annual rate of 2.2 percent from 1975 through

1980 but by only 0.7 percent from 1981 through 1987—had the same reduction continued in the 1980s, then more lives would have been saved. According to the NSWI, job safety enforcement was particularly lax under the Reagan Administration because only a third as many of the severest sanctions (willful/repeated) had been issued annually by OSHA between 1981 and 1987 as in 1980. Thus, although the number of on-the-job deaths fell from 13,000 in 1975 to 11,100 in 1987, the NSWI argues that the 1987 rate could have been lower had OSHA been subjecting employers to more aggressive enforcement (AP, 9/2/88). In response to the allegations of NSWI, OSHA asserted that worker fatalities may not decline at a steady pace and that the six-year period used to calculate the fatality rate was insufficient for determining the effectiveness of regulatory enforcement.

States, too, have joined the battle against unsafe working conditions. Twenty-five states as of 1987 had job safety and health programs approved by OSHA. During fiscal years 1985–87, states conducted a total of about 110,000 inspections annually. States' citations-per-inspection ratio was 2.32 (.35 serious; 1.97 nonserious) in FY 1985, 2.46 (.34 serious; 2.12 nonserious) in FY 1986, and 2.59 (.33 serious; 2.26 nonserious) in FY 1987. States proposed $8.3 million in penalties against violators in FY 1985, $10 million in FY 1986, and 11.2 million in FY 1987 (figures calculated from OSHA, 1988:62).

Regarding mine safety and health, during FY 1987, MSHA issued 106,360 citations after conducting 42,723 coal mine inspections (2.5:1) and issued 34,794 citations after conducting 19,886 inspections (1.7:1) of metal and nonmetal mines. Sixty coal miners died on their job during FY 1987 (down .33 percent from FY 1986), as did sixty-four other (metal and nonmetal) miners (up .38 percent from FY 1986) (U.S. Department of Labor, 1987:57–61). Besides dying in accidents, coal miners often develop the potentially fatal condition called pneumoconiosis ("brown lung"), and MSHA has a continuous X-ray health program that monitors a sample of volunteer miners for the development of that disease.

Braithwaite's (1985) study of coal mining in several countries looked at the details behind some of the most tragic mining disasters occurring between 1960 and 1981. The study concentrated on mining accidents in the United States, the United Kingdom, and Australia. Braithwaite included two other disasters as well because of their extremely high death tolls: Wankie mine (Middle Zambesi Valley, Zimbabwe, 1973, killing 425) and Bois-de-Cazier mine (Marcinelle, Belgium, 1956, killing 262). The United States' worst mining disaster during the study period was the 1972 tip slide at Buffalo Creek mine (West Virginia) in which 125 perished; the United Kingdom's worst was the 1966 tip slide at Merthyr Vale mine in Aberfan (which left 144 dead), and Australia's worst was the explosion at Box Flat mine in Queensland (killing 17) (Braithwaite, 1985:17–18). Most disasters involved an explosion of methane or coal dust.

In thirty-three of thirty-nine diasters studied (85 percent), Braithwaite (1985:20–24) found that serious violations of safety laws were uncovered in the investigations of the tragedies. In twenty-five of the thirty-nine (64 percent), it was found that a violation or violations were contributing factors (either as causes without which the disaster would not have occurred or as factors without which the disaster probably would have been less serious). Among the fourteen disasters without contributory violations, several, including the one in Zimbabwe in which 425 died, had causes that would have been violations had they occurred elsewhere or later. Among the twenty-five disasters which did have contributory violations, eighteen investigations named particular individuals responsible for those violations (foreman / deputy—six; mine manager—three; engineer, safety manager, electrician—two each; under manager, surveyor, locomotive driver—one each) (Braithwaite, 1985:25).

Braithwaite (1985:39) cites a report from one of the West Virginia mining disasters (in which twenty-two died) to sum up his conclusions about cause:

> clearly . . . in many instances men and officials in this mine, as has been true in nearly every other explosion, failed to follow known safe mining practices. The failure of supervisors and employees to follow and comply with known safe mining practices, company rules and regulations, and State and Federal laws was the basic cause of the explosion.

Penalties for fatal violations of mine safety regulations do not seem to be severe. For instance, Braithwaite (1984:89) reports that in 1981, the average fine imposed on coal mine operators was $173. Not surprisingly, the Mine Enforcement and Safety Administration's *Report on Civil Penalty Effectiveness* has concluded that nine of ten mine operators do not believe that monetary penalties are sufficient to warrant the avoidance of future violations (Braithwaite, 1985:89). Besides lacking a deterrent, some fines seem to be simply inappropriately low, given the human damages inflicted. For instance, twenty-seven miners died in the Wilberg Mine Fire of 1984. Yet the operators of Wilberg (Emery Mining, Utah Power and Light) were assessed a total of only $111,470 in penalties for thirty-four citations (which was the largest penalty given for violation of the Mine Act for a single accident). A penalty of only $77,000 against Wilberg was proposed for the nine violations which MSHA determined contributed to the accident (U.S. Department of Labor, 1987:120–21).

ORGANIZATIONAL CRIMES AGAINST THE ENVIRONMENT

Environmental pollution "amounts to [a] compulsory consumption of violence. . . ." (Geis, 1973:12). As noted, Clinard and Yeager (1980:119–21) have shown that certain industries are more likely to pollute than others, as are certain firms within industries. Recall, for instance, that the oil refining industry was responsible for almost half of all environmental violations (7.3 times its share) charged against the Clinard and Yeager sample, including more than a third (5.7 times its share) of the serious and moderately serious environmental violations.

Occidental Petroleum Company is perhaps the best known rogue in the gallery of notorious polluters, having dumped into our air, water, and ground some of the most toxic substances known to man. Occidental's most infamous case is the Love Canal (near Niagara, New York) disaster of the late 1970s, involving one of its subsidiaries, Hooker Chemical Co. Love Canal is named for the civil engineer William Love, who in the 1880s wanted to build a canal around Niagara Falls. Love's plan never materialized, and the canal was sold to Hooker in the late 1930s. The site was used by Hooker to dump hundreds of tons of chemicals and their waste for about fifteen years. In 1953, Love Canal was turned over to the local school board, which sold it to a private developer. Hundreds of houses were built directly above or near the dump site. Persons who lived at Love Canal developed extremely high rates of miscarriage, birth defects, and other health problems. More than two hundred families were forced to flee these homes (Tallmer, 1988:113). Coleman (1989:37) reports that the Love Canal disaster cost American taxpayers about $200 million.

Tallmer (1988) describes Hooker as illegally dumping chemicals "as a corporate way of life," and recounts several other dumping violations by Hooker which have affected residents and employees: Bloody Run Creek, New York (which was used to dump chemicals after Love Canal was closed); Taft, Louisiana (which has polluted the surrounding farmers' crops through smoke discharges); Lathrop, California (where a subsidiary of Hooker, Occidental Chemical, buried highly toxic wastes behind the plant for twenty-five years, causing fatal illnesses among employees and poisoned area water); Syosset and Bethpage, New York (where Hooker left hundreds of tons of vinyl chlorides and other highly toxic chemicals from its processing plant in nearby Hicksville); and White Lake, Michigan (where water contained dangerous levels of Mirex, dioxin, and Kepone— three deadly chemicals which had also been buried on vacant plant property).

Allied Chemical, identified by Sutherland as an organizational criminal recidivist forty years ago, has since been involved in an illegal toxic dumping scandal similar to those of Hooker. In particular, Allied was found guilty of illegal disposal of Kepone-related toxins (Kepone is a DDT-like insecticide) at its Hopewell, Virginia plant. The sloppy handling of the poison caused many workers to experience liver and brain damage, chest pains, personality changes, diminished ability to walk and stand, and sterility. Forty nonemployee nearby residents showed traces of Kepone in their blood. An examination of frozen seafood caught from the James River revealed that Kepone had been appearing in oysters since 1968 and in fish since 1970. Allied dumped Kepone into the Gravely Run, a tributary of the James, during the years 1966–1974 (Stone, 1988). Both Allied Chemical and Hooker Chemical knew the dangers of their deeds when they did them and attempted to hide their illegal dumping from authorities (Stone, 1988:121, 124; Tallmer, 1988:115, 118).

The world's worst industrial pollution disaster occurred December 3, 1984, when a cloud of deadly methyl isocyandate gas escaped from a Union Carbide pesticide plant in Bhopal, India. The human damage was tremendous: more than 3,300 people died within a short period; more than 20,000 were injured; and, as of early 1989, there has been a continuing death toll of at least 1 person per day since the gas leak occurred. Warren Anderson, former Union Carbide chairman, was charged with culpable homicide in the disaster, and more than 500,000 people filed a joint civil suit against Union Carbide for $3 billion. Fifty months after the disaster, the Supreme Court of India, in what may be termed a type of "plea bargain," dropped the criminal charges against Anderson and ordered Union Carbide to pay $470 million in damages as "full and final settlement of all claims" (AP, 2/14/89).

The federal agency responsible for protecting Americans from polluters such as Hooker, Allied, and Union Carbide is the Environmental Protection Agency, which since 1970 has been enforcing the nation's Clean Air and Water Acts. The major laws enforced by the EPA include the Resource Conservation and Recovery Act (42 U.S.C. Sections 6901–6991), the Emergency Planning and Community Right to Know Act (42 U.S.C. Section 11045), the Hazardous Materials Transportation Act (49 U.S.C. Sections 1801–1813), the Clean Air Act (42 U.S.C. Sections 7401–7642), the Clean Water Act (33 U.S.C. Sections 1251–1373), the Toxic Substances Control Act (15 U.S.C. Sections 2601–2654), and the Comprehensive Environmental Response Compensation and Liability Act (42 U.S.C. Sections 9601–9675). In FY 1987, the EPA referred 304 civil cases to the Department of Justice, and the Department filed 285 cases against polluters. State environmental agencies referred another 723 cases to their attorneys general and local prosecutors, almost double the number of referrals from FY 1986. During FY 1987, the EPA issued slightly more than three thousand administrative orders (as did all of the state agencies combined), and the EPA levied over $24 million in penalties. The penalties imposed during FY 1985–1987 (a total of about $68 million) constitute one and a half times the total penalties given out by the EPA during the years 1974–1984. The criminal enforcement program referred 41 cases for criminal prosecution during FY 1987, and secured convictions or guilty pleas from fifty-eight defendants who were fined a total of $3.6 million and given a total of eighty-four years in prison (EPA, 1988a: *i,*2).

The following are some examples of convictions taken from the files of the National Enforcement Investigations Center, Office of Criminal Investigations (EPA, 1988b):

- James Holland, owner of Middle Keys Construction Company, dredged and filled twelve sites in lower and middle Florida Keys between May 1980 and August 1983 and, for one site, fraudulently represented to landowners that all permits would be obtained. He was charged with eleven counts of violating the Rivers and Harbors Appropriations Act of 1899, eight counts of violating the Clean Air and Water Acts, and three counts of mail fraud. He pleaded guilty to eleven of these charges, and was sentenced to five years probation, 400 hours of community service, and was required to perform restoration at four sites. His probation was revoked almost three years after sentencing, and he was given a $10,000 fine, six months in prison, and was barred from construction activities.
- George Mills was accused of storing hazardous waste and failure to give required notification of existence of hazardous waste facilities located in Tennessee and Alabama. He was charged with four counts (two for storing and two for concealing storage). Mills entered a guilty plea and was sentenced to five years probation, a $30,000 fine and the condition that a full written account of actions and recommendations for compliance to avoid similar contraventions of environmental laws be submitted to professional journals in the field.
- K.W. Thompson Tool Company, Inc. (Thompson Center Arms) was charged with dumping cyanide, barium, potassium nitrate, and sodium hydroxide into the Cocheco River and into the ground. The Company was charged with fifty counts of pollution violations. The jury viewed the dump site and began hearing evidence in the trial. A week later, the company pleaded guilty to seventeen of the counts, and was fined $75,000. Charges against three of the company's executives were dropped.

- An automobile import and emission testing facility in Orange County, California used a mail scheme to defraud the EPA and Customs Service regarding the importation of motor vehicles not conforming to Clean Air Act emissions standards and submittal of false test data to the EPA. Albert and Garo Mardikan and Sembat Agob were charged with forty-six counts (mail fraud and giving false statements). All pleaded guilty. Albert received five years in prison (suspended to a few months), five years probation, plus 2,080 hours of community service (some of which consisted of teaching under-privileged individuals how to seek jobs), placement of twenty persons per year in a job, and restitution payment to injured parties. Garo was sentenced to five years in prison (suspended to thirty days), five years probation, plus community service. Agob was sentenced to five years in prison (suspended to twenty days), five years probation, plus 2,500 hours of community service.
- Everett Harwell (president) and Eugene Baggett (vice-president for operations), of Southeastern Waste Treatment, Inc., disposed of electroplating wastes without a permit and filed false statements with the Georgia Environmental Protection Division. They also transported hazardous wastes, failed to notify their release, and misrepresented that the wastes had been incinerated when they were poured into a city sewage system. Both pleaded guilty to a total of four counts. Harwell was sentenced to three years in prison and a $20,000 fine and Baggett was sentenced to eighteen months in prison and a $10,000 fine.
- Robert E. Derecktor, president of Derecktor, Inc. (a shipbuilding and repair yard) was charged with forty-six counts of pollution, including twenty-nine counts of discharging pollutants from drydock without a permit in violation of the Clean Water Act. Transformers from the shipyard were found to be leaking PCBs after being buried at a farm. The firm was sentenced to a $600,000 fine on its plea of guilty to twenty-six counts of violating the Clean Water Act and other laws. A third of that fine was slated for restitution to the Hazardous Waste Emergency Response Fund. Derecktor was sentenced to a $75,000 fine and five years probation.

ORGANIZATIONAL BRIBEGIVING

The last general category of organizational occupational crime that will be addressed is bribegiving. There are two basic areas of bribery that benefit organizations. First, political bribegiving encompasses outright bribes to public officials or agents and illegal political campaign contributions, both domestic and foreign, for the purpose of influencing governmental actions. (Political bribe*taking* is covered in Chapter 5.) Second, commercial bribegiving involves Firm A paying Firm B (or its employees) for favoritism in purchasing Firm A's products. Commercial bribery also involves industrial espionage—payments for confidential business information to gain market advantage (e.g., that related to trade secrets, research and development, bidding, customers).

Political Bribegiving

Johnston (1982:20) has delineated the systemic forces which create an environment that encourages political bribegiving generally, and these would be especially relevant to the encouragement of domestic (and foreign) political bribery by organizations: "(1) The fruits of governmental action are often extremely valuable (or, in the case of penalties and sanctions, extremely costly), with demand for benefits frequently exceeding supply; (2) These benefits and sanctions often can be gotten or avoided only by dealing with the government; and (3) The routine process through which benefits and sanctions are conferred is time-consuming, expensive and uncertain in its outcome." A lobbyist for the Associated Milk Producers, which illegally contributed $100,000 to President Nixon's 1972 campaign, explained that organization's rationale for such contributions: "One way a small group makes itself heard is to help politicians get into office and give him some physical help and they won't forget your favor when they do get into government. . . ." (Clinard and Yeager, 1980:157). Shortly after Nixon's reelection campaign received the contribution, the White House announced increases in dairy price supports. Political bribegiving, then, is an extremely cost-effective and time-effective way of gaining advantages with certainty. To give an idea of the scope of these activities, the Securities and Exchange Commission's disclosure drive on illegal or questionable domestic and foreign payments revealed that by 1978 at least $1 billion had been paid by more than three hundred of the five hundred *Fortune* leading industrial corporations (Clinard and Yeager, 1980:155).

Regarding outright political bribery domestically, a perusal of Ross's Roster (Table 4.1) indicates that several of America's leading firms have attempted to bribe public officials and agents. In 1978, for instance, executives of six alcoholic beverage manufacturing firms pleaded guilty to these practices—American Brands (Jim Beam Bourbon), Heublein, Liggett Group (Paddington Corp.), National Distillers, Rapid-American (Schenley), and Joseph E. Seagram (Seagram Distillers and three other subsidiaries). Seagram was again charged in 1979 with bribery of members of a state liquor control board, after which it pleaded guilty and was fined $1.5 million. In 1972, Northern Natural Gas was charged with mail fraud related to bribery of local officials to obtain right-of-way permits for pipeline construction. In 1977, Gulf Oil Company and two employees were charged with giving illegal gifts to an Internal Revenue Service agent—Gulf pleaded guilty, one executive pleaded *nolo contendre* and the other was convicted after trial. And in 1978, Tenneco Corporation pleaded guilty to mail fraud in connection with bribery of a local government official.

Outright political bribegiving to foreign officials has also been common. For instance, several aircraft manufacturers commonly made payments to foreign governments in order to secure sales, including Northrop Corporation ($30 million), Lockheed ($25 million), and McDonnell Douglas ($15.6 million). Exxon disclosed illegal or questionable payments of over $75 million (much of which went to foreign government officials). ITT admitted paying $8.7 million to foreign officials, while Xerox Corporation paid $375,000. United Brands, a major banana importer, paid $2.5 million to Honduran officials in 1974 to avoid tax increases of a penny per pound. American multinational companies have gone to great lengths to hide their foreign bribegiving, such as creating phony subsidiaries, using false or unrecorded bookkeeping entries, having recourse of third parties, and employing cash payments. In the wake of these scandals, particularly Lockheed's, the Foreign Corrupt Practices Act was passed in 1977, which outlawed bribegiving to foreign officials except in cases involving national security. Prior to the passage of that law, it had been illegal for American companies that made payments to foreign governments only not to disclose those payments to the Internal Revenue Service and the Securities and Exchange Commission. Since the passage of the Foreign Corrupt Practices Act, organizations making such illegal payments are subject to criminal fines as high as $1 million, and executives face as much as five years imprisonment and a $10,000 fine. Although bribegiving to foreign officials is seen by bribers as an accepted way of protecting American business interests abroad, it promotes unfair trade practices and can have damaging political fallout by creating negative images of America among other nations (Clinard and Yeager, 1980: Chapter 7).

Regarding illegal campaign contributions, which is the most common method of domestic political bribegiving, corporations have, since the 1907 passage of the Tillman Act, been legally forbidden from making contributions to candidates seeking a federal office. The Federal Corrupt Practices Act, passed in 1925, attempted to organize and revise the Tillman legislation and other federal laws, but it did not encompass any meaningful substantive changes. For almost a half century, the Federal Corrupt Practices Act was to a large extent powerless because it was fraught with loopholes and exceptions. Federal campaign law was completely renovated in 1971 by the Federal Election Campaign Act and its various amendments, which limited a candidate's expenditures on advertising, self-contributions, and total campaign expenditures. The Election Act also required a detailed itemization of any contributions exceeding one hundred dollars. Some of these provisions were later ruled unconstitutional by the Supreme Court, but the Court left intact the limitations on campaign spending and independent and personal contributions. As it stands now, individual candidates can receive a maximum of one thousand dollars from other individuals and five thousand dollars from "political action committees." The net effect of the Federal Election Campaign Act is to some extent negligible, because a single individual or organization can contribute to several different political action committees, each committee having the same purposes in mind (Coleman, 1989).

To avoid prosecution for illegal contributions, organizations must resort to subterfuge in order to hide their involvement, particularly through magical bookkeeping practices (e.g., false entries, mislabeled accounts, inventions of phony subsidiaries). To avoid direct payments that can be traced to the firm, organizations have been known to make "third party" contributions by secretly supplying employees with the necessary funds to give to particular candidates. For example, employees have been secretly compensated for their contributions through payment of higher salaries, "bonuses," or "reimbursements" on overstated expense accounts.

Oil corporations were one of the most visible sources of illegal contributions to Nixon's reelection campaign. For instance, five Rockefeller brothers, who owned 1 percent of Exxon stock, together made payments of over $5 million. Other secret Nixon contributions from the petroleum industry included Gulf Oil ($1.3 million), Getty Oil ($77,000), Standard Oil of California ($102,000), Sun Oil ($60,000), Phillips Petroleum ($100,000), Exxon ($100,000), and Ashland Oil ($100,000) (Clinard and Yeager, 1980:158). Several other large companies made illegal domestic political contributions: including American Airlines, Braniff International, Carnation, Diamond International, Firestone, GTE, General Dynamics, General Tire and Rubber, Goodyear, Greyhound, 3M, Northrop, Occidental Petroleum, and Singer (see Figure 4.1).

Commercial Bribegiving

As noted, commercial bribegiving encompasses two major kinds of practices: paying firms or their agents for purchasing one's products (e.g., kickbacks, rebates) and industrial espionage. Kickbacks and rebating have been normal ways of doing business for many years. After the Federal

Trade Commission disparaged the practice in 1918, several federal and state laws have specifically outlawed it. Moreover, when commercial bribery involves rebating or discriminatory pricing, then these acts can constitute restraint of trade violations. Further, some industries are subject to specific commercial bribery laws (e.g, kickbacks associated with liquor sales are a violation of federal and state laws, and paying radio personnel to play certain records is also a crime). Commercial bribegiving is particularly likely in the most competitive industries.

Many businesses routinely give substantial gifts to prospective purchasing firms (e.g., cash, "free samples," charitable contributions) or "entertain" them (e.g., lavish vacations, baseball tickets). The extent to which these gifts are excessive is the extent to which they can be seen as commercial bribegiving. Again turning to Ross's Roster (Figure 4.1), several major firms have been caught giving illegal bribes to prospective buyers: Anheuser-Busch, Arden-Mayfair, Beatrice Foods, Bethlehem Steel, Walter Kidde, LTV (Wilson Foods), J. Ray McDermott, Rapid-American, R.J. Reynolds Industries, F.&M. Schaefer, Joseph Schlitz Brewing, Joseph E. Seagram, and Seatrain Lines.

When individual purchasing agents, rather than firms, take bribes to influence their purchasing decisions, they are individual rather than organizational occupational criminals. Clinard and Yeager (1980:166–67) report several such cases from the 1970s. For example, in 1975 a Sears bicycle accessories buyer was convicted on federal charges for taking thousands of dollars from an importer of bicycle speedometers. In other cases, a purchasing agent for International Harvester set up a bogus consulting firm and collected close to $30,000 from suppliers between 1971 and 1973, and a cabinet buyer for Zenith Radio Corporation collected $100,000 in kickbacks during 1967 and 1971. Even more lucrative payoffs were given to agents of American Airlines (where an advertising buyer received close to $200,000 in kickbacks from various media sources) and the chewing gum manufacturer American Chiclets (where a purchasing agent took more than $300,000 in kickbacks from supermarket display rack suppliers).

Industrial espionage involves the theft of valuable commercial information, either directly (through bribery of double-agent employees) or indirectly (through hiring strategic personnel away from competing firms for substantial sums). A firm may spend millions of dollars developing a new product, only to have the results stolen by a competitor. One well known example involved IBM as the victim. That multinational firm charged several competitors with hiring away their key personnel because of the personnel's knowledge of IBM's trade secrets. In one such case, the engineering program manager for a new IBM system called

"Merlin" was hired by Telex Corporation with a cash bonus of $500,000. Telex was sued by IBM, and was ordered to pay restitution because Telex had "systematically" stolen some of IBM's trade secrets. In another instance of alleged industrial espionage, Mobil Oil charged Superior Oil Company with hiring away more than thirty of Mobil's employees, including a president and general manager. Mobil alleged that their former employees had undoubtedly disclosed many trade secrets for which Mobil had spent millions of dollars annually, and that Superior had intended to steal these secrets when they hired Mobil's employees (Clinard and Yeager, 1980:230–31).

In another group of cases involving industrial espionage, defense contracting firms, their consultants, and civilian employees at the Pentagon were implicated in a far-reaching bribery scheme. In 1988, several military procurement agents were charged with giving to defense contractors and their consultants confidential bidding information on Navy purchases worth more than $500 million. The FBI secretly listened to conversations among several consultants related to information on nine contracts. In one of the eavesdrops, the FBI heard defense consultant Thomas Muldoon tell another consultant (Mark Saunders), "If you can get anything, we . . . can make some money." The same day, Saunders obtained from Pentagon buyer George Stone ten "secret" bids. Saunders and Muldoon received as much as $4,000 per month apiece from one contractor alone (Litton) in the scheme. Saunders was also implicated in a conspiracy with Joe Bradley, vice president for marketing of Varian Continental Electronics, to rig the purchase requirements so Varian could beat other companies in bidding on a Navy radio system (AP, 7/1/88). Teledyne Electronics and several of its employees were charged with conspiracy and bribery in a similar scheme to get details about a Navy radar contract worth more than $100 million. And two executives of Hazeltine Corporation, a subsidiary of Emerson Electric Company, Inc., pleaded guilty in another related case (AP, 1/14/89).

A CASE STUDY OF ORGANIZATIONAL WRONGDOING: THE SPACE SHUTTLE CHALLENGER DISASTER

This chapter has reviewed a large number of crimes by organizations, as well as the various processes promoting them. A short case study concludes the chapter. Kramer (1988) has detailed the internal and external factors impinging on the National Aeronautics and Space Administration (NASA) prior to the explosion of the space shuttle Challenger on January

28, 1986. Although there have been no criminal charges and although NASA is a government agency rather than a private organization, the case nevertheless illustrates well the pressures that propel an organization into misconduct (in this case, subjecting employees to extremely unsafe working conditions).

The "official" cause of the explosion during Challenger's final flight (#51-L) was the failure of the pressure seal in the aft field joint of the right solid rocket motor. However, as Kramer (1988:8) points out, ". . . the flawed decision-making process at NASA was the more important cause." In March of 1970, President Nixon cancelled NASA's mandates for a manned Mars expedition and earth- and lunar-orbiting space stations, and ordered the development of a space shuttle, which then became the focus of NASA's short-term future. NASA was essentially forced to put all of its efforts into the design of such a vehicle, creating intense pressures to complete the prototypes and begin a heavy schedule of flights. By early 1981, NASA was being squeezed to finish the "developmental" stages of the project and declare the shuttle program "operational." Additionally, the shuttle program was to become economically self-sufficient (through satellite launching and in-flight research supported commercially) and increase its military role. In August of 1981, President Reagan declared the shuttle program "operational" after the first four orbital test flights, and announced that the program would be the nation's primary space launch system. By deeming the program "operational," Reagan put enormous pressures on NASA because his declaration implied that space shuttling was routine in operation and free of anomalies.

Because of the enormous financial outlays for America's space program since its inception, NASA needed to show that it could recover at least some of its costs through commercial operations. As a result, NASA launched satellites for a variety of commercial customers. This need to generate funds caused further launch pressures as well as competition with the European Space Agency's Ariane rocket, which also had the capability to launch satellites. NASA had to make its shuttle missions appear to the world as dependable. As the Rogers Commission (appointed to investigate the Challenger disaster) noted (1986:165):

"Pressures developed because of the need to meet customer commitments, which translated into a requirement to launch a certain number of flights per year and to launch them on time. Such considerations may occasionally have obscured engineering concerns. Managers may have forgotten—partly because of past success, partly because of their own well-nurtured image of the program—that the Shuttle was still in a research and development stage." (in Kramer, 1988:13)

Additionally, as noted, the shuttle program was being pressured by Congress, the Pentagon, and the White House to increase its military role. The external political environment, then, significantly affected NASA's organizational goals in the shuttle program. As Kramer (1988:15) notes, these pressures for accelerating flight schedules were "undoubtedly felt by the individuals who occupied positions within the organizational structure at NASA."

As NASA attempted to meet these internal pressures, several operating problems developed which compromised the certainty of safety that had been characteristic of NASA. Rather than reducing its flight schedule, NASA instead decided to proceed. When NASA discovered the faulty seal of the joint on the solid rocket motor designed by Morton Thiokol, it should have cancelled all future flights until the problem was fixed. But this decision possibly could have postponed the program for several months, and such delays had to be avoided. Although the faulty seal was considered nonserious and an acceptable risk, NASA was obviously concerned about it because the space agency made a concerted effort to rectify the problem. Flight 51-L had already been postponed three times and delayed once. The afternoon before the fatal launch, Morton Thiokol engineers voiced extreme concerns about the cold weather forecast for the next morning, because cold weather would adversely affect the known defects in the seal. Morton Thiokol engineers presented their concerns during the NASA readiness review process, and recommeded that the launch again be delayed. NASA wanted to launch, and put pressure on Thiokol management to pressure its engineers to rescind their no-launch recommendation. Thiokol finally approved the launch over the strong objections of their engineers.

As Kramer (1988:21) points out, "Rather than change the goal and delay the flight, these men resolved the strain by using deviant means, that is, lower safety standards than were acceptable." The lack of internal and external social controls over NASA caused the launch to be approved in spite of the known dangers to the lives on board; had such controls been in place, the safety threshold would have been maintained (Kramer, 1988). Not one of those who made the decision to launch was fired. And in return for a $10 million reduction in award fees, Thiokol was exonerated by NASA from any legal blame for the accident (Bancroft, 1989).

QUESTIONS FOR DISCUSSON

1. When analyzing organizational occupational crime, why is it necessary to differentiate between "official" and "operative" goals of organizations?

2. Describe the criminal liability of organizations.
3. Describe the criminal liability of persons who commit crime for the benefit of their employing organization.
4. Which structures and processes associated with organizations are criminogenic? How would you suggest that these be improved?
5. How does "strain" theory apply to crimes committed within organizations? Be sure to include strains which are both internal and external to the organization.
6. How does differential social organization increase organizational crime? Can you give any additional examples not found in this chapter?
7. Compare the works of Sutherland (1949) and Clinard and Yeager (1980) in terms of the methodology they used to study the prevalence of organizational crime. Explain the strengths and weaknesses of each approach.
8. Which structural factors did Clinard, et al. find to be most associated with organizational offending?
9. Why are regulatory agency statistics on enforcement relatively poor indicators of the totality of organizational offending? Which factors most affect those statistics?
10. The Sherman Antitrust Act of 1890 was the first of its kind in America. How have laws against restraint of trade evolved since Sherman?
11. This chapter has discussed several organizational crimes against property. What are some additional cases of misrepresentations in advertising? Price-fixing? Illegal labor practices?
12. This chapter has discussed several organizational crimes against persons. What are some additional cases of unsafe consumer product distribution? Unsafe working condtions? Environmental pollution?
13. What are the different forms of organizational bribegiving? Explain the differences among them in terms of offenders and victims.
14. Launching human beings into space has inherent safety risks. Do you believe that the adverse safety factors related to the final launch the Challenger were acceptable flight risks? If not, is any space flight "safe"? Explain.

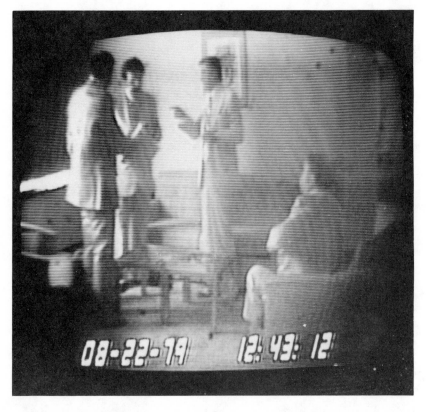

Congressman Michael Myers (second from left) discusses "the payoff" with undercover FBI agents in a videotape played at the first ABSCAM trial. Video and audiotapes shown during the trials provided Americans with an unprecedented view of public corruption in action. (AP/Wide World Photos)

F I V E

STATE AUTHORITY OCCUPATIONAL CRIME

This chapter describes crimes which occur through a person's exercise of *state authority* (a "state" can be any independent jurisdictional government entity, such as a city, a county, a state, a province, or a country). For our purposes, "state authority" refers to powers lawfully vested in persons by a state through which those persons can make or enforce laws or command others. State authority is usually empowered through the taking of a public oath. It is important to distinguish between crimes committed through state authority and other occupational crimes, because state-based legal authority carries unique opportunities to commit occupational offenses that do not exist elsewhere. Many government officials' offenses would not be possible without the legal force of their state authority.

In one sense, of course, all government employees work "for" the state or "on behalf" of it by virtue of their public employment. However, "state authority" does not merely refer to public employment-related authority to make everyday decisions on the job (e.g., hiring, purchasing). It refers specifically to a legally vested power to represent the force of state law in certain decisions.

Crimes related to the making and enforcing of laws can be committed through several kinds of state-power roles. For instance, legislators have the authority to pass laws in the name of the state, as do Presidents, Governors, and mayors. Public executives also have the legal power to make official appointments to public offices. Legislators, too, make legal judgements on public office holders when they confirm appointments and vote in impeachments. Judicial officers represent state law in their decisions about bail, guilt or innocence, sentencing, search and arrest warrants, and civil judgements. Judges also produce constitutional and other case law for the state. Criminal justice system personnel such as police officers, prosecutors, prison guards, parole officers, and regulatory inspectors often make direct decisions about enforcing the state's laws. Even bribetaking by a juror may technically fall within the spirit of the concept of state authority occupational crime. Although jurors are not government "officials" in the usual sense of the word, they nevertheless have been legally empowered through an oath to enforce the law, and they may receive some taxable income in compensation for their time.

Persons with valid military rank (or its equivalent) have the state authority to command certain persons to do certain things. In so commanding, persons with legally valid rank can commit crime directly. An example of such an offense occurred in 1988 at Pensacola Air Station, where a U. S. Navy rescue-swimmer instructor drowned a recruit by forcing him under water during a training exercise; the instructor was convicted of negligent homicide (AP, 9/24/88). Those in the military can also commit state authority crime indirectly, when they illegally order subordinates to commit offenses. Ordering military subordinates to torture and murder (as some Nazis did during World War II) or to perform other kinds of illegal acts would constitute the use of state authority for criminal activity. However, state authority would not be involved if a public employee without the equivalent of military rank were to order a subordinate to commit a crime—here, there is no legal requirement to follow such an order.

Using this spirit of "state authority," many occupational crimes by public officials would not be included under the concept. For instance, although a Senator who embezzles government funds commits a crime against the public, powers which carry the force of state law may not have been used to access those funds. On the other hand, were a Senator to accept a bribe in exchange for legislative voting influence, then the criminal opportunity would fall squarely within the concept of state authority. It may seem dubious to distinguish between a Senator who embezzles and a Senator who takes bribes, because both offenses victimize the community at large by the misuse of the public position of Senator. However, whereas the embezzling Senator needs only a trusted economic position, the bribetaking Senator needs a vested state authority to vote on legislation.

Crimes associated with the prestige of a government position should not be confused with crimes committed through the state authority of a government position. In the Watergate scandal, the obstruction of justice charges against Richard Nixon by the House Judiciary Committee and of which the President's men (e.g., Haldeman, Ehrlichman, and Mitchell) were convicted did not involve the use of state authority. The charges stemmed from attempts to bribe witnesses with "hush" money and favors; influencing through bribegiving was the crime, not bribetaking for influence. Other alleged crimes associated with the Watergate affair also had nothing to do with the exercise of state authority (e.g., burglaries of Democratic headquarters and Daniel Ellsberg's psychiatrist's office, illegal campaign financial practices, forgery of discrediting evidence against Senator Muskie). Ethical violations by elected and appointed officials are not always criminal violations, and if they are criminal, they still may not involve the use of the official's vested powers.

The House Committee accused Nixon of violating his oath of office by making false statements, withholding evidence, counseling witnesses to make false statements, and bribing witnesses with cash and favors. Nixon would be guilty of state authority crime to the extent that he used his powers as President of the United States, not the prestige of the Office, in the commission of these acts. For example, Nixon may have had a role in offering the presiding judge in the Ellsberg burglary case the directorship of the FBI in exchange for the judge's influence. There were allegations that Presidential political appointments (e.g., ambassador) were also offered in exchange for campaign contributions (Simon and Eitzen, 1982:197). These would be crimes that are facilitated through the exercise of a President's authority to make certain appointments (or nominations for them). Nixon was also accused of withholding evidence by keeping and editing the famous White House tapes. Had it been shown that he illegally withheld evidence under the powers of the Presidency, rather than in the role of individual, then he would have used his state authority in the process.

Criminal falsification of public evidence or records (including perjury) by a public employee often constitutes a state authority offense. But this is true only to the extent that the lawful validity of such information has been officially entrusted (by the state) to the word or hand of the perpetrator. A postal worker who files a false employee expense reimbursement form would be committing fraud by an individual, but the postal workers who falsified postmarks to coincide with a Super Bowl contest deadline (AP, 4/20/88) committed their crimes through a legal enforcement authority vested by the state. Similarly, a coroner who commits perjury by lying about the cause of death after an autopsy is also a state authority criminal—the coroner is directed by law to produce the legally binding, official cause of death. Many other government employees (e.g., clerks, income tax auditors, meat inspectors, customs and immigration officials, police and prison officers) directly represent the enforcement of state law when they issue legally valid documents (e.g., official reports, court citations) and give official testimony on behalf of the state (e.g., regarding an arrest or an inspection). For instance, Raymond Edwards (formerly of the Americus, Georgia, Police Department) was sentenced to four years in prison for falsifying twenty-nine sets of fingerprints and other state authority crimes. Edwards faked fingerprints by copying known sets of prints onto "lifting" tape and claiming he had found them at a crime scene. He was clearly in a state authority role when he testified for the state about the prints (Pierce, 1989).

However, an official who forges a seal to validate a document has not used state authority in doing so, because the legal validity of the document has not been entrusted to the forger's word. Additionally, if persons formally accused of state authority crime perjure themselves by denying involvement in those offenses, then the perjury is in the role of individuals rather than as representatives of the state.

There is also a difference between wielding state authority and being legally licensed. Although being lawfully licensed sometimes carries certain state requirements (e.g., in the selling of firearms and liquor), licensure does not encompass state authority. Firearms dealers, for instance, do not have the state authority *per se* to sell guns, they have only state permission to sell them under certain conditions. The issuing of official licenses, on the other hand, directly involves the use of state authority.

One also ought not confuse access to state property and state authority. Through their government jobs, almost all public employees have access to at least some state-owned goods, services and cash. Theft or embezzlement of such items, however, is rarely done through the exercise of state authority. On the other hand, a police officer who uses his or her badge to gain illegal access to an athletic event or a theft site is a state authority criminal. These rules and exclusions are meant to distinguish the particular opportunities for occupational crime associated with the use of state authority that are not possible without such legal powers.

Knotty problems are bound to arise in deciding whether a public employee's occupationally related crime is based on the exercise of state vested powers to "make or enforce laws or to command others." There is even a question in some cases about whether a person's behavior was or was not as an official. A case in point is when, toward the end of President Reagan's second term, a special prosecutor was appointed to decide if Edwin Meese was acting as an official when he was involved in certain allegedly unethical financial transactions as Attorney General. Those involved in the "Iran-Contra Affair" were in state authority positions, but such authority may not have been used to complete their deeds. In some cases, then, whether certain offenses by government employees are accessed through what is termed here as their "state authority" will be a matter of opinion. There are, however, many clear examples of state authority crime, some of which will now be presented under five general categories: Genocide and Torture; Police Brutality; Civil Rights Violations; Theft; and Bribetaking. These categories help to organize the discussion, and are not meant to be exclusive or exhaustive.

GENOCIDE AND TORTURE

When persons in higher level government positions employ policies of genocide and torture through their state authority to command others, those acts often are not readily classified as "crime" because the officials who command these acts usually define them as noncriminal. According to our definition in Chapter 1, if an act is not defined as criminal, then it technically may not be viewed as occupational "crime" because it is not criminally punishable by the state.

However, even if torture and genocide are not defined as criminal in the jurisdictions in which they occur, they nevertheless might be regarded as violations of international law or treaty. An article in the 1948 *United Nations Universal Declaration of Human Rights*, for instance, specifically prohibits torture: "No one shall be subjected to torture or to cruel, inhuman, or degrading treatment or punishment." In regard to genocide, as a specific response to the atrocities during World War II, the United Nations, also in 1948, outlawed genocide through international treaty. That document defines genocide as:

"any of the following acts committed with the intent to destroy, in whole or part, a national, ethical, racial, or religious group, as such:
  (a) Killing members of the group;
  (b) Causing serious bodily or mental harm to members of the group;
  (c) Deliberately inflicting on the group conditions of life calculated to bring about its physical destruction in whole or in part;
  (d) Imposing measures intended to prevent births within the group;
  (e) Forcibly transferring the children of the group to another group."

Forty years after the United Nations drafted this treaty, America finally ratified it, joining more than ninety other nations. Genocide is now punishable under the force of United States law.

Genocide and torture are most often employed systematically by government officials as instruments to preserve and maintain the power of the state, although they may be camouflaged as legally justifiable corporal and capital punishment (such as in the outlawing of dissidence). But torture and genocide can also be practiced through state authority by individual government officials acting by themselves. Each series of brutalities varies according to the level of official knowledge and decision, and the degree of repetitiveness. Before one can say that these crimes are occurring as the result of a systematic governmental policy, then, there must be a definition of "systematic." That definition, of course, could be unique to the definer. Moreover, levels of officials' internal and external accountability vary situationally. This variance will affect the overall probability of genocide or torture taking place systematically, because opportunity to commit these atrocities may or may not be blocked by checks and balances in the political system.

There is a very fine conceptual line between genocide and torture. To illustrate, the United Nations statute against genocide cited above also encompasses torture, for genocide includes "causing serious bodily or mental harm to members of the group." Torturing to death also may be employed as a method to reach the end of genocide. Nor can there be doubt that mental harm caused by anticipation of death, such as that experienced by Jews in Nazi concentration camps, is torture. Indeed, torture and genocide may often be indistinguishable.

Without attempting a precise definition of "systematic" torture and genocide, we can point to a few historical instances that would qualify by most definitions. The campaign by the Nazis to extirpate the Jewish people (and other racial and religious groups), the Stalinist purges of the 1930s (involving 40 million victims), and the systematic extermination of opponents to Idi Amin in Uganda in the 1970s are obvious twentieth century examples.

Regarding torture by itself (Green, 1981b), Amnesty International has formulated a working definition of it as "the systematic infliction of acute pain in any form by one person on another, or on a third person, in order to accomplish the purpose of the former against the will of the latter" (Amnesty International, 1975: 35). This definition does not designate the official position of the torturer, but others have proposed that only public officials and their agents can be torturers. For example, the United Nations defines torture as those sufferings "inflicted by or at the instigation of a public official. . . ." (United Nations, 1975:13). Only torture by officials is relevant to the present discussion.

The Amnesty International definition is problematic because it is not clear what constitutes "acute pain in any form." First, human thresholds to physical pain differ. Second, "mental pain" is often culturally determined; forcing a devout member of some religious group to engage in taboo behavior could cause more mental pain than forcing a less orthodox member to do so. The provision about infliction of physical and mental pain in the United Nations' definition of genocide is similarly problematic.

The infliction of severe physical pain—by shooting, beating, electric shock, surgery, extreme heat and cold, suffocation, and burning of the flesh—is easily identifiable as intentional physical torture. Less severe forms of inflicted pain, however, are not as readily established as deliberate. Partial sensory deprivation, physical exhaustion, and significant (but not complete) deprivation of adequate nutrition may result from deliberate attempts at torture by authorities; but they may also indicate only an inability to provide adequate prison conditions. The deliberateness of the inflicted psychological pain may also be masked, because the causes of such pain can range from routine semi-isolation for security purposes to the more obvious systematic production of chronic anxiety through threats of physical violence. The infliction of physical and mental pain by authorities, then, may or may not deliberately aim to break the victim's will and may be more or less severe, depending on the methods used and the subject's threshold for pain.

Torture by governmental officials has four major motivations. First, it can be used to extract confessions and information about confederates. This torture is sometimes practiced by police and military officials and is not part of an overall coordinated plan. However, torture motivated by a desire for information can also be used by officials as part of an overall policy to ferret out dissidents. Second, officials may use torture for personal gain. Such instances are usually individually motivated. As an example, prisoners in Arkansas were threatened with whippings if they did not pay prison officials (Murton and Hyams, 1969).

Third, torture is used as an operant conditioner (see discussion in Chapter 3). Torture can be used to coerce the victim into a compliant behavioral or belief pattern by making the victim afraid of reexperiencing the torture. This is commonly known as specific deterrence. Fourth, torture can also be employed as an operant conditioner by serving as an example to others, to coerce those others into a compliant behavioral or belief pattern. This is commonly known as general deterrence. These latter two motivations are usually part of an overall coordinated governmental policy to quell opponents, but they can also be used by individual prison personnel for disciplinary purposes. Mental torture can also be inflicted systematically for deterrent purposes. Attempts by the California Department of Corrections (during the period 1965-1971) to coerce politically active prisoners into displaying compliant behavioral patterns—through systematic manipulation of sentence length (Wright, 1973)—has many of the elements needed to qualify as an example of deterrent-based mental torture.

Gathering reliable information on state-authorized torture and genocide is difficult because governments are reluctant to admit its use. Although reliable aggregate information on torture and genocide does not exist, case-by-case data have been gathered through international organizations, most notably Amnesty International. Skillful interview work is needed to document the details of each incident and to determine the reliability of sources, because accusations of torture and genocide can be fabricated by persons who wish to discredit an incumbent regime or an individual official. Unfortunately, case-by-case research is of little help in estimating the total incidence of torture and genocide because it is underrepresentative.

Victim surveys, too, hold little promise for providing a more accurate picture of the incidence of torture and genocide. There are two basic methodological problems with these population surveys. First, there is a potential sampling bias because there may be few persons in the general population who were tortured, or threatened with torture or death (known as a low "base rate"). Available base rates are small to begin with anyway, because many torture and genocide victims are killed or imprisoned and obviously cannot be found in the general population. Second, there is a strong potential for response bias because the intimidation of torture and genocide may be effective, and victims and their acquaintances may fear reprisal and, therefore, will not report torture or murder. Even randomized response models are rather hopeless here because of the potential for very low base rates.

Any explanation of torture and genocide would have to include logistical, social structural, and individual psychological items. Logistically, to carry out torture and genocide, state authorities must possess the manpower and technology to dominate victims. They must have loyal military or civilian police and needed weaponry, and they must be in a position to control the flow of information about their actions. History suggests that even the modern conventional war machines of the superpowers may not be able to dominate a citizenry that has its own armed physical power, as the American experience in Vietnam and the Soviet experience in Afghanistan demonstrate.

On the social structural plane, genocide and torture might be least likely to occur in societies in which most persons share several statuses in common (Eisenhauer, 1981). Under such conditions, there is less chance of singling out a group that has a unique status. Genocide and torture might be most common when status differentials, particularly those of a political nature, are more pronounced.

Psychological studies may provide answers regarding the willingness of one person to inflict injury and death on another. Research on persons actually carrying out torture and genocide should examine whether such persons have dispositions congenial to the their use. However, ordinary citizens have been shown to develop dominant personalities while temporarily in the role of prison authority (Zimbardo, 1972), so disposition to commit these acts may be partially a function of role socialization. Perhaps direct obedience is the reason behind an individual's infliction of torture and genocide. The classic studies by Milgram (e.g., 1963; 1965) demonstrated that almost all persons are willing to inflict some degree of pain on another person if commanded to do so by the proper authority.

Because voluntary obedience to a command to torture can take place so readily in the civilian population, such obedience appears even more likely in a well disciplined police or military force—subordinates will seldom question orders, even if they are morally opposed to them.

Other research might examine the effect of group socialization on role performance. Sutherland's ideas about differential association discussed in Chapter Three may be relevant to explain the behavior of persons who inflict torture and genocide, by indicating why they possess definitions favorable to committing atrocities against other human beings. Captain William Calley, the only soldier convicted of the 1968 murders of men, women, and children at the My Lai massacre during the Vietnam War, indicated that his actions were part of a normative system developed by the military and transmitted to soldiers through learning, which promoted a lack of "attachment" to the feelings of the Vietnamese people:

> "If I have committed a crime, the only crime that I have committed is in judgement of my values. Apparently, I have valued my troops' lives more than I did that of the enemy. When my troops were getting massacred and mauled by an enemy I couldn't see, I couldn't touch; that nobody in the military ever described as anything other than communism. . . . They didn't give it a race, they didn't give it a sex, they didn't give it an age. They never let me believe it was just a philosophy in a man's mind. That was my enemy out there and when it came between me and that enemy, I had to value the lives of my troops, and I feel that that is the only crime I have committed." (Esper, 1988)

Torture and genocide may be more likely to occur under the two forms of social disorganization identified by Sutherland (anomie and differential social organization). When the population of a country is in political transition and turmoil—an anomic state—there may be a breakdown of standards about which means are allowable to justify various political ends. Regarding differential social organization, the Calley quote shows that the United States military seems to have had an organized normative system that promoted genocide during the Vietnam War. Issues of psychological make-up and group socialization are not limited to persons who actually carry out torture and genocide, but pertain to all officials implicated in their use.

Criminal prosecution of highest-level political torturers and murderers from within the country is difficult unless the offending regime is ultimately overthrown, in which case torturers and murderers can be brought to trial. Prosecution of offending regimes from outside the country is almost impossible unless nations organize to invoke international sanctions, such as in the prosecution of Nazi war criminals at Nuremburg. Laws forbidding relations with offending regimes—for example, the United States Foreign Assistance Act of 1976—are of little use unless invoked and joined by the community of nations. Even if a few powerful nations invoke such laws, offending regimes may meet their economic and military needs from states not participating in the sanctioning.

POLICE BRUTALITY

As noted, the difference between individually motivated police brutality and "systematic" policies of brutality depends on the definer. For citizens, the phrase "police brutality" conjures up situations in which individual police officers commit unnecessary acts of violence against innocent and defenseless people. Reiss (1968) has identified the gamut of behaviors most likely to be viewed by the public as brutality: (1) the use of profane and abusive language; (2) commands to move on or get home; (3) stopping and questioning people on the street or searching them and their automobiles; (4) threats to use force if not obeyed; (5) prodding with a nightstick or approaching with a pistol; and (6) actual use of physical force or violence. Prisoners, too, perceive abusive language, unnecessary searches, and the threat and use of physical violence as brutality, when such acts are committed by prison guards and officials.

Exactly what constitutes brutality or unnecessary force in a given situation is a function of subjective judgment, and often depends on one's role in the incident. "Unnecessary" or "improper" force by the police in a given situation also has been defined by Reiss (1968). If force were to be used in one or more of the following ways, he argues, it would constitute unnecessary force:

- If a policeman physically assaulted a citizen and then failed to make an arrest; proper use involves an arrest.
- If the citizen being arrested did not, by word or deed, resist the policeman; force should be used only if it is necessary to make the arrest.
- If the policeman, even though there was resistance to the arrest, could easily have restrained the citizen in other ways.
- If a large number of policemen were present and could have assisted in subduing the citizen in the station, lockup, and in the interrogation rooms.
- If an offender was handcuffed and made no attempt to flee or offer violent resistance.
- If the citizen resisted arrest, but the use of force continued even after the citizen was subdued.

From randomly observing police patrol practices during a seven-week period in Boston, Chicago, and Washington, D. C., Reiss (1968) and his assistants found thirty-seven cases in which force was used improperly according to the above criteria. In all, forty citizens were assaulted. In fifteen cases, no one was arrested. Of the fifteen persons, eight had offered no verbal or physical resistance whatsoever; seven had. An arrest was made in twenty-two cases, thirteen of which involved force at the station house when at least four other officers were present. In two cases, there was no verbal or physical resistance to the arrest, but force was still applied. In two other cases, the police applied force to a handcuffed subject in a field setting. In five of the cases, the suspect resisted arrest, but force continued to be used after he had been subdued. The most remarkable thing was not that the police committed these acts, but rather that the acts were committed with full knowledge that the officers were being watched by observers who could document the behavior.

The following are some specific illustrations of police brutalities (Inciardi, 1987:285):

- During the detention of a suspect arrested for assault on a police officer, detectives periodically kicked the suspect in the stomach, groin, and kidneys. Eight police officers participated. The suspect was later taken to a hospital. The official report stated that he had "fallen down a flight of stairs."
- When police arrrived at a burglary scene, a suspect was taken to the roof of a twelve-story building, hung over the side by a rope fastened to his belt, after which he confessed to the offense.
- Two officers entered a bar to question the bartender about the location of a suspect. A patron accidentally bumped into one of them. After the patron insulted the police, both officers hit him in the head and stomach, breaking several of his bones.
- The police observed a drug dealer dropping envelopes into a sewer. The police began pushing the man with their batons. After raising his arms in self-defense, the dealer was tripped to the street and arrested for assault.
- An alleged armed robber was taken to the police station for interrogation. When the suspect refused to confess, his clothing was stripped, and a wire coat hanger was wrapped around his testicles, after which he admitted the robberies.

Police brutality also often involves the unnecessary use of deadly force. In *Tennessee vs. Garner* (36 CrL 3233, 1985), the Supreme Court of the United States found that the use of deadly force falls under the Fourth

Amendment to the Constitution regarding search and seizure, because it involves the seizure of a person. The Court ruled that the use of deadly force is legal only if it is necessary to prevent the escape of an individual who can reasonably be believed to pose a danger of serious bodily harm or death to innocent persons. Any use of deadly force that does not conform to the Court's prerequisite, then, may be deemed unnecessary, and can be prosecuted criminally as assault or homicide.

Much of the unnecessary violence perpetrated by police against citizens has been attributed to the "Policeman's Working Personality." This personality is nurtured through the law enforcement job, and has been claimed to include the elements of authoritariansim, suspicion, racism, insecurity, hostility, and cynicism (Skolnick, 1966). Because police are expected to establish authority immediately in a given situation, they sometimes resort to physical force to achieve that authority, and their personalities may develop into authoritarian ones. Because police are constantly exposed to danger on the job, they are likely to become suspicious about those who are not part of the police fraternity. Suspicion and authority, coupled with hostility and insecurity, can easily promote the use of unnecessary force. Moreover, police officers tend to have a cynical view about the social value of many citizens with whom they come in contact. Poor training and unclear departmental policies about the use of deadly and nondeadly force further escalate the possibility of brutality by police.

Some of the attitudes associated with the police working personality are taught by other officers, and therefore Sutherland's differential association might be used to explain brutality by individual officers. In some cases, there may exist an excess of definitions favorable to the justification for criminal brutality that have been learned by officers who employ it, and such learning may include the various techniques at inflicting brutality and covering up such deeds (e.g., carrying extra "throw-down" weapons to plant on unarmed suspects who have been shot by the police). In Sutherland's terms, some groups of police officers may be "differentially socially organized" around conduct norms that promote excessive force. In a 1978 survey of police officers, only 12 percent stated that they would report cases of police brutality "every time," while 42 percent would report it "sometimes," 37 percent would report it "rarely," and one in ten (9 percent) would "never" report it (Barker, 1978). A lack of formal sanctions (e.g., criminal conviction and punishment) and informal sanctions (e.g., losing the job) meted out to brutality inflictors would produce an absence of operant conditioning and normative validation against excessive use of force.

Officers who do not believe in the correctness of brutal behavior may change their views of it through employing various techniques of neutralization, so that it is seen as acceptable. For instance, appeals to higher loyalties seem relevant as a technique here, because the police sometimes neutralize their brutality by claiming that the court system fails to punish adequately. "Necessity" and "denial of victim" may be other neutralization techniques used by individual officers to render brutal behavior acceptable. After a period of time, of course, such neutralizations may develop into a police normative system that encourages brutality.

CIVIL RIGHTS VIOLATIONS

There are two basic avenues for criminal charges against the police for the unnecessary use of force. First, individual police or prison officials can be criminally charged through normal indictment processes (grand jury or prosecutor) with violation of state assault and homicide statutes. Second, persons acting under "color of law" (including the state authority to enforce law) can be charged with a federal criminal violation for intentionally restricting an individual's constitutional or other civil rights, under Title 18 of the United State Code (Section 242), which states:

"Deprivation of rights under color of law"

"Whoever, under color of any law, statute, ordinance, regulation, or custom, willfully subjects any inhabitant of any State, Territory, or District to the deprivation of any rights, privileges, or immunities secured or protected by the Constitution or laws of the United States, or to different punishments, pains, or penalties, on account of such inhabitant being an alien, or by reason of his color, or race, than are prescribed for the punishment of citizens, shall be fined not more than $1,000 or imprisoned not more than one year, or both; and if death results shall be subject to imprisonment for any term of years or for life."

Additionally, Title 18 United States Code (Section 241) considers a *conspiracy* to violate civil rights as a federal crime if it occurs under color of law. Title 42 of the United States Code (Section 1983) allows individuals to recover monetary damages from persons who, under color of law, deprive them of their rights. However, conviction under Title 18 (Sections 241 or 242) does not necessarily entitle one to recover monetarily under Title 42 (Section 1983).

Many government officials, particularly those in law enforcement, have been charged with violation of Section 242. In Georgia, for instance, a sheriff and his deputy were guilty of violating this statute because they allowed members of the Ku Klux Klan to beat victims (the statute also covers ommission to act) (*U.S. vs. Lynch*, 189 F2d 476, 1950). A police officer who arrests or searches an individual, knowing that there is no legal basis for such search and seizure, is also guilty of this offense (arrest—*U.S. vs. Ramsey*, 336 F2d 512, 1964; search—*Irvine vs. California*, 347 U.S. 128, 1954). The FBI has been implicated in a series of illegal searches and wiretaps which clearly constitute violations of Section 242 (for Fourth Amendment encroachment), although no such charges were ever filed. In 1975, for instance, that agency was shown to have illegally opened private mail for over twenty years in at least eight major cities (as many as 42 million pieces of mail during 1959 through 1966 in New York City alone) (Roebuck and Weeber, 1978:111).

The willful exposure of individuals to cruel and unusual punishment by prison or jail officials, a violation of the Eighth Amendment, also constitutes a federal crime under Title 18 U.S.C. (Section 242). For instance, an Arkansas prison official who willfully beat a prisoner for the purpose of imposing illegal summary punishment was considered to have an intent to deprive the inmate of his Eighth Amendment consititutional rights (*U.S. vs. Jackson*, 235 F2d 925, 1956). In West Virginia, a deputy sheriff's failure to protect persons detained by him from group violence or to arrest members of a mob who assaulted the prisoners constituted a violation of his common law duty to preserve the peace, and his derelictions in this respect came squarely within the provisions of the statute (*Catlette vs. U.S.*, 132 F2d 746, 1943). A similar case in Michigan found a county police officer liable for allowing a prisoner to be beaten by other inmates (*U.S. vs. Georvassilis*, 498 F2d 883, 1974).

One need not be a government official *per se* to be criminally liable under Section 242; rather, one need only be acting under official authority. For example, railroad police in Illinois who assaulted a group of vagrants were liable because, through state law, they possessed the same authority as city police (*U.S. vs. Hoffman* 1974, 498 F2d 879). Similarly, a private detective, who was sworn as a peace officer, was found liable for beating a confession out of a suspect, because, at the time of the beating, he was acting as a peace officer and not as a private detective (*Williams vs. U.S.*, 1951, 341 U.S. 97). The reckless use of deadly force by a police or prison official, however, does not in itself constitute a violation of Title 18 U.S.C. Section 242, unless it can be shown that there was an intent to punish or otherwise deprive the victim of a constitutional right.

Police and prison officers are not the only persons acting under state authority to be prosecuted under Section 242. Prosecutors, for instance, who, while acting within the scope of their state authority to initiate and prosecute a case, willfully deprive an accused person of any rights are subject to criminal punishment under Title 18 U.S.C., Section 242 (*Imbler vs. Pachtman*, 1976, 424 US 409). If voting authorities enforce election laws maliciously, then they are subject to liability under Section 242. If an official makes it difficult for individuals to register to vote, or purposely fails to count votes, such acts can be considered crimes under this statute (by precedent, *U.S. vs. Classic*, 1941, 313 US 299; *U.S. vs. Stone*, 188 F. 836, 1911).

THEFT

Simple theft from the government by its employees involves employee theft by an individual rather than state authority theft. However, persons are often presented with opportunities for theft or access to theft sites through the exercise of their state authority to enforce the law (e.g., theft from fire or burglary scenes, theft of suspects' and prisoners' confiscated property and evidence). In a ghoulish example of opportunistic theft accessed through state authority, New York City police admitted to taking money from corpses in their charge. They also admitted to stealing house-keys from corpses that were later used to burgle the deceaseds' homes (Knapp, 1973:184). Opportunistic theft by police can even turn into looting. The following two accounts demonstrate how New York City officers took advantage of their official access to burglary scenes (Knapp, 1973: 186):

> "Me and my partner went in the back of the building [where] a door was open. We went in. There was about six or seven radio cars out front. A lot of cops was inside. Everybody was stuffing clothes down their pants, in their shirt, up their sleeves. Everybody looking fat because they were stuffing so much clothes in their pants. And my partner was telling me that the owners usually take it out on their income tax. Usually declare—say—more was stolen than was actually taken. Or, they would take it out on their insurance."

> "[M]en in police uniforms emerge[d] from the [meat] packing company carrying large, paper-wrapped packages which they loaded into the [patrol] car. In the next few hours, four other police cars . . . half of the precinct . . . responded to the site. Police officers . . . were seen putting packages from the company into their cars. . . . [P]ackages [were transferred] into two private automobiles . . . which were registered to . . . patrolmen."

Inciardi (1987:273-75) has documented several other accounts of opportunistic thefts by public safety employees in various cities:

- While searching a purse snatching suspect, a police officer found seventy-two diamond rings. The officer turned in only seventy of them.
- While dusting a burglary scene for fingerprints, one officer removed a man's gold watch that the burglar had overlooked. He then stated that the victims had theft insurance.
- Contraband was seized after raiding the premises of a local receiver of stolen goods. Several televisions, radios, and musical instruments were put in a private automobile. Officers later divided the booty.
- Police divided $18,000 in cash that they discovered while searching the premises of a dead man.

In addition to opportunistic theft, public safety employees can also steal through planned theft. Here, they would have access to information or to property by virtue of their official authority. The police are trusted with the locations of empty stores and homes, and often know where valuable or unattended property can be found. Police have also been known to seek out particular drug dealers and then rob them of money and drugs (Knapp, 1973).

In a major case of thefts facilitated by state authority, guards at the Mississippi State Penitentiary used their official status to smuggle low denomination Postal Service money orders into the prison, where the orders were altered by inmates to reflect a higher payable amount. The altered money orders were then sent to unsuspecting "pen pals," primarily widows and elderly women. The pals were persuaded to cash the money orders and forward the proceeds to friends and relatives of the inmates, or to guards at the prison. The Postal Service lost in excess of $2 million in the caper, and approximately a third of the forty persons convicted in the scheme were guards (U.S. Attorney General, 1987:75).

Another case of planned theft through the use of state authority involved the falsification of odometer readings by Laurel County (Kentucky) clerk C. A. Williams. Williams and his brother pleaded guilty to charges of conspiracy to alter odometer readings in a multistate auto title laundering and odometer tampering scheme. Investigations by the Kentucky State Police and the FBI revealed that as many as 1400 car titles with false odometer readings passed through the Laurel County Clerk's office during a five-month period (U.S. Attorney General, 1987:74-75).

There is evidence that techniques of neutralization sometimes are employed by public safety officers who steal from suspects or crime and fire scenes when they perceive such behavior as being contrary to their values. For instance, thefts in two of the above scenarios were neutralized because the victims either had insurance or could deduct the loss from income taxes (denials of injury and victim). As in the case of brutality neutralizations, the acceptability of theft may eventually become a regular part of an officer's conduct norms.

POLITICAL BRIBETAKING

The state authority occupational crimes discussed thus far have, for the most part, inflicted harm on discernible victims or groups of victims (e.g., assault, theft). Bribetaking for influence, however, is a state authority offense that diffuses its harm throughout an entire populace. It is perhaps the quintessential violation of public trust. The practice is by no means a modern phenomenon—John Noonan's encylopedic *Bribes* (1984) documents its occurrence over the past four millenia.

Legal Aspects

By the beginning of the seventeenth century, only judges and witnesses could be criminally charged for taking money for their influence in court. Legislators were criminally chargeable for bribetaking by the eighteenth century. By the middle of the twentieth century, virtually all government officials and employees were potential criminal bribetakers, either explicitly by statute or implicitly by court precedent (Noonan, 1984: Chapter 18). The *corpus delicti* for bribetaking has moved beyond the concept of an overt agreement to peddle state influence. As Noonan (1984:580) has noted, "Contract—the rule of reciprocity reached by private agreement—was replaced in government and out of government by law protecting duties defined by [public] status." Currently, then, virtually any public employee who peddles authority or influence over state matters for a price can be convicted for bribetaking.

Not all laws against bribetaking for influence involve the payment of cash; many statutes also include explicitly or implicitly the taking of favors. However, there may well be some difficulty in interpreting what constitutes a "favor." For instance, if Congressman Smith agrees to vote "yes" on Congresswoman Jones's bill in exchange for Congresswoman Jones's "yes" vote on Congressman Smith's bill, then the agreement technically might fall under the umbrella of the payment of favors for state influence. Additionally, intent to be influenced is not a necessary element of bribetaking under many statutes; bribetaking often requires only the acceptance of something "for" or "because of" an official's act. Thus, even a policeman's acceptance of a free cup of coffee from a restaurant, for "official" presence at the establishment, might be considered a form of criminal bribetaking under a strict interpretation of some statutes. Modern bribetaking laws—which include the payment of nonpecuniary rewards, then, may technically permeate even the customary behavior of state employees who use their authority in good faith.

Offenses against bribetaking (or its attempt) by persons who are acting "for or on behalf of" the United States are found primarily under Title 18 U.S.C., Section 201. Roles "for or on behalf of" the United States certainly include those which exercise what has been termed here as a "state authority," such as federal police and prison officers, federal judges, and federal elected and appointed officials. Section 201 also includes bribery of persons who are making decisions on behalf of the United States which do not involve the exercise of state authority, such as purchasing and hiring by federal employees in their normal administrative roles. This statute also punishes persons who, acting either individually or on behalf of an organization, bribe or attempt to bribe any of these agents of the United States. A conviction under Section 201 carries a penalty of as much as 15 years in prison and a fine equal to triple the amount of the bribe.

Federal obstruction of justice statutes (Title 18 U.S.C., Chapter 73) outlaw giving bribes to persons influential or material to a federal trial, hearing, or investigation (e.g., witnesses, jurors, prosecutors, judges). Obstruction statutes primarily punish the bribegiver. Bribetakers who use their official influence are generally punishable under Section 201 rather than Chapter 73. However, bribetaking to obstruct state and local law enforcement against organized illegal gambling is a specific obstruction offense under Chapter 73 (Section 1511).

Nonfederal state agents who take bribes are punishable under similar local bribery and obstruction of justice laws, as are their bribegivers. Both federal and nonfederal public agents who take bribes can also be charged with the following federal offenses, depending upon the circumstances: extortion, interstate travel to commit a crime, mail and wire fraud, tax evasion, and racketeering.

The Hobbs Act (Title 18 U.S.C., Section 1951) was passed by Congress in 1946 to combat robbery and extortion that interfere with interstate commerce. Bribery has been considered synonymous with "extortion" under Hobbs, although bribery is not mentioned explicitly. Subsection (b)(2) of the Hobbs law defines extortion as those acts which obtain the property of another with the other's consent, when such consent was induced by ". . . wrongful use of actual or threatened force, violence, or fear, or *under color of official right*" (emphasis added). Extortion under color of official right is considered to be the wrongful taking by a public officer of money or property not due him or his office, independent of whether such taking was accomplished by force, threats, or use of fear (*U.S. vs. Adcock*, 558 F2d 397, 1977). Even if the bribetaker did not have the official authority to do the deed requested by the briber, the taker is still guilty because the briber believed that the taker had such a power and the taker accepted the bribe under the auspices of having the power. Interpretations of the Hobbs Act currently see no difference between accepting bribery and kickbacks (or conspiring or attempting to secure them) for state influence on the one hand and extortion under color of official right on the other hand. Violation of Hobbs carries a penalty of as much as twenty years in prison and a $10,000 fine. This federal statute has jurisdiction over many nonfederal bribetaking officials because misuse of a public position can affect interstate commerce. The Hobbs Act seems to be enforced; Ruff (1977) reports that by the mid-1970s, over three hundred bribetaking officials were being prosecuted annually under the Hobbs interpretation of extortion.

The Travel Act of 1961 (Title 18 U.S.C., Section 1952) made it illegal to travel or promote travel from one state to another in order to accomplish any one of several federal and state criminal offenses, explicitly including bribery (subsection (b)(2)). If a bribetaker or bribegiver causes (or attempts to cause) another person to cross state lines or uses the federal mails or interstate wires to complete a bribe in any way, they are guilty under the Travel Act, and are subject to as much as five years in prison and a fine of $10,000. A party is also punishable if he or she travels interstate for matters related to the bribe. Bribery of persons in both public and private roles is punishable under the Travel Act.

In addition to violating the Travel Act, any bribetaking that touches the mails or interstate wires in the process of proposal, payment, distribution, or carrying out the agreement of a bribe may also be a violation of federal mail fraud (Title 18 U.S.C., Section 1341) and federal wire fraud (Title 18 U.S.C., Section 1343) statutes, depending upon the circumstances. Although bribetaking officials are defrauding their constituencies by not exercising honestly their state authority (which they have promised to do through oath when they were elected or appointed), to be guilty of fraud a bribetaking must encompass some tangible *financial* victimization of another party (*McNally vs. U.S.*, 107 S. Ct. 2875, 1987). Thus, a bribetaker who agrees to introduce a given piece of legislation is not necessarily guilty of fraud because there may be no financial victimization. However, an official who takes a bribe to favor one contractor over others is guilty of fraud because there would exist a financial victimization to the others who were not awarded the contract. In short, when bribetaking involves only a political harm, rather than an economic harm, then the taker is not guilty of fraud (see Bradley, 1988). Bribetaking officials can also be prosecuted for evading federal and state income tax if they do not in a timely manner report payments (cash, goods, services) from bribes as ordinary income.

The Racketeer Influenced and Corrupt Organizations Act (Title 18 U.S.C., Chapter 96), or RICO, was passed by Congress in 1970 to battle all conceivable dimensions of "organized" crime. RICO Section 1962 outlaws using a pattern of racketeering activities to invest in or gain control of an enterprise which engages in or affects interstate commerce. Section 1962 also prohibits persons from using a pattern of racketeering activities while in association with any enterprise that engages in or affects interstate commerce. Conspiracy to commit these acts is also punishable under RICO. "Racketeering activity" specifically includes bribery (public and private bribetaking and bribegiving) chargeable as a felony under state and federal law. In addition, "racketeering activity" comprises many other felonies (e.g., murder, kidnaping, extortion, arson, robbery, gambling). RICO "racketeering" explicitly includes bribery and other instances that fall within the federal crimes previously discussed: Section 201, the Hobbs Act, the Travel Act, federal mail and wire fraud statutes, and federal obstruction of justice laws. Persons can be charged with each of these offenses and with RICO. RICO penalties provide for as much as twenty years in prison, a $25,000 fine, forfeiture of any gains from or interests in racketeering enterprises, and triple damages for any person harmed by a RICO offense.

To be guilty under RICO, one must practice a "pattern of racketeering" to the extent that it affects an "enterprise." A "pattern" must comprise at least two racketeering events within a ten-year period, excluding the time the perpetrator was incarcerated (Section 1961.5). Racketeering acts must be connected with each other by some common scheme, plan, or motive so as to constitute a set of related events. A public agent who takes bribes from two different entities within a ten-year period or from the same entity on two different occasions during that time period is guilty of a RICO offense. Even the acceptance of two installment payments on a single bribe within the specified period constitutes a "pattern of racketeering" under RICO. And there is ample precedent to indicate that governments are "enterprises" which are affected by bribetaking and which affect interstate commerce. Moreover, acquittal of state bribery, obstruction of justice, or other charges does not preclude one from being charged under RICO. Indeed, RICO has created the federal legal power to ferret out virtually all political bribers and bribetakers in the United States.

Having discussed some of the legal aspects related to bribery for state influence, we shall now turn to two of the more infamous cases of it—the Knapp Commission Report on police corruption in New York City and the "ABSCAM" scandal.

Bribetaking by Police—The Knapp Commission

New York's *Knapp Commission Report on Police Corruption* (1973) is perhaps the best known collection of cases involving bribetaking by police officers. The investigation by the Commission was the result of information about police corruption brought to light by former New York City detective Frank Serpico in 1967. The Knapp Commission, chaired by Whitman Knapp, was in operation from 1967 through the end of 1972. The Commission found pervasive corruption practices throughout virtually all lower ranks (through lieutenant) of the New York City Police Department, as well as among some selected higher officials. Of course, not all police officers in these lower ranks were involved in blatant corruption, but most at least accepted gratis meals and services, and did not take steps to prevent what they knew or suspected as corrupt police activities.

The Commission differentiated two major forms of bribetakers: "meat eaters" and "grass eaters." Grass eating refers to passively accepting bribes when "appropriate" situations present themselves, and is the most common form of bribetaking. Meat eaters, on the other hand, are the relatively few police officers who aggressively seek out situations they can exploit for financial gain, including gambling, drugs, and other serious offenses which can yield substantial bribes totaling thousands of dollars. For instance, one highly placed police official told the Commission that $5,000 to $50,000 payoffs to meat eaters were common, and one narcotics bribe amounted to a quarter of a million dollars.

There are two general types of bribes taken by the police: "pads" and "scores." The pad refers to regularly scheduled (e.g., weekly, monthly) bribes in exchange for nonenforcement of the law, and pertain to entities which operate illegally all or most of the time. Illegal gambling operations are probably the largest source of pad payments. Ostensibly legitimate businesses such as construction contractors, bars and liquor stores, and those with large numbers of motor vehicles (e.g., parking lots, taxicabs, trucking firms) are often involved in "pad" payments—they operate in fixed locations and are subject to many statute and code infractions written by the police. Plainclothes detectives generally received larger pad payments than uniformed officers. Some detectives collected monthly or biweekly pads amounting to as much as $3,500 from each of the gambling establishments within their jurisdiction. The monthly share (or "nut") per officer ranged from $300 or $400 in midtown Manhattan to $800 in the Bronx, $1,200 in Brooklyn, and $1,500 in Harlem. Supervisors' nuts often were a share and a half. Newly assigned plainclothes officers did not receive their shares until after a few months (to ascertain whether the newcomer was an informant), but received "severance pay" upon leaving the area. To illustrate the long term benefits of paying the nut, the Knapp Commission (1973:153) reported that one trucking firm paid $15,000 a year to police to avoid being ticketed, while another firm of similar size which did not participate in police payoffs received approximately $50,000 to $60,000 in annual parking fines.

Uniformed officers assigned to street duties were not found to receive cash payments on the large and organized scale of plainclothes officers, but received small payments regularly, usually under $20. One's assigned area of uniformed street patrol affected the number and sizes of payments—an officer assigned to guard City Hall, for instance, had less opportunity to exercise authority for a bribe than, say, an officer who patrolled an area where prostitution, drugs, and gambling were rampant.

A "score" is a one-time bribe that an officer solicits from (or is offered by) a citizen for not enforcing the law. For instance, a police officer can "score" from a motorist (for not writing a traffic citation) or from a narcotics peddler (for not making an arrest). In one score, the motel room of a "narcotics dealer" (actually a federal undercover agent) was raided by two detectives and a uniformed patrol officer. They found $12,000 in cash in the room and demanded $10,000 to avoid an arrest. The detectives, who received $8,000 from the "dealer," paid a sort of finder's fee to another detective who alerted them to the "dealer's" presence (all officers involved were arrested). In another score, a restaurant owner was threatened with the arrest of his daughter on drug charges and the placing of his grandchildren in a foundling home if he did not pay $6,000 to police. The police returned a few months later and demanded an additional $12,000. The restauranteur then notified officials about the threats, and arranged for the arrest of the officers.

The possibility for a "score" does not end with the arrest. Many officers were implicated in the solicitation of payoffs for nebulous court testimony that would result in the dropping of charges. Additionally, narcotics officers were known to take bribes in exchange for information about an impending arrest, for the results of telephone wiretaps or other confidential police information, and for interceding for known dealers or addicts by attempting to influence the justice process. Scores were also solicited to expedite the processing of licenses and the processing of impounded vehicles. In addition to bribetaking, the Commission uncovered several other illegal practices committed by New York City police officers. For instance, officers planted (or "flaked") drugs on the persons of suspects to increase the severity of the charges—clearly a civil rights violation under Title 18 U.S.C., Section 242. Officers also admitted to many cases of opportunistic and planned theft, including drugs, money, and property confiscated from suspects.

"Gratuities," variants of the "pad," refer to free meals, free goods and services, and cash "tips" received by officers. Gratuities were "by far the most widespread form of misconduct the Commission found. . . ." (Knapp, 1973:170). The most universally accepted gratuity was the free meal offered by restaurants, luncheonettes, bars, and hotels. Officers typically dined only at establishments which gave free meals to the police. Several thousand free meals were consumed by the New York officers each day, and the sheer numbers of gratis meals often posed problems for many establishments. Those that did a particularly large police business either offered a discount or charged a token price, usually 50 cents. Officers assigned to the stationhouse even sent radio cars to get free food for their consumption. One precinct had a list describing which restaurants gave free food on certain days. One restaurant owner, after raising the police price for a two-dollar chicken dinner from gratis to 50 cents because of so many police demands for free food, soon found his delivery cars being ticketed by angry police for as much as $600 in fines in a week.

Liquor, too, was often given to officers for consumption on and off the premises while they were on and off duty. Three patrol sergeants in one precinct, for instance, regularly spent their entire tours going from one bar to another. Rooms, meals, and liquor were also solicited from many New York hotels, including the more luxurious ones. The Statler-Hilton, for instance, gave $1,500 worth of free meals to higher ranking officers in one month.

Christmas "tips" from various establishments were collected by officers anually and in an organized fashion. Typically, lists would be drawn up at each precinct enumerating the businesses expected to give money at the end of the year. The lists, which usually comprised ten to fifteen establishments, were then given to various officers, each of whom was to go to those on his list. Collection was either in the form of a flat fee (to be divided later at the precinct) or in the form of payments to individual officers. Lieutenants and sergeants, as well as higher ranking officials, had a "list" system that was separate from their subordinates. The Christmas pad in the Seventeenth Precinct, for example, netted each man $400 or $500, sums which were augmented by individual payments of about $200 (Knapp, 1973:177).

Gratuities were also given for the performance of normal duties. City marshals usually tipped five dollars for help in handling an eviction. Foreign consulates, too, often tipped with money, jewelry, and liquor the officers assigned to protect them. Police were also tipped to escort managers of legitimate businesses to the bank with their day's receipts—ranging from "a couple of packs of cigarettes to $4" (Knapp, 1973:179). Proprietors of burgled stores often paid officers $5 for responding to their call for help.

The Knapp Commission concluded that the intense group loyalty to fellow police officers is often a hindrance to anti-corruption efforts. Two principal characteristics emerge from this group loyalty. First, hostility toward outside interference is enhanced by the already hostile attitudes toward the public associated with the police officer's "working personality." Second, police group loyalty promotes intense pride in the department as a whole. Unfortunately, this mixture of hostility and pride can be a serious impediment in the attack on police corruption, because it fosters a refusal to admit that a problem of graft exists.

Bribetaking by Elected Officials—"ABSCAM"

The first statute punishing bribetaking by a member of Congress appeared in 1852, but no convictions were obtained before the twentieth century. As of 1970, only ten members of Congress had been convicted of crimes involving bribery, and most of them received relatively mild censure. Two received Presidential pardons, some returned to their practice of law, one was sentenced to a day in jail and another was sentenced to probation. During the 1970s, there were several more prosecutions of members of Congress for bribetaking or variants of it, but sentences continued to be light (e.g., fine only, probation, three months in jail) (Noonan, 1984: 601-604). Lackadaisical efforts to prosecute bribetakers in Congress ended in 1978 with "ABSCAM." Much of the following discussion of ABSCAM is from Noonan (1984: 604-19).

"Abdul Enterprises" was a fictitious company set up in March of 1978 with money provided by the Federal Bureau of Investigation. The firm allegedly represented two rich Arabs, Kambir Abdul Rahman and Yassir Habib, who wanted to invest large sums of money in the United States, and did not particularly care about violating official rules in the process of such investment. The credibility of the backdrop for the firm was predicated upon the general beliefs that, first, Arabs had money to invest, and second, that foreigners were generally less likely to be concerned with American laws.

The FBI paid an experienced confidence man, Melvin Weinberg, to play the major character for Abdul during the sting. Weinberg's role in ABSCAM was described by Noonan (1984:606) as "A swindler formerly outside the law, he now swindled swindlers who had prospered in American society. A criminal, he turned lawmakers into lawbreakers like himself." The allegedly oil-rich Abdul Enterprises originally lured thieves trying to sell stolen art, securities, and other items. One of the forgers with whom the "firm" was dealing proposed that the Arabs build a casino in Atlantic City. The forger assured Abdul Enterprises that a New Jersey casino gaming license could be arranged without much of a problem. The "friend" that could arrange for the license was Angelo Errichetti, the mayor of Camden. Thus, the first politician who took the bait in ABS-

CAM was not specifically targeted by the authorities; Errichetti's involvement seems to have been serendipitous.

Through Errichetti, other government officials were introduced into ABSCAM and then bribed. Ultimately, the trap ensnared a member of the New Jersey Casino Commission; members of the Philadelphia City Council; public agents for sewer contracts in Connecticut, New York, and New Jersey; several middlemen; and several members of the United States Congress.

Errichetti brought to Abdul Enterprises U.S. Representatives Michael Myers (D-NJ), Frank Thompson (D-NJ) and Raymond Lederer (D-PA), all of whom accepted bribes in exchange for introducing a private immigration bill to allow the fake Rahman and Habib to stay in the United States. Thompson brought in Congressman John Murphy (D-NY), who also pledged support for such a bill in exchange for cash. Errichetti also recruited U.S. Senator Harrison Williams (D-NJ), a 23-year veteran of Congress. Williams agreed to influence the United States government in its purchase of contracts from a titanium venture allegedly financed by the fake Arabs in exchange for a large lump of stock in the titanium company (the titanium venture never existed). Other middlemen unwittingly netted U.S. Representatives John Jenrette (D-SC) and Richard Kelly (R-FL). Kelly later tried to argue in court, quite unsuccessfully, that he actually planned to turn the bribers over to the FBI at a later date, and that he spent some of the bribe money only to convince the bribers that he was earnestly involved with them.

The crimes by these public officials and their middlemen were captured graphically on video and audio tape by the FBI. Never before had Americans seen public corruption in action so vividly. Bribes in ABSCAM were as high as $100,000.

Aside from the moral questions raised by Congress and the public about whether the government's trickery during ABSCAM was fair to the bribees, there were legal questions about the chicanery that became significant for the defendants themselves. One legal objection raised was that the government entrapped the offenders by offering sums of money; without such an offer the bribe would not have occurred. The government demonstrated, however, that the bribees were willing to take the bribes on their own and not as the result of government persuasion—none of the entrapment claims were supported by juries.

A second series of legal objections to the tactics of ABSCAM revolved around due process of law considerations. Senator Williams's defense argued, for instance, that the government's activities in the sting exemplified the egregious state abuses protected by the due process clauses of the U.S. Constitution; the judge disagreed. Another judge presiding over the Philadelphia councilmen's trial, however, accepted the due process violation argument, but was reversed on appeal. After Kelly's "double-agent" claim was rejected, his defense argued that since he had refused the initial bribe offer, any additional bribe offers would not have been made if the briber was not actually an undercover agent. The point was that any person other than an agent would not have pursued the additional offer because of a fear of exposure. Without this realistic restraint, Kelly argued, the FBI's conduct was unfair. The judge agreed and dismissed Kelly's jury verdict, but his conviction was reinstated on appeal.

A third series of legal questions arose regarding the farcical premise of Abdul Enterprises and its representatives. Myers's defense claimed that he could not have deceived the "Arabs" into believing that he could get them special immigration status, because the "Arabs" knew that they were actually American FBI agents and therefore could not be so deceived. Similarly, Williams argued that his "bribe" was stock in an imaginary company; therefore, the FBI agents knew they were giving Williams something of no value in exchange for something he could not do. However, the courts rejected these arguments by centering on the bribee's state of mind. If the bribee takes something thought to be of value, a bribe has been taken. If the bribee makes the giver believe that the taker has the power to effect the agreement of the bribe, a bribe has been solicited. In short, the pretense of a bribe constitutes a bribe.

All told, Jenrette, Kelly, Lederer, Myers, Thompson and Williams were convicted of bribery, and Murphy was convicted of the lesser offense of taking money for an official action. Kelly, Lederer, Myers, and Williams were also convicted of violating the Travel Act, while Thompson and Williams were convicted of criminal conflict of interest. Violations of the RICO and Hobbs Acts were not prosecuted by the government. Kelly received eighteen months in jail, Jenrette two years, and the remainder three years. Jenrette, Lederer, Murphy, Myers, Thompson, and Williams were fined, ranging from $20,000 (Murphy) to $50,000 (Williams). Jenrette, Kelly, Murphy, and Thompson lost reelection, Lederer resigned, Myers was the first person expelled from the House of Representatives for bribe-taking, and Williams finally resigned from the Senate under intense pressure (Noonan, 1984: 604-619).

The legal and moral messages sent by the ABSCAM scandal to wielders of public power were identical: persons entrusted with state authority are expected to keep themselves beyond temptation. This expectation is not unrealistic, as South Dakota's Senator Larry Pressler demonstrated during ABSCAM. Pressler was offered a campaign contribution by Abdul Enterprises in exchange for a promise to help the Arabs with a private bill. Pressler, recorded on tape, refused to promise anything in exchange for such a contribution. ABSCAM may well have also sent a very different type of message to those in public office, one based on deterrence: the next person who offers you a bribe may be a federal undercover agent.

State Bribery and Differential Social Organization

For many, it is difficult to understand how a sacred public trust can be corrupted. Indeed, single bribes can amount to substantial sums, and therefore one may point to avarice (or "strain") as a motivation for bribe-taking. However, the lure of money would not explain why some officials choose to become corrupt and others do not. In both cases of pervasive bribery we have discussed—ABSCAM and the New York City Police Department—there is evidence that persons become corrupt through occupatonal differential association.

The Knapp Commission's materials demonstrated that participation in scoring, padding, and other forms of bribery was learned through association with other officers; these activities were common practice and common knowledge. Much of the testimony before the Commission indicated that officers were "taught" (e.g., Knapp, 1973: 100) or "learned" (e.g., Knapp, 1973:102) how to participate in the corruption system. Taken together, the Knapp Commission evidence clearly indicates that the occupational social system of the New York City Police Department was socially organized around bribery and other forms of corruption.

In the ABSCAM cases, the evidence of differential social organization is more inferential. Bribetaking did not appear as an accepted practice in Congress or other specific government positions; rather, it seemed to be an accepted practice in given locales. New Jersey, according to Lincoln Steffens, had always been corrupt (Noonan, 1984). The ABSCAM roles of Errichetti, Myers, Thompson, Williams, and others have done little to detract from that criminal image of the Garden State. Errichetti once boasted to Abdul Enterprises early in their dealings that he could "give" them Atlantic City (Greene, 1981: 126). This statement indeed may have been true, in which case the mayor of Camden was a major operator in a system of corrupt politics. Errichetti easily produced for the FBI other officials he knew would be willing to take a bribe, many of whom were from his geographic area. And various techniques of bribery designed to camouflage offenses and offenders were commonly used by the players (e.g., a middleman or "bagman," the avoidance of literal references to cash). Because of the close collusion between many of those involved, especially those involved with Errichetti, it seems more likely that these protective techniques were learned rather than invented independently by each of them.

The point of this discussion on differential social organization is not to single out New Jersey politics or the New York City Police Department.

Not all officials exposed to corrupt occupational systems will become corrupt. Nor is it necessary to associate with other bribetakers in order to become one. The point is that some officials may learn to practice corruption from their occupational associations, just as individuals in certain industries learn from their cohorts the attitudes favorable toward occupational crime and the techniques necessary to commit those offenses.

QUESTIONS FOR DISCUSSION

1. Why is it difficult to differentiate between the concepts of "torture," "genocide," and "police brutality"?
2. State authority crimes are sometimes committed by persons who have the power to define their actions as noncriminal. Which factors affect the exercise of such self-definitions?
3. The police, because of the danger and authority involved in their everyday work, tend to isolate themselves from other citizens. Should the attitudes associated with police work (e.g., suspicion, authoritarianism) be discouraged, or are they necessary for safety?
4. What formal and informal mechanisms would you implement to control police uses of excessive force? One must be careful here to limit the use of force without denying its use.
5. Discuss problems in enforcing criminal civil rights violations under Title 18 United State Code, Section 242.
6. Private companies often subject their workers to periodic polygraph examinations to discover dishonest employees. Should police officers be given regular polygraph examinations regarding theft or bribetaking on the job? What about biological tests for the use of illicit drugs? What positive and negative ramifications might such testing produce specifically for members of a police department?
7. Is it permissible for police officers to accept certain noncash gratuities, such as free or discount meals and services? What are the undesirable outcomes of a policy that allows police to accept free meals?
8. What reforms would you suggest to reduce bribetaking by police?
9. How "fair" were the government actions used to incriminate those implicated in ABSCAM? Should the government continue stings similar to ABSCAM? If so, do you believe that it is fair to randomly approach politicians and offer them a bribe?
10. Why is it difficult to prove that an official has been "bribed" with a campaign contribution?
11. Describe the legal relationship between the various federal bribery crimes discussed in this chapter (i.e., Title 18 United States Code, Sections 201, 1341, 1343, 1951, 1952, 1962).

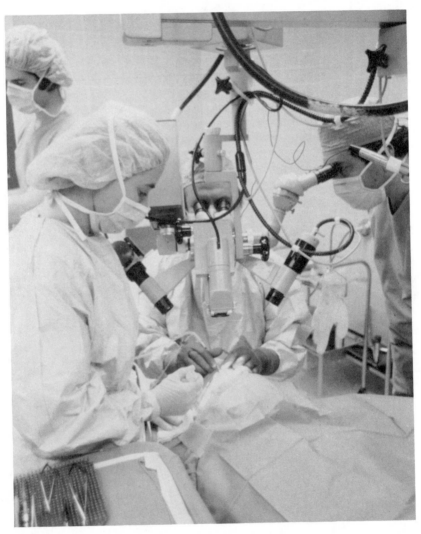

Surgeons perform a cataract operation. Over one third of all eye surgeries are estimated to be unwarranted. (Harry Wilks / Stock, Boston)

S I X

PROFESSIONAL
OCCUPATIONAL CRIME

The *Oxford American Dictionary* (1980:533) defines the word *profession* as: "an occupation, especially one that involves knowledge and training in a branch of advanced learning." Professions also are distinctly characterized by self-regulation. As Freidson (1970a:71-72) notes, professions have been given "the right to control [their] own work . . ." and to deem "outside evaluations illegitimate. . . ." Although there may be "professionals" in all occupational areas, the traditional conception of professional has been limited to careers such as human and veterinary medicine, psychology, law, pharmacy, and accountancy.

Crime in the professions is conceptually distinct from other occupational offending because the professions invariably require some sort of oath or ethical commitment that bestows upon these practitioners a special trust on which the persons they serve believe they can rely. For example, the Hippocratic oath states, "I will adopt the regimen which in my best judgment is beneficial to my patients, and not for their injury or for any wrongful purpose." In another example, the American Psychoanalytic Association's *Principles of Ethics for Psychoanalysts*, Section 6, states, "Except as required by law, a psychoanalyst may not reveal the confidences entrusted to him." These kinds of special trusts set the professions apart from other occupations.

Clients readily share their innermost physical, mental, and financial problems with professionals, who are often perfect strangers. Generally, a client's trust in a professional involves a belief that the professional will do what is in the best interests of the client rather than what is in the professional's best interests. Because crime by professionals in their professional capacity often involves a violation of this special trust, it may be seen as particulary deceitful. Professionals are also entrusted by the state with certain legal responsibilities, such as the signing of death certificates, the dispensing of prescriptions, and various fiduciary duties.

Overall, there seems to exist a public trust in the integrity of professionals. In a 1981 Gallup poll (*U.S. News*, 1982), the public was asked to rate the honesty and ethical standards in various occupations. Clergy was ranked highest, followed by druggists, dentists, and doctors. Less than 10 percent believed the latter three were unethical. Although lawyers fared worse, ranking twelfth (a quarter of those surveyed believed attorneys had low ethical standards), they were regarded higher than politicians (Senators, Congressmen and state officeholders) and business executives. In another poll eight years after Gallup's, however, more than a third of over one thousand people believed that the prestige of doctors had decreased during the previous decade (*Time*, 1989a).

The existing data on the incidences of crimes in the course of professions are poor, largely because they are primarily based on proactive enforcement by investigators. Available figures more accurately reflect enforcement agency policies and budgetary constraints than they do the universes of professionally related offenses and offenders. For instance, medical insurance fraud and fee-splitting by physicians and improprieties by lawyers are usually brought to light only through an audit or by a chance occurrence. And there is some evidence that legal authorities are more lenient with at least some professionals than they are with other kinds of offenders. As one federal agent notes:

"U.S. attorneys are extraordinarily kind to doctors, because even if they are crooks, theoretically they're still providing some useful services for the community. There's a double standard for doctors because there aren't many other categories of white collar criminals that are looked upon as a community of people who save lives." (Jesilow, Pontell and Geis, 1985:161)

Even when offenders in the professions are discovered and an attempt is made to prosecute them, there is often tremendous difficulty in establishing criminal intent to commit the crimes of which they are accused. The self-regulating intraprofessional ways of handling violators through peer processes often avoid official prosecution, which results in a further lack of official information. While it is certainly true that some crimes by professionals come to the attention of the authorities through victim complaints (e.g., double-billing medical patients, embezzlement from clients by lawyers, sexual assaults on patients), many victims remain unaware of their victimization (e.g., unnecessary surgery, adulterated prescriptions). On the whole, unfortunately, most of the information available on crimes by professionals in their professional capacity is piecemeal.

There often is a fine line between intentional criminality on the one hand and "a difference of professional opinion" on the other hand. Because of mutual professional respect and an interest in keeping the integrity and public image of the profession intact, intraprofessional pronouncements of criminal violation may be restricted to only the grossest abuses. Moreover, because professional colleagues often define which professional behaviors are criminal, such definitions may become self-supporting. For instance, individual failures among physicians to prosecute colleagues for mercy killing can develop into a collective absence of operant conditioning or normative validation (see Chapter 3) within the profession against euthanasia, encouraging its further use.

MEDICAL AND MENTAL HEALTH PROFESSIONS

There are numerous criminal acts that can be commited by doctors who treat human beings (physicians, osteopaths, chiropractors, podiatrists, dentists, psychologists, psychiatrists, etc.) through occupational opportunity. Fee-splitting, prescriptions drug violations, fraudulent medical insurance claims, aggravated assault (unnecessary surgery or other needless painful treatment), and sexual assault are the "common crimes" among medical professionals. Criminal homicide (murder and manslaughter), through illegal abortion and euthanasia, have also been committed by doctors and nurses in the course of their occupations. Other professionally related criminal violations would include fraudulent reports and testimony in criminal and civil court cases (including the falsification of death certificates and other official documents) and failure to report certain treatments to authorities (e.g., for gunshot wounds, child abuse). Veterinarians who inflict unnecessary surgery or treatment on animals are guilty of at least two offenses: cruelty to animals and fraud. The professions can facilitate individual crimes as well, such as price fixing (e.g., fees and laboratory tests) and tax evasion (physicians have been more than ten times as likely to be indicted for income tax evasion than their representation in the population) (Gross, 1967:635-36).

Crimes By Doctors Against Persons

Unnecessary Surgery and Treatment.   Willfully committing unnecessary surgery is both a crime against property (fraud) and a crime against the person (assault, mayhem, or criminal homicide) (see Lanza-Kaduce, 1980; Stroman, 1979). Upon reexamining 1,356 patients recommended to undergo major surgery, researchers at Cornell Medical School found that one in four of the operations was not needed (Berger, 1988:43). Given these figures, of the approximately 35 million surgical operations performed in the United States in 1985, as many as 4 million may have been unwarranted. In terms of the particular body parts subject to high amounts of unnecessary maiming, 36 percent of eye surgeries, half of all pacemaker implants, 31 percent of gall bladder removals, a third of hysterectomies, 29 percent of prostate surgeries, 43 percent of hemorrhoid operations, and 32 percent of knee surgeries have been estimated to be unwarranted. The Public Citizens Health Research Group estimates that more than $10 billion is spent each year on unnecessary surgical procedures (Berger, 1988:43-45). In terms of public outcry, Cullen, Clark, Link, Mathers, Niedospial, and Sheahan (1985) report that, among those they surveyed, about two persons in five (42 percent) favored a prison term for a physician who performs an unnecessary operation.

The following is a particularly horrifying example of unnecessary surgery, in which the offending physician was sentenced to four years in prison:

> "[A] California opthalmologist was convicted [in 1984 for] subjecting poor patients to unneeded cataract surgery in order to collect Medicaid fees. In one instance, he totally blinded a 57-year-old woman when he operated needlessly on her one sighted eye. Oddly, if the patients had private insurance or were well off, the surgery was done skillfully and successfully; benefit program patients simply were treated in a more slipshod fashion." (Jesilow, et al., 1985:153)

> "[He] was convicted of performing unnecessary eye operations that left 14 patients with impaired vision. . . ." (Pontell, Jesilow, Geis, and O'Brien, 1985:1029)

Regarding unnecessary treatment, "U.S. Senate investigators, 'shopping' some of [New York City's] 'mills' with feigned ailments, usually described as a cold to the physicians, found themselves subjected by 85 different doctors they visited to 18 electrocardiagrams, eight tuberculosis tests, four allergy tests, hearing and glaucoma tests, and three electroencephalograms" (Pontell, et al., 1985:1030). Many unnecessary surgeries and treatments are performed to defraud, while others are the result of diagnoses by incompetent doctors. Regarding the latter, a past president of the Federation of State Medical Boards has estimated that "as many as one in nine . . . physicians are repeatedly guilty of practices unworthy of the profession" (Lewis and Lewis, 1970:25). *The New York Times* has reported widespread cheating on state qualifying examinations for physicians, and alleged that as much as $50,000 has been paid for copies of examinations prior to the official date of the test (Lyons, 1984). Many physicians awarded fraudulent degrees in various Latin American countries are currently practicing medicine in the United States. Foreign-educated doctors constitute approximately a quarter of all practicing physicians in the United States, but they were overrepresented (36 percent) among physicians sanctioned for abusing public health insurance claims (Pontell, et al., 1985:1030).

Estimating the incidence of assault and fraud through needless treatments and surgery by doctors is difficult for researchers because persons are rarely aware that they have experienced such victimization. When victims have realized that unnecessary treatment has been given, they often seek redress in civil rather than criminal court because they are "more interested in compensation than vengeance, and prosecutors are responsive to such feelings" (Jesilow, et al., 1985:153). Yet, even when unnecessary treatment allegations are presented for criminal prosecution, it is difficult to prove intent, because, as noted earlier, there is often a fine line between criminal fraud and assault on the one hand and a "difference of professional opinion" on the other hand.

Because the line between criminal intent and the permissible exercise of professional judgment is so vague, the best source of reliable information on the incidence of intentional unnecessary treatment may be self-reports by the offenders themselves. They are the ones who should know whether their actions were needless. The example given for a randomized response approach in Chapter 2 might be used by researchers to attempt to estimate the number of unnecessary surgeries and treatments (as well as other crimes committed by professionals), because it guarantees anonymity and thereby alleviates respondent fears of reprisal for admitting abuses. However, such a self-report method would not be feasible unless physicians were to view their behavior objectively. Here, they would have to perceive honestly their unwarranted treatment as fraudulent.

Another method for estimating the amount of unnecessary surgery and treatment may be found in direct observational study. Methodologies analogous to Jesilow's "sick" car battery study (see Chapter 2) have been suggested. Contrived illnesses would be described to doctors to ascertain whether they would render unnecessary treatments. This is much like the tactics of the U.S. Senate fraud investigators described above. There are two major problems with such an approach, however. First, subjecting a research team to the risks of unnecessary treatments would be unethical. Similar ethical objections would be raised by animal rights organizations, were such a method proposed to identify veterinarians who prescribe unnecessary surgery and treatment. Second, just as the courts have had difficulty proving intent because of the ambiguity of professional judgement, so too would the researcher.

Such a methodology has been tried on psychiatrists (Rosenhan, 1973). Rosenhan placed eight "sane" persons into twelve mental hospitals. The patients made an appointment and complained about hearing "empty, hollow, and thud" voices. All but one was diagnosed as "schizophrenic" upon admission (the pseudopatients lied only about the voices, their names and occupations; no other social and family histories were faked). Other than the feigned hallucinations at admission, the pseudopatients "ceased simulating *any* symptoms of abnormality" after entering the hospitals (Rosenhan, 1973). The hospital stays ranged from seven to fifty-two days (averaging nineteen days). The gist of Rosenhan's conclusion was that the professional mental health personnel could not determine that these persons were in fact "sane"; rather, they relied upon their initial diagnosis and treated the patients according to their schizophrenic labels (those so diagnosed were discharged with a diagnosis of "schizophrenia in remission").

Shortly after the piece was published in *Science*, several complaint letters to the editor were written in regard to the method of the study. One letter (Hanley, 1973:360) was concerned with the possible "risks" of the "reckless experiment" (e.g., the possibility of subjecting patients to "lumbar puncture, skull x-ray series, and radioisotope brain scans," all of which are feasible treatments for "isolated auditory hallucinations"). Many other letters pointed out that the doctors acted in good faith because they treated patients based on symptoms they believed to be true. As Fleischman (1973:356) noted, "Most physicians do not assume that patients who seek help are liars; they can therefore, of course, be misled." Similarly, Ostow (1973:360) notes, ". . . simulators sought admission to psychiatric hospitals. It is so rarely that this is done by anyone who is not indeed mentally ill that that alone must be taken seriously by a conscientious admitting psychiatrist as suggestive of illness." In short, pseudopatient studies are for the most part out of the question because they can be risky, unfair, and subject to conflicting interpretations about "intent" to render unnecessary treatment (see Bulmer, 1982 for additional discussion about the ethics of pseudopatient studies).

It is not necessary to determine the extent of unnecessary treatment (or other professional offending) in order to understand the factors leading to such behavior. As noted in Chapter 2, counting need not precede theoretical explanation of wrongdoing—the aim should be to explain *processes* leading to illegal behavior. For instance, Keisling (1983:30) describes the processes leading to a physician's desire for affluence, which may necessitate unneeded treatments to support such a lifestyle:

". . . fee for service medicine subtly corrupts its own practitioners. Motives for medicine are many and complex but the strongest is the desire to be a healer. . . . Unfortunately, the feelings of dominance that inevitably accompany the healer's role frequently overpower whatever native idealism a doctor might have brought to his profession. . . . As he gets older, he also begins believing that the same power and respect he commands in the office or operating room should extend into the community, where the badges of success and status, instead of centering on the value of one's work, center on material possessions and social standing. And as the fee for service system combines with the doctor's revered status to make these things so accessible, what increasingly becomes important are not the satisfactions of medicine itself but the benefits that result from practicing it. For these doctors, stories of million-dollar incomes do not provoke outrage, but envy" (in Jesilow, et al., 1985:159-160).

Such desires for affluence, coupled with high practitioner and malpractice insurance costs, may place a financial "strain" on doctors to render unnecessary treatments.

As Sutherland's ninth point of differential association indicates, however, doctors who are similarly strained do not always choose to maim and defraud patients as a means for meeting their high overhead and living expenses. Ethical socialization about whether unnecessary treatment is acceptable physician behavior (differential association) may explain why some commit it and others do not. A "professional dominance" (Freidson, 1970b) often prevails in the minds of physicians, which "supports informal professional norms which encourage some doctors to exploit [patients]. The behavior which enables a doctor to engage in fraud probably is at least partially learned from others in the profession in most instances, and professional values may effectively neutralize the doctors' conflicts of conscience" (Pontell, Jesilow and Geis, 1984:411).

There undoubtedly are cases in which the professional values that neutralize the wrongfulness of unnecessary surgery or treatment are not internalized, and the physician needs to avoid feelings of guilt for such behavior. "Condemnation of condemners" or "appeals to higher loyalties" may be invoked by physicians who choose to believe that ordering unnecessary tests is acceptable because it insulates them from potential malpractice claims which would allege that every possible avenue for diagnosis was not considered by them during treatment. For instance, a medical fraud investigator claimed that medical review boards are sensitive to self-defense against malpractice: "[Medical review boards will] say, 'Oh well, you know, it's malpractice time and I can understand why he might have ordered unnecessary tests'" (Pontell, et al., 1984:413). Or, "denial of victim," "denial of injury," and "condemnation of condemners" may be collectively utilized by individual physicians who believe that they are not justly compensated by insurance companies for their work. In support of this claim, a recent survey of California doctors has shown that inadequate reimbursement and denial of reimbursement for services are "critical" problems in the state's governmental health insurance program (Pontell, et al., 1984:409). More telling, however, is the response by a hospital's Board of Directors which reelected to their Board a physician who was at that time in jail for submitting fraudulent insurance claims: "Yeah, but you know [government health insurance] doesn't pay very much anyway." The extent to which these neutralizations are learned from colleagues and internalized as acceptable behavior is the extent to which differential association is a relevant explanation rather than neutralization theory.

Control theorists might argue that some physicians have less "attachment" to the sensitivities of their patients than other physicians, as evidenced by: (a) the 80 percent higher hysterectomy rate south of the Mason-Dixon Line; (b) Des Moines residents' 100 percent higher open-heart surgery rate than that of Iowa City residents; (c) San Diegans' two-thirds higher open-heart surgery rate than that of their fellow Californians in Palo Alto; (d) a 400 percent difference in elective surgery rates across Kansas; and (e) a 400 percent difference in hernia operation rates and a 1,000 percent difference in pacemaker operation rates across Massachusetts (Berger, 1988: 46-47).

Additionally, control theorists might see purposeful unnecessary surgery and treatment by doctors as a matter of perceived risk, because physicians may believe they are insulated from prosecution because of their "social position and the inadequacies of program policing" (Pontell, et al., 1984: 411). As one investigator of physician fraud and abuse notes, however,

"A lot of doctors don't believe that we have computer records that will show one whole year's history right in front of us. I don't think they believe we have that or they wouldn't cheat the way they do. The bottom line is that they have egos, and they think that welfare recipients are stupid. That's their biggest mistake because there are a lot of bright people on public assistance and we go out and interview these people. . . . They feel that those people pitted against them in the courtroom are never going to be believed. But they are believed. That's the part they don't understand. These recipients will go into the courtroom . . . tell their simple little story, and the doctor's going to fall. They just don't believe that." (Pontell, et al., 1984:411-12).

Sexual Assault on Patients.   In addition to committing assault on patients by subjecting them to unnecessary treatments and surgeries, doctors also at times commit willful sexual assault against their patients. Taking sexual advantage of patients, especially when patients are unaware of the assault because of anesthesia or otherwise are incapable of giving informed and willful consent, is a particularly heinous form of violating that special trust between professional and client. In addition to issues of occupational criminality by professionals, sexual assault on patients by doctors also raises issues of sexual harassment, exploitation, and domination (almost invariably by men over women) at the workplace.

In a study by the *American Psychologist*, less than one in ten therapists said that they were "never" sexually attracted to their patients, while exactly half claimed that they were sexually attracted to patients at least "sometimes" (*U.S. News*, 1988a). Kardener, Fuller and Mensh (1973), through an anonymous self-report questionnaire, investigated the incidence of patient sexual contact by male physicians in the course of their practice. Among their 460 respondents (1000 questionnaires were distributed), 59 acknowledged having sexual contact with patients according to the following specialities: obstetrics/gynecology, 18 percent; general practitioners, 13 percent; internists, 12 percent; and psychiatrists and surgeons, each 10 percent. An overwhelming majority of the 460 doctors responding condemned such behavior.

Because sexual exploitation of clients is clearly a strong violation of medical ethics (as well as the ethics in other professions), there is little support for a learning hypothesis such as differential association. Therefore, professionals who violate this norm need to neutralize their behavior so that it is not seen as unprofessional. Kardener, et al. (1973) identified what are probably neutralization techniques among their respondents: "demonstrates doctor's effectiveness to his patient," "supports and reinforces a patient's sexual appeal," and "stimulating the clitoris helps a patient relax." The compulsive behavior involved in patient sexual abuse would certainly be explained by the control theorists' emphasis on self-gratification.

Many episodes of patient sexual abuse have been documented. For instance, a seventy-one-year-old Minnesota therapist was charged with sexually abusing a seventeen-year-old boy by whipping him on his buttocks, hands and feet while the boy was naked. He was also accused of whipping recovering alcoholics as part of their "treatment" (AP, 6/10/87). In another case, an Augusta, Georgia gynecologist was convicted on two counts of battery for touching patients in "sexual ways" during their examinations. This was the second round of accusations against this particular physician, and five women testified that they were sexually assaulted (AP, 5/13/88). And Michael Koplik, a dentist convicted of sexually assaulting a heavily sedated patient, was sentenced in July of 1989 to treat six AIDS patients who had been refused treatment elsewhere (*Time*, 1989b).

In another well publicized case, described in the *American Journal of Psychiatry* (Burgess, 1981), a gynecologist used his physical examinations to masturbate at least sixteen patients for an average of twenty to thirty minutes. Although eight of the ten women who described sexual arousal had orgasms, none reported any subjective pleasure associated with their physiological response. Most were humiliated but uncertain about how to deal properly with such an assault, knowing, but not absolutely positive, that what was happening to them was not part of the regular examination. Ten of the women described feelings of physical discomfort and pain during the internal examination.

Only three of the victims tried to end the examination, either by asking the physician to stop or by physically changing position. Eight patients allowed the doctor to continue until he was finished. After the incidents, the women generally felt their powerlessness in dealing with the incident. Although "unaware" of their exploitation during the assault, afterwards they felt degraded and upset with themselves for their inability to respond. Although many believed they should press charges against the doctor, there was a perception about their credibility vis-a-vis the doctor's ("What good would it do—my word against his" and "doctors are so well protected").

Most of the patient-victims immediately changed physicians, though others returned for several more visits. Those who continued to see the doctor after he assaulted them did so because of necessity (serious medical need or because they could not find another doctor to take them in the late stages of preganancy). Other gynecologists in the area tended to ignore their colleague's behavior ("I've heard lots of complaints but I have no facts," "[You are] not the only one [to complain about his methods]"). In some cases, the offending doctor was used to treat the other gynecologists' patients while they were on vacation, which was perceived by the victim-patients to be a betrayal by their new doctor.

Criminal Homicide.   Criminal homicide (murder, manslaughter) also has been committed by persons in the medical profession inadvertently through negligence or incompetence, and sometimes purposefully, such as in the cases of illegal abortion and euthanasia. Because of their professional knowledge, doctors and nurses can sometimes kill with impunity for their own benefit by making their victim's death appear to be natural. Even Lombroso (1911:58), himself a physician, noted that "[h]omicide with the aim of getting the benefit of life insurance, is an example of a new form of crime committed by some physicians, and favored . . . by new advances in scientific knowledge" (in Jesilow, et al., 1985:155). In such a case in Albany, Georgia in 1988, Karen Paschal, a trained nurse, allegedly tried to murder her pediatrician husband, Thomas, by injecting Pavulon (a muscle relaxant) into his intravenous tube while he was in the hospital (she pleaded *nolo contendre* and was sentenced to probation). When offenses such as these occur outside of regular medical practice, they should be considered professionally facilitated rather than as occurring in the course of occupation.

Nonspontaneous Abortions. Prior to the Supreme Court's 1973 decision in *Roe vs. Wade* (410 U.S. 113, 1973), nonspontaneous abortions were illegal in the United States, except for states which allowed abortion in rape and incest cases and those which permitted it if it was believed to be medically necessary to save the mother's life. The pre-*Roe* California Theraputic Abortion Act also allowed a legal abortion for the mental well being of the mother (see Packer and Gampell, 1959). Here, because of the exercise of professional opinion about the operation's necessity for the physical or mental well being of the mother, such a pre-*Roe* abortion is another instance in which the application of criminal definitions is controlled intraprofessionally.

There seems to be no information available about the number of physicians who have performed illegal abortions on their patients. However, a self-report study of 388 obstetricians by Lader (1965) prior to *Roe* found that about one in ten admitted that he or she illegally referred patients to abortionists, and respondents guessed that about one in seven of their colleagues did likewise. Illegally performing an abortion or illegally referring someone to an abortionist may be caused by "ideological and humanitarian impulses of physicians pushing them into law-breaking" (Jesilow, et al., 1985:157) Thus, an appeal to higher loyalties (i.e., the procedure is necessary for the mental or social well-being of the pregnant woman) may act as a technique of neutralization that allows doctors to view their illegal abortions of fetuses as professionally acceptable behavior. It should also be noted that under illegal abortion conditions, trained physicians can make an excellent income from performing black market operations (Schur, 1965), so there exist financial motivations to perform them in addition to humanitarian ones.

Euthanasia. Euthanasia, or mercy killing (which could conceivably include some nonspontaneous abortions), may also be the result of humanitarian impulses, because it is usually believed to be done for the benefit of the patient. Euthanasia typically has been legally treated as criminal homicide in the United States. However, there seems to be no case of a medical professional convicted of murder or manslaughter for having killed to end the suffering of a patient (Fletcher, 1968). There also seems to be no case in which a physician has been convicted for withdrawing or omitting therapy (Sanders, 1969). That juries tend to be sympathetic toward euthanasia committed by the victim's relatives (Sanders, 1969) illustrates the overall lenient attitudes of the criminal justice system toward mercy killings.

Euthanasia is another of those offenses in which intent is difficult to determine because violations of the law are interpreted in terms of professional opinions. Unless the medical community asserts that a given instance of euthanasia was not within the realm of acceptable medical practice, the doctor being scrutinized is not guilty of homicide. While there is no dispute that the purposeful mercy killing decisions of physicians are the immediate causes of death, there can be a considerable legal question about whether such decisions are the true (or "proximate") causes of mercy deaths. The medical community seems to be polarized on the issue of euthanasia ethics, but, as Crane (1975) has found through surveys of about 3,000 physicians (which included pediatricians, internists, and neurosurgeons), doctors are increasingly invoking a "social" interpretation of death (the potential for patient's and family's quality of life) rather than a clinical one (brain death).

The decision to practice euthanasia revolves around three major types of cases: (1) the conscious terminal patient; (2) the irreversibly comatose patient; and (3) the brain-damaged or severely debilitated patient whose chances of long-term survival in his or her present state are good (Crane, 1975:2). Crane (1975:2-3) presents the following polarized positions on mercy killing:

For:
"[T]he life of the dying patient becomes steadily less complicated and rich, and, as a result, less worth living or preserving. The pain and suffering involved in maintaining what is left are inexorably mounting, while the benefits enjoyed by the patient himself, or that he can in any way confer on those around him, are just as inexorably declining." (Morison, 1971:696)

Against:
"It is ethically wrong for a doctor to make an arbitrary judgment, at a certain point in his patient's illness, to stop supportive measures. The patient entrusts his life to his doctor, and it is the doctor's duty to sustain it as long as possible. There should be no suggestion that it is possible for a doctor to do otherwise, even if he were to decide that the patient were 'better off dead.' " (Karnofsky, 1960:9)

The official medical policy about treating patients is clear: Treatment ". . . should be continued as long as life, defined in physiological terms, can be preserved" (Crane, 1975:204). However, as noted, Crane's research indicates that an informal system of counternorms to this official policy has developed, a system which allows physicians to make decisions about death based on social rather than physiological prognoses. Techniques of neutralization such as appeals to higher loyalties (minimization of suffering for patients and their families) or denials of injury, victim, and responsibility (the patient will die anyway) may encourage the practice of mercy killing in individual cases among individual doctors. Yet, the fact that doctors increasingly are invoking criteria other than physiological death for prolonging life points to an internalization of such ethics, which are probably learned through socialization in medical school and from colleagues (differential association). Control theorists who assume that the basis for crime is self-gratification will have trouble explaining euthanasia because the motivation for this crime is to end another's suffering rather than to enhance personal gratification.

Turk's (1969) theory of criminalization, discussed in Chapter 3, is applicable to the explanation of the absence of prosecution against doctors who may, in fact, be criminally practicing euthanasia. Recall that a congruence between the legal and social norms of authorities is probably the greatest variable promoting prosecution of crimes. Apparently, authorities' social norms do not hold the legal norms against mercy killing to be of great importance; if they did, more open conflict between criminal justice authorities and physicians would have resulted over euthanasia laws, as well as a greater number of criminal prosecution of physicians.

According to Turk, norm violators' power relative to that of authorities affects the probability of their behavior being criminalized. Doctors wield considerable power in our society by controlling the absolutely essential commodity of human medicine. Their very high status is well recognized, as is the collective power embodied in the American Medical Association. Physicians favoring euthanasia also have demonstrated "sophistication" and "realism in conflict moves" with authorities by promoting their position through respectable lobbying organizations such as the Euthanasia Society and the Foundation for Thanatology. Such organazations have made legal inroads toward redefining mercy killing as ethical medical practice (e.g., "living wills"). The reduction of the criminality associated with euthanasia, then, will continue as long as the offenders possess enough power to control the definition of the offense.

Sutherland would argue that criminal euthanasia most likely would occur under the two conditions of social disorganization. First, there may be a "differential social organization" promoting euthanasia within the ranks of physicians. Second, an "anomic" lack of rules about its appropriateness, part of the present period of normative transition from clinical to social criteria of death, would encourage euthanasia. Criminal euthanasia may become a relatively common practice unless concrete standards are established inhibiting its use; otherwise physicians will employ loose legal interpretations of the situations in which it is considered appropriate.

There may well be an inverse relationship between the extent of euthanasia and the medical resources available. Pontell (1984) has described such a "system capacity" hypothesis in criminal justice, in which the incarceration rate is inversely related to prison overcrowding. For Pontell, incarceration increases as overcrowding decreases and vice versa—incarceration is merely a function of available prison space. Similarly, if available medical resources (physicians, equipment, hospital space) are in short supply, doctors may opt to expend the resources they have on patients who have the greatest chance for a high quality of life. If, on the other hand, there is an abundance of doctors and hospital space, there may be a tendency to expend on patients whatever resources are available, even if the prognosis for a decent quality of life is bleak. A medical "system capacity" hypothesis would predict a greater amount of extended treatment for those with poor social prognoses when there are sufficient available medical resources than when such resources are more heavily utilized. However, testing this hypothesis empirically may be difficult because the researcher would have to create valid measures of both availability of medical resources and the incidence of euthanasia.

On an individual patient basis, the practice of euthanasia may be inversely related to "financial capacity." If a patient can afford prolonged treatment or has adequate insurance to cover its costs, withdrawal of treatment may be less likely than in situations in which the patient cannot pay. Here, the decision for mercy killing is based on profit/loss considerations rather than on humanitarian ones. Along the same line, a doctor's personal financial "strain" may encourage him or her to prolong treatment of a well-resourced patient rather than withdraw it. In this case, ironically, "strain" would be a motivation *not* to commit the crime.

Crimes by Doctors Against Property

Fee-Splitting.   Generally, fee-splitting "involves a kickback, usually to a general practitioner who refers patients to a surgeon or specialist" (Jesilow, et al., 1985:158). The referral can be for necessary or unnecessary patient care. "Pingponging" refers to the needless referral of a patient to another physician for additional treatment. Sutherland (1949:12) made specific reference to this illegal practice in his *White Collar Crime*: "The physician who participates in fee-splitting tends to send his patients to the surgeon who will split the largest fee rather than to the surgeon who will do the best work." Sutherland (1949:12) indicated in his monograph that two-thirds of the surgeons in New York City were estimated to have participated in fee-splitting, and that more than half of the physicians in a north central state who answered a questionnaire favored fee-splitting.

Fee-splitting "restricts competition, militates against excellence, inflates health costs, and increases the number of unneeded operations, inevitably maiming and killing some patients" (Jesilow, et al., 1985:158). As Whitman (1953:24) has noted, ". . . fee-splitting . . . kickbacks range as high as . . . 70 percent [and] the less skilled the surgeon, the higher the kickback he must give in order to get business [so] split-fee cases gravitate to the highest bidders, the worst surgeons." The fact that fee-splitting is conspiratorial by definition and certain professionals resort to fee-splitting as a normal part of their occupation supports Sutherland's idea that professionals learn to do what they do through differential association. Violators may be differentially socially organized around definitions favorable to violation of fee-splitting laws. Just as with the case of unnecessary surgery and treatment, the financial "strain" caused by the high operating costs of a medical practice and the quest for a higher income may be motivations for physicians to engage in fee-splitting.

Fraudulent Medical Insurance Claims. Fraudulent submission of insurance claims for medical services is integrally related to many unnecessary surgeries and treatments and fee-splits because fees are often charged (and claimed from an insurance company) for services that should not have been performed. In addition to pingponging, physicians also "family gang" (needlessly request to see members of a patient's family), prolong treatments, bill for physician services when nonlicensed personnel performed the task, or double-bill insurance companies for services (Pontell, Jesilow and Geis, 1982:118; 1984:406). There is also a type of medical insurance fraud in which claims are made for services that were never performed (e.g., examinations, tests, X-rays without film). The former is known as "overutilization" or "abuse" and the latter is simply fraud. Although fraud is easier to prove legally than abuse, both kinds of insurance claiming are criminal.

Because medical insurance companies pay claims on a fee-for-service basis, fraud is easily accomplished by doctors. Needleman and Needleman (1979) have characterized the fee-for-service system as a "crime facilitative environment." A report by the Inspector General's Office in the Department of Health and Human Services estimated that about $2 billion may be lost to fraud and abuse in the the federal Medicare program alone (Wilson, Geis, Pontell, Jesilow,and Chappell, 1985:27).

Pontell, et al. (1985) found a total of 147 physicians who were either suspended or excluded from the Medicaid and Medicare programs for fraud in a period between 1977 and 1982. Twenty-two physicians in 1978, twenty-three in 1979, thirty in 1980, twenty in 1981, and forty-nine in 1982 were sanctioned, but such figures are more a reflection of enforcement efforts than they are of the number of these offenses. About a third (36 percent) were foreign school graduates; among domestic schools, four colleges accounted for eighteen of the violators and fifteen schools each had two violators. California-trained doctors accounted for more than a quarter of all violators (28 percent) while those earning degrees in New York accounted for almost one in five of the violators (17 percent). The top five violating specialties were: general and family practitioners (27 percent), psychiatry (18 percent), general surgery (11 percent), internal medicine (8 percent), and obstetrics/gynecology (7 percent).

Geis, Jesilow, Pontell, and O'Brien (1985:233) point out that some medical specialties, by nature, facilitate apprehension for fruadulent insurance claims. Anesthesiologists, and particularly psychiatrists and psychologists, are easier targets for insurance fraud investigators because such specialists bill on the basis of time rather than on the basis of services (e.g., examinations, injections, treatments). There are several methods which can be used to document overcharging for time spent with patients. Practitioners who bill for more hours than are in a day's work are caught relatively easily by a computer. Additionally, investigators have documented the hours spent with patients by photographing and timing traffic in and out of offices and waiting rooms, and then comparing the observed time of treatment with the hours billed. Undercover investigators have also sought treatment themselves and, using a contrived insurance indentification card, determined whether the doctor billed the insurance company for the correct amount of time. Psychiatrists also have been known to dispense drugs to patients or have sexual contact with patients or former patients, and then to charge the insurance company for therapy time.

In the previously cited survey by the *American Psychologist* (n = 465), only about a third (37 percent) of the psychologists stated that they "never" alter a diagnosis to meet insurance criteria. Almost one in ten (8 percent) stated that they altered diagnoses "very often" or "fairly often" for that purpose. Over a quarter (27 percent) said they did so "sometimes" (*U.S. News*, 1988a). Geis, Pontell, Keenan, Rosoff, O'Brien and Jesilow (1985) have presented detailed information about two cases of "peculating psychologists" in California:

• The practitioner billed the insurance carrier for office visits with family members who were never treated. He procured insurance cards from several family members and filed claims for sessions not given. In addition to filing false claims, the practitioner also precluded members of the family from seeing other doctors because their insurance cards had been confiscated by him. He was ultimately charged with twenty-four counts of filing false claims and one count of grand theft. He plea bargained with a guilty plea to one count of filing false claims, which was a felony, and he was given three years probation, ordered to pay $3,975 in restitution, given a $5,000 fine, and suspended from participating in the state's insurance program for the period of his probation.

- The practitioner billed the insurance company for therapy sessions performed by his wife, who was not licensed, and had billed for services at a residential facility far in excess of the number of working hours in the day. Also, he had taken insurance cards of family members of patients he was treating. In addition to a sentence much like that given in the above case, he was also dismissed from his tenured position at a California college for immoral conduct and dishonesty.

Of the eight psychologists studied, the average age was fifty-six and all were male. All had children, five were married at the time of the interviews, and five were in practice by themselves. They had been working as psychologists for an average of twenty-two years, and the majority had remained at the same site for most of their career. These were not young professionals struggling and "straining" through the early years of establishing a practice, nor was there noticeable evidence that insurance fraud was part of socially shared norms among psychologists. Instead, the evidence presented seemed to support neutralization theory. The respondents seemed to have resorted to all of the techniques of neutralization in one form or another. Through criticism of the insurance program and its enforcement tactics, the respondents justified their behavior and kept their noncriminal self-image intact:

- I felt I was getting raped in terms of fees. They were paying $27 a session when the going rate was something like seventy-five dollars. It was a farce because they didn't want anyone to do therapy with Medicaid.
- I think if your're not paid enough there's a tendency to feel you're being taken advantage of and wanting to make amends for it a little bit. . . . People do feel they have to make up for all the hell they go through.
- There should be more controls over the recipient [client] than over the professional, and I think they would be saving themselves more dollars and doing themselves a justice.

- I don't even know what [business] goes on in my outer office. I don't want to drain my energy doing that. . . . Now they've (state authorities) got us all paranoid.
- [Insurance] drains you with all its regulations and details. You spend so much time on the clerical work that you would prefer to put into more creative work.

All but one of the offenders remained in practice, and the one who did not was on disability status at the time of the study. More surprisingly, four of the seven who remained in practice reported an increase in the number of patients they treated. Essentially, there seemed to be no lasting business effects from the sanctions.

THE LEGAL PROFESSION

Lawyers, as professionals, also have abundant opportunities to commit crime in the course of their occupation. Offenses can be committed by attorneys for their own benefit (e.g., overbilling clients for time, embezzlement of funds entrusted to them) or for the benefit of their clients (e.g., falsification of documents). Some crimes they commit are particular to their profession, such as contempt of court by an officer of the court and violation of a client's legal confidence.

There are several aspects of service delivery related to the practice of law which offer tremendous opportunity for abuse and fraud. As Blumberg (1984:196) explains:

"Legal service lends itself particularly well to confidence games. Usually, a plumber will be able to demonstrate . . . that he has performed a service by clearing up the stuffed drain, repairing the leaky faucet or pipe—and therefore merits his fee. He has rendered . . . a visible, tangible boon for his client in return for the requested fee. . . . In the practice of law there is a special problem in this regard, no matter what the level of the practitioner or his place in the hierarchy of prestige. Much legal work is intangible either because it is simply a few words of advice, some preventive action, a telephone call, negotiation of some kind, a form filled out and filed, a hurried conference with another attorney or an official of a government agency, a letter or opinion written, or a countless variety of seemingly innocuous and even prosaic procedures and actions."

A question arises, then, about the worth or value of such activities. For instance, how much is a lawyer's service worth if he or she, through some simple advice over the telephone, saves his client several thousand dollars in taxes? The advice may only have taken a few minutes, but the resultant benefit to the client was substantial. The client would readily pay an hour's fee of up to $300 to that attorney for such advice.

This intangible fee-for-service system further promotes overcharging clients because much of the work done by attorneys (except for court appearances and client conferences) takes place behind office doors outside the purview of the client. When an attorney informs a client that an arduous negotiation with the opposing party has been completed, and then sends a bill for four or five hours of work, the client is in no position to dispute the charges.

In addition to defrauding clients through their fees-for-service, lawyers sometimes also violate fiduciary duties. The following are just a few such cases reported recently in the newspapers: (1) Joel Steinberg, a New York City attorney, arranged for the adoption of a child for one of his clients, and then illegally adopted the infant himself (this fact was brought into the national spotlight after Steinberg was accused of beating the child to death) (AP, 12/6/88a); (2) in 1987, Thomas Barefoot, an Indiana lawyer, was indicted on three felony charges of theft for allegedly diverting more than $6,600 in clients' funds for his own use (AP, 6/30/87); and (3) disbarred Georgia attorney William Braziel, Jr. pleaded guilty in 1988 to stealing $371,000 from various clients, and was sentenced to six years of imprisonment (AP, 2/2/89). Attorneys, in their capacity as professionals, have also violated individuals' constitutional rights and have been charged criminally for those transgressions under Title 18 U.S.C, Section 242 (see Chapter 5). Prosecutorial abuse of civil rights has already been discussed. Regarding defense attorneys, in one case a public defender was convicted under Section 242 for attempting to exact money from those he represented and their friends by asserting that an adequate defense could not be mounted otherwise (*U.S. vs. Senak*, 527 F2d, 129, 1975). The aforementioned crimes represent blatant offending by lawyers, but there are also more subtle ethical violations that they can commit.

Ethical Violations in the Legal Profession—The Carlin Study

Lawyers are informed of their ethical obligations through several sources: canons of professional associations, statutory requirements, court rules governing their behavior, court decisions in disciplinary cases involving lawyers, and the definition and interpretation of legal ethics found in textbooks and other publications. There are also unwritten norms, customs, and practices that have evolved. These ethical obligations relate to dealings with clients (e.g., confidentiality, conflicts of interest, overcharging, neglect) and colleagues (e.g., deceiving, solicitation of cases, breaking agreements), and the administration of justice (e.g., concealment of evidence, false representation, unfounded claims) (Carlin, 1966).

Carlin (1966) has investigated how members of the New York City Bar accept the various ethical standards of their profession. Carlin asked 800 lawyers their opinions regarding hypothetical situations which represented ethical conflicts. He found that some norms are generally accepted by almost all attorneys; he termed these "bar norms." Other ethical norms were accepted only by some of the respondents ("paper norms"). Third, Carlin identified a group of ethical standards which were accepted by most of the members of large firms, but far fewer members of smaller firms ("elite" norms). Thus, the overall pattern that emerged was a "norm hierarchy"—a large majority of attorneys accepted a basic framework of rules, but other standards were differentially accepted.

As an example of an almost universal acceptance of a bar norm, over four-fifths of the attorneys disapproved of police payoffs (large firm—87 percent, medium firm—83 percent, small firm—82 percent, and individual practitioners—83 percent). Telling a client who wishes to make a bribe that such an action is "risky but your own business" is an example of an elite norm. Sixty-two percent of large firm attorneys rejected this practice, while those in smaller organizations were less likely to condemn it (medium firms—46 percent, small firms—42 percent, individuals—39 percent). As an example of a paper norm, attorneys were generally likely to have their actions governed by consideration of their contingency commission, for only one in five large firm attorneys disapproved of this practice, as did only about a tenth of smaller firm attorneys ("contingency" commissions are paid only in the event that a client wins the case). Overall, about two-thirds of the large firm attorneys and about half of those in medium firms accepted more than the bar norms, while individuals and those in small firms, for the most part, accepted only the bar norms.

In addition to measuring respondents' acceptance of various norms, Carlin also determined their actual adherence to ethical standards by tabulating self-reported past and projected future ethical violations. He found occupational status, as measured by firm size, to be strongly associated with more ethical behavior. Carlin also concluded that the lower the status of the client (income, size of business), the less likely the attorneys were to act ethically, even in regard to higher-level, more demanding bar norms. Moreover, the more unstable an attorney's practice, the more likely he or she would endorse ethical violations. Further, the greater a lawyer's opportunity to exploit a client (by gaining financially to the client's detriment), the more he or she was likely to violate ethical norms. This was true especially among attorneys with lower status clients. Lawyers were also influenced by clients pressuring them to violate ethical standards—the more pressure, the more violations.

Lawyers, then, do not have a strong consensus about what they can and cannot do. Although there are certain norms to which almost all attorneys adhere, there is a large amount of occupational anomie in the legal profession which contributes to ethical transgression. This anomie and the loosely defined fees-for-service associated with the legal profession combine into a criminogenic occupational structure.

THE CONFLICT BETWEEN PROFIT AND PROFESSION

Professions can be lucrative occupations. Many persons enter the professions in order to make a great deal of money. Quinney (1968), in his study of retail pharmacists, identified the occupational role conflict between professional ethics and profits. He interviewed eighty pharmacists from Albany, New York, twenty of whom had been sanctioned by state authorities for prescription violation and sixty of whom had not. He hypothesized that there is a role strain among pharmacists between a business and a professional orientation. Pharmacists have to resolve the dilemma by adapting to an "occupational role organization," which refers to the "relative orientation of the retail pharmacist to both professional and business roles" (Quinney, 1968:213). After measuring respondents' occupational role organizations, Quinney found that only 16 percent of the total group were oriented to a "professional role," 20 percent were oriented to a "business role," 45 percent were oriented to a hybrid "business-professional" role, and 19 percent were indifferent. However, among violators, 75 percent were oriented principally toward a "business" role, almost four times the rate of the total group. All of those claiming to have "professional" occupational role organizations were nonviolators.

Quinney then discusses prescription violation as a matter of "differential orientation." Occupational role conflict causes a structural strain within the profession and differential orientations among pharmacists to various roles may cause some to violate. Although Quinney's research provides no insight into the important question of how occupational role organizations are developed, his approach is helpful in predicting which professionals generally are more likely to turn to occupational crime for monetary gain by identifying those who adopt "business" rather than "professional" occupational role organizations.

QUESTIONS FOR DISCUSSION

1. Why is professional occupational crime a distinct form of offending?
2. Explain how fee-for-service structures facilitate crime in the professions. How would prepaying professional services (e.g., a yearly fee) help to curb fraud in the professions?
3. Explain how self-regulation can both encourage and discourage professional occupational crime.
4. Why is the existing evidence on the incidence of professional occupational crime piecemeal rather than representative of those crimes and criminals?
5. Discuss the ethical and methodological problems involved with pseudopatient studies.
6. Techniques of neutralization were identified among doctors (e.g., appeals to higher loyalties in the cases of euthanasia and illegal abortion, condemnation of condemners in the case of insurance fraud and abuse). Which specific neutralization techniques might be invoked by lawyers? Pharmacists?
7. Discuss euthanasia as a criminal offense. If you do not consider it to be criminal behavior, which criterion would you use for committing euthanasia (physiological brain death or the social quality of life)? If you choose the social quality of life, should it be in relation to the patient or the patient's family? Why?
8. Discuss occupational anomie in medicine and law. Why is anomie criminogenic in those professions?
9. What are the implications of "medical system capacity" as it relates to patient treatment?
10. How does occupational anomie affect a profession's ability to regulate itself?

Jim and Tammy Bakker greeting the press, before the scandals that destroyed their PTL ministry. In 1989, Bakker was sentenced to forty-five years in jail for defrauding his congregation. (AP / Wide World Photos)

S E V E N

INDIVIDUAL
OCCUPATIONAL CRIME

It was noted earlier that occupational crime by individuals as individuals is a catch all category that includes all occupational crimes other than those committed for organizations by their employees or by persons in their capacity as government authorities or professionals. This category undoubtedly includes the largest number of occupational crimes and criminals, and therefore the present discussion will have to be confined to relatively few instances. Crimes against property (e.g., employee theft, embezzlement, fraud, personal income tax evasion, insider stock trading) constitute the bulk of individual occupational crime, but there are also many occupational crimes against persons that are committed by individuals (e.g., sexual molestation on the job, knowingly selling unsafe consumer products such as contaminated food, or recklessly endangering others by driving public transportation while intoxicated).

EMPLOYEE THEFT

Incidence

Estimates of the amount of revenue lost through the varying forms of theft of cash, goods, and services by employees are difficult because there is such a great amount of this activity that remains undetected or unpublicized. Employee thefts can be relatively petty, such as the pilfering of pencils or the charging of personal long distance telephone calls to an employer. Or, sophisticated employee thefts can net thousands of dollars. Annual losses due to employee theft have been estimated to be anywhere from at least $6 billion (Adler, 1977) to as much as $10 billion (Pope, 1978), and are believed to total much more than the aggregate losses from street crime (Jaspan, 1974). *Finance* magazine, reporting on a survey by the U.S. Chamber of Commerce, asserts that about half of those who work in plants and offices steal to a greater or lesser extent, and that about 5 percent to 8 percent of employees are said to steal in volume (Broy,

1974:42). In another estimate, store employees were thought to account for almost half of all thefts from retailers (DeMott, 1984). According to Adler (1977:6), 30 percent of all business failures are the result of employee dishonesty.

Employee theft of funds, property, and services is usually divided into three categories: larceny, embezzlement, and fraud. "Larceny" is the simple taking of something. "Embezzlement" refers to the theft of something with which one has been entrusted. "Fraud" refers to the theft of something through the use of false pretenses. Thus, the theft of money from a cash drawer to which one has authorized access would be embezzlement, but theft from another's cash drawer to which one does not have authorized access would be larceny. The filing of a false report regarding reimbursable employee expenses or the number of hours worked would be an example of theft under false pretenses.

Cash, merchandise, supplies, or services such as telephone calls can be taken from almost any job site. However, many employee thefts are more elaborate than simple taking, as internal theft specialist Harvey Yaffe has indicated (Adler, 1977): there is the waiter or waitress who fails to charge for an extra drink or an appetizer, hoping to build a bigger tip; the movie ticket-taker who hides tickets without tearing them in half, returns them to the box office to be sold again, and then splits the profits with the cashier; the usher who, for a bribe, shows patrons to more expensive seats; the employees who hide stolen goods in the trash and split the profits with the garbage collector; and the claims adjuster who fraudulently legitimates self-fabricated claims. One of Yaffe's bolder thieves was the manager of a midwestern supermarket, who built an extra check-out lane in his store and set up his own cash register. Each day, he would open up the register and do several hundred dollars worth of business—$70,000 in just a few months. Other sizable employee thefts include that of the cleaning woman at the Neiman Marcus department store in Dallas who stole 343 dresses valued at $686,000, and that of a warehouse employee who stole 65,000 beer bottles, which he redeemed for five cents each (*Time*, 1986).

Rates of employee theft based on available agency-generated data are impossible to determine. As noted in Chapter 2, the *Uniform Crime Reports* are virtually useless for determining occupationally related thefts. Besides, as also noted in Chapter 2, agency-generated data usually do not reflect unverses of offenders or offenses, and may not even reflect representative proportions of these categories. This is especially true in cases of employee theft, because the victimized employer often seeks some sort of unofficial resolution to the problem, such as dismissal or restitution payment. Embezzlement is the one offense category in the *UCR* that probably includes the largest proportion of theft-from-employer cases, but because so few people are involved in the crime (a low "base rate"), even the slightest changes in arrests for embezzlement will translate into relatively large increases or decreases. Keeping these problems in mind, Table 7.1 presents *UCR* race, gender, and age data on persons arrested for embezzlement during 1986. Table 7.1 indicates that arrested male embezzlers constitute almost twice the number of female arrestees for that offense. And, men and women 22 to 29 years of age are much more likely than those of the same gender in other age groups to be arrested for embezzlement, constituting together a third of all persons apprehended for the offense.

Although national victim surveys used to include business victimizations (e.g., Hindelang, 1976), the only two offenses investigated were robbery and burglary. Regarding self-report data, Adler (1977) notes that 76 percent of surveyed employees of a drug store chain admitted stealing one hundred dollars or more within the previous six months, and Horning (1970) found that 85 percent of his eighty-eight subjects admitted purposely stealing goods from the electronics assembly plant in which they worked. Such self-reported theft rates, however, are not necessarily applicable to the work force outside the populations studied. Hollinger and Clark (1983), interviewing a more representative sample of about nine thousand employees in several sectors, found that approximately a third of their respondents admitted to stealing from their employer within the past year (thefts were generally nonserious and infrequent).

Franklin (1976) conducted an in-depth study of internal theft from nine branch stores of a large retail organization over a seven-year period. Her study included embezzlement, fraud, and theft. In an employee population averaging more than 5,000 persons over the seven-year period, a total of 447 known cases of theft were discovered. Thus, less than 2 percent of the store employees were caught stealing each year. The most frequent months for theft were November and December, which involve increased hiring of part-time employees for the holiday season and the requirements of present-giving. Although persons 18 to 22 years of age made up 12 percent of the employees, they constituted almost seven in ten violators (69 percent), while those 23 to 28 years of age accounted for another 14 percent of the thieves. More than four of five thefts, then, were attributable to those aged 18 to 28. Blacks were almost twice as likely to commit theft (38 percent) than their representation in the employee pool (20 percent), while males were 37 percent more likely to commit offenses (55 percent) than their representation in the store's work force (40 percent). Three-quarters (76 percent) of the crimes involved theft of cash or merchandise, 4 percent involved the misuse of equipment, and 20 percent involved the alteration of records. Sales personnel were most overrepresented among thieves—they were responsible for two-thirds of the thefts, but constituted only

Table 7.1 Persons Arrested for Embezzlement According to Race, Gender, and Age, 1986

Race			Percent of Total
Total White		7,356	70.1
under 18		516	4.9
18 and over		6,840	65.2
Total NonWhite		3,139	29.9
under 18		179	1.7
18 and over		2,960	28.2
Total		10,495	100.0

Gender			Percent of Total
Total Male		6,678	63.6
under 18		414	3.9
18 and over		6,264	59.7
Total Female		3,822	36.4
under 18		282	2.7
18 and over		3,540	33.7
Total		10,500	100.0

Age			Percent of Total
15 and under	Male	81	0.8
	Female	32	0.3
16–17	Male	333	3.2
	Female	250	2.4
18–21	Male	1,155	11.0
	Female	921	8.8
22–29	Male	2,365	22.5
	Female	1,432	13.6
30–39	Male	1,687	16.1
	Female	782	7.4
40–49	Male	701	6.7
	Female	299	2.8
50–59	Male	291	2.8
	Female	80	0.8
60 and over	Male	65	0.6
	Female	26	0.2
Total		10,500	100.0

SOURCE: *Crime in the United States 1986,* Federal Bureau of Investigation; Washington, D.C.: U.S. Government Printing Office, 1987. From Tables 34–38. 10,473 Agencies Reporting; Estimated population 198,488,000.

two-fifths of the employees. Managers and clerical personnel were most underrepresented, accounting for less than 6 percent of thefts but 28 percent of employees. Regarding the amounts stolen, more than half of the thefts involved less than sixty dollars, and another 15 percent were valued at 61 to 150 dollars. Less than one in twenty (4.7 percent) involved more than a thousand dollars, one of which concerned the theft of more than thirty-five thousand dollars. Those who worked for the company for a year or less constituted seven in ten violators. Only about two in five were prosecuted.

Computer-Related Employee Pilfering

Computer technology has created new opportunities to steal from employers. "Computer crime" is defined by the Bureau of Justice Statistics (1979:v) as "any illegal act for which knowledge of computer technology is essential." Computer crime is especially menacing because it can be committed from a great distance and evidence of intrusion can be erased. Any of the millions of business and personal microcomputers, which are becoming faster, smarter, and cheaper, have the potential to be used as instruments of crime against employers and others. The U.S. Army estimates that the chance of being detected for computer crime is about 1 in 100, and the chance of being prosecuted for it is about 1 in 22,000 (Thornton, 1984).

Examples of computer crime against employers include the nineteen-year-old bank programmer on the West Coast who ordered the computer to transfer $4100 (one hundred dollars from each of forty-one accounts) into an account set up for his wife under a fictitious name (Pope, 1978). In a 1980 case, San Francisco's Wells Fargo Bank lost $21 million in a year, allegedly to two sports promoters who, with a bank employee's help, used a computer for illegal transfers (Thornton, 1984). Sheridan (1979:69) reports that a dishonest computer operator in New Jersey diverted $20 million worth of oil from an Exxon Corporation refinery to a barge docked nearby. A study of government computers by the Department of Health and Human Services uncovered 172 cases of fraud and abuse by employees (Thornton, 1984). One employee diverted $24,000 in unauthorized benefit checks to himself over a five-month period. In another case, three clerks were able to steal $150,000 worth of food stamps by computer. Computer theft against employers can also be for the purposes of extortion, such as in the case of the computer programmer who "kidnapped" several programs he had developed and attempted to extract $100,000 in ransom from his employer for their safe return (Sheridan, 1979:70).

Explanations for Employee Pilfering

Criminals need not "learn" specific techniques for the taking of cash. Even in more sophisticated thefts, such as embezzlement, specific theft techniques and attitudes toward stealing are not necessarily learned from others (Cressey, 1953). Klockars's (1974:125) study of a professional fence (a dealer in stolen goods), however, indicates that employee thieves sometimes are taught specific pilfering techniques. In the following passage, Klockars's fence explains how he told truck drivers the best ways to steal:

> See, I school my drivers, I mean, if they got an overload, that's a free thing, a gift. They can bring it to me just like it's legitimate. But stealin', I tell 'em, they just gotta use their heads. You pick a day when it's rainy an' cold an' the shipper's rushed. That's when you wanna throw on an extra carton. Or the same goes when you're deliverin'. If the guy's got five trucks waitin' he ain't gonna count what you got. It don't make sense to steal from your own truck either, if you can just as easy pick up a couple a cartons where somebody else unloaded 'em. Oh, I school my drivers; show 'em how to go about doin' things, you know.

Theories other than differential association, however, are probably more powerful for explaining employee theft. Studies by Cressey (1953), Horning, (1970), Zeitlin (1970), and Mars (1974), presented in Chapter 3, found that the various techniques of neutralization facilitated employee theft. Denials of injury ("the company can afford it"), denial of responsibility ("I was only 'borrowing' the money"), and condemnation of condemners ("my employer does not pay me enough wages") were commonly used by the offenders in these studies. Benson (1985) has also alluded to Minor's "metaphor of the ledger" neutralization technique in his study of embezzlers. Three of the four embezzlers he studied "referred explicitly to extraordinary circumstances and presented the offense as an aberration in their life history" (p.595). Although Benson's subjects admitted their responsibility and did not deny the victimization and injury associated with their thefts, their involvement was still couched in terms of being uncharacteristic of their otherwise law abiding behavior. A classic example of an emplyee thief's "appeal to higher loyalties" neutralization technique is the case of "Robin HUD," Marilyn Harrell. In 1989, Ms. Harrell, a private escrow agent for the Department of Housing and Urban Development, admitted to diverting more than $5 million in government funds to poor people, stating "I justified my actions inwardly only by reminding myself that I followed a higher law in an attempt to ease suffering" (AP, 6/17/89b).

"Strain" theory may account for some of the motivations to steal from employers. Moreover, "strain" as a motivation for employee theft may be mixed with Minor's (1981) neutralization technique of "necessity." As noted in Chapter 3, Cressey (1953) identified the first step on the road to embezzlement as a perceived immediate need for money, terming this condition an "unsharable financial problem" (see Clinard, 1953 for a critique of this concept). However, when Franklin (1976:113) sought to ascertain the reason for employee thefts among 169 persons (mostly long term employees), only a third were coded as "needed money." In contrast to actual need as a motivation, Gibbons (1973) has observed that some embezzlements develop as attempts to sustain standards of living for which legitimate income is insufficient. Similarly, Nettler's (1974:74) study of six major embezzlements in Canada revealed that "desire and opportunity generate theft more frequently in these instances than does a financial difficulty. . . ." Only one of Nettler's embezzlers, an attorney, had stolen to meet current financial obligations. Zeitz (1981) reached similar conclusions about the lack of offenders' pressing financial problems in her study of female embezzlers. Cressey, too, later admitted that though an "unsharable financial problem" could be important to the process of embezzlement, it was "not critical" (Laub, 1983:138).

Zeitz (1981) found that the female embezzlers she interviewed most often claimed the needs of their family as a justification for stealing, rather than a pressing financial problem. Similarly, in her study of the court records of convicted embezzlers, Daly (1986) found that when a need for money was claimed as a motivation, females were about twice as likely as men to cite the needs of their family as a justification for their embezzlement; males were much more likely to mention business needs. However, there may be other factors besides the character of neutralizations which affect the employee offending rates of males and females. For instance, Box (1983) points out that because female workers are often supervised more closely than males in the same position, lower female rates of employee theft can be expected.

CONSUMER FRAUD

In addition to being committed against employers, fraud, or theft through the use of false pretenses, can also be committed to cheat consumers in the course of an occupation. In *The Popular Practice of Fraud*, T. Swann Harding (1935:25) documented consumer fraud as early as the first century A.D., when Pliny the Elder told of the adulterated honey on the market and of the fortification of wine with gypsum, lime, pitch, rosin, wood ashes, salt, sulphur, and artificial pigments. Pliny also denounced the fraudulent pharmacists of his day, and provided tests for detecting food and drug adulterations.

It is rather commonly held (e.g., Coleman, 1985:135; Litman and Litman, 1981:647) that the axiom of *caveat emptor* ("let the buyer beware"), which insulates fraudsters from prosecution, is an "ancient" or "old" legal doctrine. However, such adjectives are misleading because, as Hamilton (1931:1169) found, there is no hard evidence in legal precedent to suggest that this doctrine has much of a long history, other than a few scant references to it. Rather, as Geis (1988:14) put it, *caveat emptor* was adopted "only when social conditions and power relations existed which allowed the pretense that there was such a sacred common-law doctrine."

Although it had been going on for a very long time, consumer fraud was not recognized as a criminal offense until the *Carrier's Case* in 1473 (Hall, 1952:1-33; Geis, 1968a:9). The *Carrier's Case* for the first time included within the definition of theft the appropriation of goods by a middleman. The defendant in the *Carrier's Case* had been hired to carry bales of wool to Southampton, England. Instead of fulfilling this obligation, he transported the bales to another place, where he stole the contents. This particular crime, more accurately conversion rather than fraud, represents the first time cheating a customer became defined as criminal larceny.

Harding (1935) has compiled hundreds of cases of fraud throughout history (see also Comstock, 1880). One of Harding's (1935: 31-32) more humorous involved London's James Graham, who, in the late eighteenth century, invented a "Magneto-Electrico" bed, guaranteed to produce offspring for even the most "barren" of couples. Graham claimed, "Any gentleman and his lady desirous of progeny, and wishing to spend an evening [on this bed] . . . may, by a compliment of a fifty pound bank note, be permitted to partake of the heavenly joys it affords by causing immediate conception. . . ." Consumer fraud was so rampant during the early nineteenth century that Frederick Accum, a noted London chemist, felt compelled to write in 1820 his *Treatise on Adulterations of Food and Culinary Poisons, Exhibiting the Fraudulent Sophistications of Beer, Wine, Spiritous Liquors, Tea, Coffee, Cream, Confectionery, Vinegar, Mustard, Pepper, Cheese, Olive Oil, and Pickles.*

The possibilities for fraud against consumers are virtually limitless, because it can occur whenever goods or services are sold. Consumer fraud is an individual occupational crime to the extent that its gains accrue directly and knowingly to employees (e.g., those working on commission) or to the owners of a business. Even in cases in which the perpetrators unknowingly commit consumer fraud, such as when goods are sold with unintentionally erroneous promotional materials (Hopkins, 1980), the seller can, through strict liability, be held criminally responsible for the offense. It has been estimated that consumer fraud accounts for about *one in every six dollars* of revenue derived from criminal activity in the United States (Pennsylvania Crime Commission, 1980:6, cited in Hagan, 1986:16).

Some frauds against consumers might be seen as relatively petty individually, such as slightly overweighing meat or produce through adjustment of scale calibration. Relatively petty gains, however, can aggregate into substantial losses to a community. For instance, in a recent organizational crime, Chrysler Corporation was ordered to pay more than $16 million in restitution to some 39,500 consumers in forty-six states who had purchased cars that had odometers disconnected while they were driven from forty to three hundred miles each by Chrysler executives (AP, 8/24/88). And as noted in the chapter on professionals' crime, unnecesary treatments and surgeries have not only maimed and killed, but have cost consumers as much as $10 billion each year (Berger, 1988:45).

Fraudsters have also been known to prey on consumers' humanitarian and charitable instincts. In a nationwide telephone solicitation, 100,000 Americans were duped into buying inferior lightbulbs, the profits from which allegedly aided disabled workers. The bulbs, marketed under the brand name "Torch," were overpriced by about 300 percent. An investigation by the State of New Jersey revealed that some of the bulb sellers' disabilities, which had been "certified" by licensed physicians, included obesity, acne, hay fever, and nervousness (Flaherty and Cohen, 1979).

Tricksters sometimes take advantage of people when they are most vulnerable, such as during bereavement. In Cross Plains, Tennessee, funeral director Bobby Wilks was charged with burying persons with trash in their coffins or without a coffin at all. After unearthing several graves, families found bottles, newspapers, discarded flower arrangements, and bags of hair in the caskets. One corpse had "an old metal flowerpot on top of his head." One family paid for a vault to be installed over a casket, but none was found when the grave was disinterred. Two caskets were found buried on their sides and one was left with an arm hanging out of it (AP, 10/15/88).

Clergy fraud, too, has duped thousands. In December of 1988, a federal grand jury indicted PTL (Praise the Lord) founder Jim Bakker and his former top aide, Richard Dortch, on twenty-four counts of fraud. Bakker and Dortch were charged with mail fraud, wire fraud and conspiring to defraud the public through the sale of lifetime partnerships in the ministry's Heritage Village theme park. The indictments alleged that in 1983 and 1984 Bakker and Dortch announced the construction of a vacation park at Heritage USA that was to include a lavish hotel, and the lifetime memberships were sold to help finance the projects. Lifetime partners were to receive free lodging at the complex in exchange for large contributions. Bakker and Dortch allegedly made false statements to induce the public to buy the partnerships, collecting over

$150 million. They promised that the funds would be used to build several hotels, but by March of 1987, only partial construction had been completed. Bakker and his wife received about $3.5 million in "bonuses," while Dortch received over $500,000. Three months after Bakker left the PTL because of allegations about sexual misconduct, the minstry filed for bankruptcy (AP, 12/6/88b). In 1989, Bakker was convicted and sentenced to serve forty-five years in prison, and to pay a fine of $500,000.

Compassionate instincts have also been preyed upon by politicians. In December of 1988, political maverick and three-time fringe presidential candidate Lyndon LaRouche, Jr. was convicted on several counts of mail fraud for cheating supporters who gave him loans totalling more than $30 million. The jury that convicted him believed LaRouche never intended to repay the loans. One of the victims, who lent the LaRouche organization $112,000 to finance an anti-drug abuse book, was later asked by the organization to try to obtain a bank loan so she could supply more money (AP, 12/17/88). LaRouche received a fifteen-year sentence, while his fund raiser (William Wertz) and his legal advisor (Edward Spannaus) were each sentenced to five years (AP, 1/28/89).

Consumer fraud can also be indirect. In a two-year undercover operation by the FBI, dubbed "Pharmoney" (U.S. Attorney, 1985), fraudulent representations were made by pharmaceutical wholesalers to drug manufacturers that goods purchased were intended for distribution to hospitals, nursing homes, clinics, foreign countries, and international non-profit organizations, so that the wholesalers could obtain low purchase prices. These drugs were then sold to regular consumers at a substantial profit. Persons charged included not only those who obtained the drugs fraudulently from the manufacturers, but also several individuals who bought the drugs from wholesalers knowing that they had been originally acquired through fraud. Indicted were owners and employees of hospital pharmacy management firms, national and regional pharmaceutical wholesaler employees, managers of retail drug store chains, neighborhood pharmacists, physicians, sales representatives of the drug manufacturers, and other brokers and middlepersons.

In addition to defrauding consumers by overcharging them, many in Pharmoney were also charged with adulteration and misbranding. According to the indictments, drugs were "shucked" or removed from their original packaging because the time limit of their usefulness had passed, because they were for nonpublic consumption, or because they were manufactured outside of the United States beyond federal Food and Drug Administration control. Some of the defendants were also charged with the removal of the word "sample" imprinted on individual capsules through scraping or through application of chemicals such as acetone, fingernail polish remover, and rubbing alcohol.

Fraud is also common in service delivery. One of the most frequent kinds of fraud affecting large numbers of consumers is found in the auto repair industry. Here, mechanically inept customers must rely on the judgement of persons who are "experts," which puts them at the mercy of repair shops. According to a 1979 government survey, American motorists were overcharged an average of $150 per car per year for repairs. Of each dollar spent, fifty-three cents were wasted because of unnecessary repair, overcharging, and services never performed or performed incompetently (Blumenthal, 1979).

Academic researchers, too, have been known to commit a type of "consumer" fraud by falsifying scientific results. Faking research is obviously an ethical violation of the canons of science (e.g., "disinterestedness," see Merton, 1942), and it also is criminal if university and research grant monies have supported such research or if job promotions are based on fraudulent research accomplishments. Cheating in science is relatively rare, however, because it is more difficult for a scientist to dupe his or her expert peers than it is for, say, an automobile mechanic to dupe a layperson (for a historical account of fraud in science, see Merton, 1973:309-316; Altick, 1951:Chapters 2 and 6). Harriet Zuckerman (1977:98) believes that, "Taking . . . forgery, data manipulation, data suppression, and plagiarism—willful acts of deceit—the known cases number perhaps several hundred in a cumulative population of research scientists, which, over the generations, number something on the order of more than a million, each at work over a span of years." Since many "honest mistakes" have often gone unnoticed for some time, it is quite likely that a good deal of purposeful scientific fraud has also gone undetected.

One of the best documented chicaneries in science is the 1912 "Piltdown Man" forgery by Charles Dawson, who had ground down the teeth on an ape jaw and cobbled the mandible to a human skull. His purpose was to make the skull appear to have come from a more primitive being than those known previously. More recently, Dr. Robert Slutsky, a radiology researcher at the University of California (San Diego), was found by his peers to have forged results in as many as sixty of his papers (AP, 11/29/87). In another recent case, paleontologist John Talent accused India's Viswa Jit Gupta of obtaining fossils of invertebrates that are readily available in curio shops and academic collections and then claiming to have found them in the Himalayas. Talent and his colleagues believe that there are more than one hundred other discrepancies in Gupta's findings. For example, Talent asserts that the site where Gupta supposedly obtained fossils had undergone geological deformation that was incapable of allowing such fossils to survive intact. Talent also claims that some of Gupta's fossils most closely match those that could only have been unearthed at sites in the State of New York (Allman, 1989). The "publish or perish" pressure in many American universities may strain an individual to the point of forging data or plagiarizing the works of others. In an effort to reduce the pressures to publish, Harvard University recently announced a new policy of taking into account only a select few of a candidate's best research papers when considering a scientist for hiring, tenure, or promotion. Fortunately, the belief in conventional scientific values is a strong impetus behind resistance to scientific cheating, and such beliefs are constantly reinforced by colleagues and professional associations.

In perhaps the most colossal fraud in modern history, mentioned in Chapter 4, Equity Funding Corporation of America duped its high-finance customers out of about $2 billion. According to The *Equity Funding Papers: The Anatomy of a Fraud* (Seidler, Andrews, and Epstein, 1977), EFCA would make loans to customers for the purchase of its life insurance policies. However, the firm soon began to lose money. To generate cash, EFCA then sold the policies to other insurers, receiving about $1.80 for each dollar in life insurance premiums sold in the first year. All subsequent life insurance premiums would go to the reinsurers rather than EFCA. Such transactions, then, became only a temporary solution to the company's cash flow problems. A further "solution" involved fraudulently inflating EFCA's assets in order to secure loans, which were used to acquire other companies with real assets. As this inflationary method of fraud came to an end, EFCA then began to falsify life insurance policies and sell the bogus policies to the reinsurers. EFCA even "killed off" nonexistent persons in order to obtain full beneficiary value on some of the fake policies. In all, some fifty-six thousand false policies were sold to reinsurers and at least $120 million in assets were fabricated. When EFCA fired one of its workers, he became disgruntled and told the story to an outsider, who in turn told the authorities. Eventually, twenty-two people pleaded guilty, and the crimes' mastermind, EFCA founder Stanley Goldblum, was sentenced to eight years in federal prison.

A compilation of publicized case studies such as Equity Funding makes interesting reading. Accurately determining the overall incidence of consumer fraud, however, is extremely difficult. As noted, agency-generated information on fraud, such as that found in the *Uniform Crime Reports*, does not distinguish between occupational and nonoccupational circumstances. Victim-generated information on consumer fraud (e.g., McCaghy and Nogier, 1982; Ennis, 1967) is probably unreliable because, first, many victims may be unaware of a fraud and therefore underreport it. Second, consumers who claim fraud victimization may have merely made an unwise, but legal, transaction, and therefore overreport it. As noted, in Ennis's (1967:108) pioneering victim survey, staff attorneys considered almost two-thirds (63 percent) of "victim"-respondent claims about consumer fraud to be "doubtful."

Three research teams have quite cleverly used direct observation to determine the prevalence of consumer fraud in various aspects of the automobile industry. First, in Jesilow's (1982:122) auto repair fraud "car battery" study (see Chapter 2), about one shop in ten (34/313) was considered to be "dishonest" because the mechanic declared what was in fact a chargeable battery to be unchargeable. Second, Tracy and Fox (1989) took several cars that had body damage to a representative sample of repair shops in Massachusetts to obtain estimates for the cars' repairs. The auto body repair estimates were significantly higher when the repair shops were told that the car was insured than when they were told that the car was not covered by insurance. This held true regardless of type of car, extent of damage, gender of driver, and location of repair shop.

Third, Braithwaite (1979) went to twelve used car lots in Queensland, Australia and noted the mileage on a systematic sample of used cars, and then contacted the immediately previous owners (whose names were a matter of public record) to verify how much mileage was on the cars when they were sold to the dealer. Because of existing research and because persons seem likely to remember their car's mileage at the time they trade for a new one (since it is a key factor in the trade-in value), Braithwaite considered former owners' responses about existing mileage to be valid. After accounting for "test drive" and other acceptable increases in mileage (up to one thousand) during the time the car was in the dealer's possession, Braithwaite (1979:104) found that over a third (thirteen of thirty-five, or 37 percent) of the cars appeared to have odometer readings rolled back. The average discrepancy was about ten thousand miles and the greatest rollback was fifty-three thousand miles. He cautions that this 37 percent rate is probably an underestimate because other cars may have had the mileage reduced, but had been driven to the point where the deficit was almost overcome. Based on the total number of used cars sold in Queensland, the rate translated into an estimate of over seventy thousand odometer rollbacks each year.

In more severe figures from the United States, Carter (1988) reports that there is a 50 percent chance in Georgia of buying a used car that has had its odometer rolled back and that the average rollback in that state is thirty thousand miles. Because for each ten thousand miles rolled back the consumer pays an extra $300 to $500, consumer loss on each illegal car in Georgia averages as much as $1,500.

Braithwaite (1979) interviewed a sample of twenty used car dealers, excluding the lots he used for direct observation (their managers would not cooperate). The responses help to explain some of the illegitimate practices in the used automobile industry in light of some of the theories discussed in Chapter 3. Braithwaite's respondents continually pointed out that in the past, before consumer protection measures were instituted, rollbacks were common because of strong competitive market pressures. A similar conclusion was reached by Leonard and Weber (1970), who found that automobile manufacturers provide such slim profit margins on new cars that dealers have to resort to overcharging for repairs and for used cars in order to stay in the business. Braithwaite's (1979) subjects, too, felt that in some significant ways the manufacturers use their market power to maximize their profits on new cars, while at the same time minimizing dealer profits on them. Most dealers strongly supported the view that the intense competition in the "cut-throat game" of used car sales created pressure to violate the law. Thus, there seems to be strong support for strain theory as a motivation for automobile dealer fraud.

Salesmen and managers did not appear to become dishonest because of differential association within the industry; fraud was not necessarily a socially shared value. Rather, most respondents said that honest people are simply weeded out of the business by dishonest competition. Some illegitimate techniques, however, are common practice and may have been learned as part of the trade.

One dealer made no effort to defend odometer fraud, stating emphatically that it is a product of "poor character." Most, however, tended to neutralize the wrongfulness of what they did. For instance, Braithwaite (1979:119) points out a denial of injury in the following response defending rollbacks:

> People pay too much attention to the mileage reading on a car. There might be a car with a low mileage reading but all sorts of faults and another perfect car with a high mileage reading. It doesn't matter what the mileage reading is, but how good the car is. . . . So if you turn the mileage reading back of a car in perfect order, you are encouraging the people to buy a good car.

Condemnation of condemners was the most common neutralization technique. Dealers unanimously believed that the public tries to cheat them at least as much as customers accuse dealers of cheating the public. One of Braithwaite's (1979:119) dealers stated, "They think because you are a used car dealer you are a liar. So they treat you like one and lie to you. Can you blame the dealer for lying back?" Here, Braithwaite sees the development of a "self-fulfilling prophecy." A self-fulfilling prophesy refers to something that is in fact false, but becomes true because of a belief in it as being true. Because customers believe the used car dealer is dishonest, they are dishonest in return. This, in turn, forces the dealer to actually be dishonest.

INDIVIDUAL INCOME TAX EVASION

Willful personal income tax evasion is an offense in which the taxpayer has deliberately cheated the government, and it is punishable by both civil and criminal penalties. It is included under the concept of occupational crime because, as noted in Chapter 1, were it not for legally derived income, persons would not be able to evade income tax. Of course, income derived illegally is also taxable. Al Capone and other criminals, including drug traffickers, have been convicted for evading taxes. The present discussion, however, includes only offenders who evade tax payments on legally derived personal income. Tax evasion encompasses failure to file a tax return and filing a false tax return (underreporting income or overstating deductions).

The Internal Revenue Service publishes information on its enforcement of income tax laws in its *Annual Report* (IRS, 1988:22). During fiscal year 1987, 242 persons were prosecuted for fraudulent tax shelters, and 94 were convicted; 243 were prosecuted for illegal tax protesting, and 275 were convicted; 185 were prosecuted for violation of the Bank Secrecy Act (which requires that cash deposits and withdrawals over $10,000 be reported by banks), and 116 were convicted; and 1,860 were prosecuted for "all other" offenses not related to drug trafficking income, of whom 1,391 were convicted. Note that the number of convictions can exceed the number of prosecutions because convictions may include cases from previous years, and persons prosecuted may not have come to trial by the end of the fiscal year.

The IRS also reports the probability of going to prison among those sentenced: 59 percent for fraudulent tax sheltering; 62 percent for illegal tax protesting; 39 percent for violation of the Bank Secrecy Act; and 57 percent for "all others" not related to evading taxes on drug trafficking profits. Although the probability of going to prison is relatively high for those sentenced, the number of convictions for criminal tax evasion seems relatively small, given about 103 million individual tax returns filed in 1987 for the tax year 1986 (IRS, 1988:50). The criminal conviction rate, then, would be about one in forty thousand returns. Common sense and empirical data (see discussion below on self-reports) tell us that a much greater proportion of taxed individuals willfully overstate deductions, underdeclare income, or fail to file.

In one violation of the Bank Secrecy Act, a former bank investment officer was sentenced to five years in prison, fined $250,000, and assessed

$9,700 in prosecution costs for her part in a conspiracy to hide $36 million through San Diego banks and a currency exchange. The IRS intercepted more than $11 million in fictitious claims for multiple refunds during FY 1987. A Florida man was arrested in one such case for filing 350 fictitious tax returns, claiming in excess of $1.5 million in refunds. In another scheme, a father and son filed hundreds of fraudulent tax returns to try to cheat the government out of almost $6 million; both were sentenced to prison (IRS, 1988:22). In 1988, John Galanis was sentenced to twenty-seven years in prison for his part in several phony oil- and gas-drilling tax shelter schemes, known as Transpac Drilling Venture, that created more than $172 million in fraudulent tax writeoffs for about 2,500 investors. In addition to leaving one bank insolvent, Galanis gained control over another bank, and caused Utah banking officials to have to take over even another bank. He also stole $3.9 million from three California mutual funds. Eleven others pleaded guilty in Galanis's various schemes (AP, 9/29/88).

The agency-generated data on tax violations in the IRS *Annual Report* also include victim-generated data, because the victim in this case is that agency. One researcher (Groves, 1958) attempted to observe directly income tax compliance among landlords in Wisconson by interviewing tenants about rents paid, and estimating deductible expenses. Groves found that some landlords underreported their net rental incomes by as much as half, and some did not report any such income.

Regarding self-reported tax evasion, Mason and Calvin (1978) sampled eight hundred households in Oregon to ascertain levels of compliance with state and federal tax laws. About one in four respondents (24 percent) admitted to practicing at least one form of evasion—5.3 percent admitted overstating deductions, 14.5 percent admitted underreporting taxable income, and 8.5 percent admitted failure to file a tax return (these total more than 24 percent because violators could commit more than one form of evasion). This figure is about three times the 8 percent admitted evasion rate found for Oregonians in Tittle's (1980:128) three-state self-report study discussed in Chapter 2 (11.2 percent of his entire sample admitted past tax cheating). As high as the Mason and Calvin 24 percent figure might seem, however, it is not as high as in other countries. For instance, Vogel (1974) estimated a 34 percent willful tax noncompliance rate from self-reports in Sweden.

The demographic differences between evaders and nonevaders also were investigated by Mason and Calvin (1978). They found that persons with lower incomes were more likely to fail to file a return and that about a third more men than women (57 percent to 43 percent, or 1.3:1) admitted to any one form of violation. They also report that young people are more likely to admit underreporting income than are older persons. The directions of these results agree with Tittle's (1980) findings for income, gender, and age (see Table 2.2).

Tittle (1980:188-89) has attempted to ascertain whether some of the theories discussed in Chapter 3 can account for respondents' projected *future* probabilites of committing the offense. For differential association, he used a composite scale which included the number of acquaintances known to be tax evaders, the number of acquaintances caught for tax evasion, the number of youthful acquaintances who were in trouble with the law, the frequency of church attendance, and the number of others thought likely to commit tax evasion if given the chance. The findings indicated that, holding other theoretical variables constant, the composite scores reflecting pro-cheating definitions had a strong relationship with individuals' belief that they would be evading taxes in the future. Tittle's (1980:66) analysis also reveals some independent partial support for a differential association hypothesis. Among those who admitted tax evasion within the previous five years (N = 217), two in five (39 percent) did not consider this method of cheating the government morally wrong and about half (51 percent) did not consider it a "serious" offense.

Evaders who adopt the attitude that their offenses are not morally wrong or serious may do so to help neutralize their guilt before committing the crime. As noted in Chapter 3, Smigel's research showed that persons are more willing to steal from the government than from other people, because it "can afford it" (i.e., denials of injury and victim). Other research suggests that there may also be a "condemnation of condemners," whereby the tax system is seen as unfair (Strumpel, 1969) or the government is not seen as representative of the people (Conklin, 1977:99). Evaders also have been known to mitigate the gravity of their offense by claiming that everyone cheats on taxes to some extent (Benson, 1985:594). In terms of *post factum* rationalization, there is a tendency to deny responsibility for the offense because of an ignorance about complex tax laws. Benson (1985:594) interviewed six evaders about their crimes, and three skirted responsibility for the offense, saying they merely had made simple errors. Deliberate intent to steal from the government for personal benefit was denied:

I didn't cheat. I just didn't know how to report it.

I didn't take the money. I have no bank account to show for all this money, where all this money is at that I was supposed to have. They never found the money, ever.

My records were simply one big mess. That's all it was. If only I had an accountant, this wouldn't have happened.

Another of Benson's (1985:594) evaders disclaimed criminal intent through an "appeal to higher loyalties":

I'm not a criminal. That is, I'm not a criminal from the standpoint of taking a gun and doing this and that. I'm a criminal from the standpoint of making a mistake, a serious mistake. . . . The thing that really got me involved in it is my feeling for the employees here, certain employees that are my right hand. In order to save them a certain amount of taxes and things like that, I'd extend money to them in cash, and the money came from these sources that I took it from. You know, cash sales and things of that nature, but practically all of it was turned over to the employees, because of my feeling for them.

As always, financial "strain" may be a motivation to commit an occupational crime in individual cases, but there seems to be no study investigating evaders' financial needs immediately prior to evasion. To find at least indirect support for strain theory, Tittle (1980) measured respondents' perceived deprivation of opportunity to reach desired goals. Persons frustrated in goal attainment were *not* more likely to project a future probability of evading taxes. Nor did Tittle find that alienation from the social order affected projected probabilities of future evasion (1980:188-89).

In terms of the Hirschi-Gottfredson (1987) control theory, the opportunity to commit personal income tax evasion would seem to be available to anyone who is subject to filing a tax return, although some persons may have more opportunities to evade taxes than others. Persons who have their wages and salaries reported to the government by an employer, for instance, have less opportunity to evade than persons who are self-employed. Holding opportunity constant, control theory predicts that persons will have the same criminality rates given equal tendencies toward self-gratification and equal perceptions about the threats of formal and informal sanctions. A "belief" in the legitimacy of social rules is one factor that keeps self-gratification in check. In support of this control notion of belief, Tittle (1980:188-89) found that measures of greater "moral commitment" to the social order were independently tied to fewer projected future instances of tax evasion.

In support of the importance of sanction threat, Tittle (1980:188-89) found that greater formal and especially informal sanction fears were also independently associated with fewer projected future instances of tax cheating. In a similar finding from the opposite side, Mason and Calvin (1978) report that the most powerful variable explaining evasion in their sample was the evaders' beliefs that they would not be caught. A sanction threat theory of tax evasion is also supported by Schwartz and Orleans

(1967), who found that honest taxpaying is more forthcoming when prosecution threats (or appeals to conscience) are made than when a neutral appeal or no appeal is offered. Thus, although the true probability of criminal conviction for willful tax evasion may be small according to the IRS figures cited previously, the perceived threat of formal and informal sanctions, which is the more important variable (Gibbs, 1975:7), has an effect on individual decisions to evade. Tittle (1980:193) cautions, however, that even though his results confirm that fear of sanctions, anti-evading associations, and moral commitment operate to mitigate projected future involvement in income tax evasion, the results do not necessarily suggest that any one of these items is convincingly potent as a predictor of conformity.

SECURITIES CRIME

The practice of "churning" refers to the buying and selling of stock in order to generate commissions for the stockbroker rather than to maximize the client's profits. A client who has given the broker complete discretion to buy and sell is especially vulnerable to "churning." The broker sells his or her services on the basis that they are in the best interests of the client, when, in fact, they sometimes are not. In one case of alleged churning, two sisters each gave Drexel Burnham Lambert discretionary accounts of $500,000 in 1981 and 1982. After two years, their assets had shrunk to about $70,000 after more than 1,400 trades that netted the firm and its brokers $400,000 in commissions (Work, 1986).

Brokers have also been known to underrepresent investment risks in order to induce a client to buy securities. Some brokers mix the "discretionary" accounts of customers with their own accounts, and assign winning trades to their personal ledgers and the losing transactions to the customers' accounts. Blumrich (1986:42) compiled the number of complaints against stockbrokers lodged by irate customers with the Securities and Exchange Commission—they had increased from slightly under 7,000 in 1982 to almost 16,000 in 1986. And in 1985, the National Association of Securities Dealers received 2,054 customer complaints about stock brokers (Work, 1986).

Shapiro (1984:18-19) has detailed other securities violations. Clients order stock purchases, but the broker converts the payment for personal use without buying the stock. Brokers also use customers' stock for collateral on personal loans, or simply cash in a client's stock by forging the client's name. Brokers have also cashed in their clients' accounts without authorization, and forged the proceeds check. Shapiro's analysis of investigatory records of criminal stockbrokers reveals "the usual [reasons for stealing]: expenses generated by divorce, alimony, and family illness; repaying loan sharks for gambling debts; extravagant living; liquor or cabaret bills; purchase of a new home . . . [and saving an] insolvent firm."

"Insider trading" is another kind of securities crime committed by individuals. Insider trading refers to buying or selling securities while in possession of material nonpublic information that was wrongfully obtained or the use of which would be wrongful. Obtaining such information wrongfully would include theft, bribery, misrepresentation, or espionage through electronic or other means. Wrongful use includes a breach of duty to maintain information in confidence. Persons expected to retain securities information in confidence include issuers of stocks and commodities, securities holders, traders in securities, governmental entitities, persons engaged in analyzing and disseminating information concerning securities, and persons who obtain confidential information from these sources (SEC, 1987). Insider trading is viewed as harmful behavior because it represents a form of unfair competition.

During fiscal year 1986, the Securities and Exchange Commission levied $41.9 million in fines and penalties for insider trading (Cauley, 1986). During fiscal year 1987, the SEC obtained court orders requiring defendants to disgorge $70.1 million of profits obtained through insider trading, and levied $62.6 million in civil penalties under the Insider Trading Sanctions Act of 1984. Insider trading and other securities matters resulted in a total of seventy-two criminal indictments during fiscal year 1987 (SEC, 1988:6). To help identify insider trading violations, the SEC conducts an ongoing "stock watch" through monitoring the major stock exchanges (New York, American, and NASDAQ) by sophisticated on-line computers. Those exchanges also have self-policing market surveillance programs.

Several recent cases of insider trading have been featured in the media. Probably the most infamous offender was Ivan Boesky, who bought stock in Fischbach Corporation in 1984 based on confidential information. Boesky was implicated by Dennis Levine, whose insider trading case launched a host of probes into the industry. Boesky, once considered Wall Street's leading speculator in stocks of potential takeover targets, shocked the securities industry in November of 1986 when he pleaded *nolo contendre* to civil charges levied against him by the Securities and Exchange Commission. In November, 1986, the SEC disclosed that Boesky had agreed to pay $100 million dollars in its civil case, the largest amount ever levied by the SEC. He was also banished from the industry. Boesky further pleaded guilty to one felony count of insider trading, for which he received a three-year prison sentence. He was charged with only one count even though he was known to have committed several other offenses (e.g., manipulating stock prices, unlawful takeover activity, and false record keeping), because he gave evidence to prosecutors about his confederates (AP, 12/18/87).

One of those implicated by Boesky was Martin Siegel, a merger specialist with Kidder Peabody and Company, a subsidiary of General Electric. Siegel allegedly received $700,000 from Boesky in return for trading information (SEC, 1988:11). The Kidder firm was charged with using Siegel's insider trading information in a civil suit by the SEC in 1987. The material information was allegedly passed on to Kidder by Siegel, who had learned it from an arbitrageur at an investment bank. Kidder pleaded *nolo contendre* and was fined $13.6 million (to disgorge profits) and $11.6 million (double penalty under the Insider Trading Sanctions Act) (SEC, 1988:11). The U.S. attorney in the case decided not to charge the firm criminally because it had cooperated in the investigation (AP, 6/4/87), but Siegel pleaded guilty to criminal charges of illegal trading and paid $9 million in civil penalties (*U.S. News*, 1988b).

Boesky also implicated Michael Milken of the Drexel Burnham Lambert investment firm. The SEC charged the Drexel company, Milken, and five others in a 184-page indictment for offenses related to insider trading, rigged takeovers, falsified transactions, and the destruction of records. All told, more than sixty people were indicted on the basis of investigations launched after the Boesky affair. In addition to Siegel at Kidder and Milken at Drexel, top management from Wall Street giants such as Goldman-Sachs, Merrill Lynch, Paine Webber, and E.F. Hutton were also charged. Based on the pervasiveness of the insider trading scandals of 1986-1987, a differential social organization (see Chapter 3) which favored that offense appears to have permeated Wall Street.

The U.S. Government has started to use the Racketeer Influenced and Corrupt Organizations Act (RICO), which was discussed in Chapter 5, to target insider traders. Former U.S. Attorney Rudolph Giuliani has effectively used RICO against insider traders such as Drexel Burnham Lambert and Princeton/Newport Partners. Giuliani employed RICO to force Princeton/Newport to liquidate and Drexel to plead guilty to six felonies (and pay a $650 million fine). While SEC convictions can include triple damages on insider-trading profits, RICO penalties are much more severe (recall that the law provides for forfeiture of the convicted person's total racketeering gains, triple victim damages, and incarceration for as long as twenty years). Giuliani gave Drexel a choice: settle or face indictment under RICO (which would involve multiple civil suits with damages of hundreds of millions of dollars, freezing much of Drexel's assets, and federal prison terms). Drexel settled (AP, 12/25/88). Six Princeton/Newport executives, however, chose differently, and they were convicted of a total of sixty-three counts of securities fraud, including RICO (Paltrow, 1989).

Securities violations are also monitored by the Commodity Futures Trading Commission. During fiscal year 1987, the CFTC's Division of Enforcement instituted eleven injunctive actions and twenty administrative proceedings against alleged violators of futures trading laws, and aided in the prosecution of sixteen criminal cases (CFTC, 1988). For instance, John Flynn was fined $25,000 and had his trading privileges revoked for failing to pay an earlier imposed penalty and for trading on the New York Cotton Exchange after being forbidden to do so. Scott Dial traded his own account ahead of those of his customers when he knew that within an hour he and others would be trading a large block of customer orders; he was barred from future trading after entering a *nolo contendre* plea. Edward Liu was suspended from trading futures for five years and fined $5,000 after he was found to have failed to file required information about his reportable positions and having traded while failing to file those reports. And, in addition to problems with the SEC mentioned above, Kidder Peabody and Company was fined $35,000 after pleading *nolo contendre* for failure to keep proper records and other violations (CFTC, 1988:27-40).

During the summer of 1989, forty-six commodities traders and brokers working at the Chicago Board of Trade and the Chicago Mercantile Exchange were indicted by federal grand juries for cheating customers. The indictments, which grew out of a two-year investigation, were based on evidence gathered by federal agents who infiltrated the trading floor and secretly recorded conversations. The charges alleged that traders skimmed customers' profits by falsifying the cards on which trade information is kept and by tampering with the exchanges' systems for timing trades. Brokers also participated in "front running," in which they used advance knowledge of customers' orders to enrich themselves. Besides securities crimes, the indictments included charges of RICO violations, tax evasion, mail fraud, lying to federal agents, and conspiring to defraud the Internal Revenue Service (Berg, 1989). Various reforms have been suggested to avoid securities violations in the future, including video surveillance of the trading areas, ethics courses offered by the various exchanges, and closer monitoring of trading activities (Richter, 1989).

SOME INDIVIDUAL OCCUPATIONAL CRIMES AGAINST PERSONS

Chapter 4 discussed crimes against persons committed by individuals for the benefit of their organization (e.g., willful distribution of unsafe consumer products, unsafe working conditions, environmental pollution). Chapter 5 reviewed these offenses when committed in a capacity as government official (e.g., torture and genocide, police brutality), and Chapter 6 considered them when committed by professionals (e.g., unnecesary surgery). In addition, there are criminal homicides and assaults (including sexual assault) committed by individuals as individuals in the course of an occupation. However, such individual occupational crimes against persons are not differentiated in agency-generated, victim-generated, or self-report information on crimes against persons generally. Therefore, the discussion here is limited to a few examples gleaned from the mass media.

In Georgia, an unlicensed exterminator was charged with manslaughter in the death of a seven-month-old boy resulting from overspraying the victim's home with chemicals. The offender supposedly mixed a three-gallon container of the solution, using a pint and a half of insecticide; normally, this would have been enough to make five hundred gallons of solution (Pierce, 1987). In another instance of manslaughter, engineer Rick Gates was accused of running a stop signal and driving three freight locomotives into the path of a speeding passenger train at 120 miles per hour— Amtrak's deadliest crash. In exchange for a guilty plea to one count, the State of Maryland dropped fifteen other charges of manslaughter by locomotive. In addition to killing 16 people, the crash injured more than 170 others. Gates failed to heed stop signals allegedly because he was under the influence of marijuana and alcohol (AP, 2/16/88).

Regarding occupational sexual assault, 68-year-old Carl Eakins was sentenced to a twenty-year prison term for sexually assaulting mentally handicapped adults in Evansville, Indiana. Eakins, a bus driver for the local Association for Retarded Citizens, admitted to molesting three of his passengers in addition to others during the twelve years he worked for ARC (AP, 5/29/87). There have also been a number of sexual assault cases related to child day-care centers. In one such instance, day-care center teacher Margaret Michaels was convicted on 115 charges of sexually assaulting, endangering, and terrorizing twenty preschoolers. Among other things, she had the children perform sex acts on her and did the same with them. She was also found to have smeared peanut butter and jelly on her genitals before having sex with one of the children. Other charges stated that she played the piano while naked in front of the children, made them take part in a nude pile-up, defecated in front of them, and even had one child urinate on her (AP, 4/16/88).

At the Florida School for the Deaf and Blind, four persons pleaded guilty in 1988 to sexual or physical abuse of handicapped students. Another employee was charged with twenty-seven counts of abuse against nineteen boys. In addition to these abuses, there were three mysterious deaths, including one girl who was scalded. A preliminary report issued by the State of Florida stated that there was some support for the presence of abuse in the scalding death (*The Reporters*, 1988).

Child sexual abuse also has been alleged at the West Point military academy. At the academy's West Point Child Development Center, parents of eleven children aged thirteen months to three years claimed that two civilian female employees sodomized and fondled the infants. Although a brief FBI investigation cleared the suspects, at least four of the alleged victims vividly described acts of physical and sexual abuse in a small utility closet. Ten parents filed a civil suit charging the U.S. Government with inaction and negligence, asking $100 million in damages (*Newsweek*, 1985b). And in 1988, evangelist Mario "Tony" Leyva was convicted of two counts of child sodomy in Roanoke County, Virginia; he had used his traveling ministry for many years to gain access to young boys. Leyva and two other pentecostal ministers were also indicted by a federal grand jury in Roanoke for allegedly shipping numerous young boys throughout the South and Midwest for use as prostitutes (AP, 9/23/88). In another clergy-related child sexual assault case, Grace Baptist Temple Church minister Henry Bazil Waters was convicted on three counts of child molestation in Statesboro, Georgia in February, 1989. Waters claimed unsuccessfully that his fondling of three boys was an effort to save the youths from a life of depravity by showing them how not to be sexually abused (AP, 2/17/89).

Given the limited anecdotal information available in these cases of individual occupational crimes against persons, it is not possible to apply systematically the theories discussed in Chapter 3, as we have done in other parts of the chapter. However, the emphasis in the Hirschi-Gottfredson theory on self-gratification would seem particularly applicable to the sexual abuse and drug cases.

QUESTIONS FOR DISCUSSION

1. What are the similarities and differences between defrauding employers and defrauding consumers?
2. Explain the theoretical relevance of techniques of neutralization to thefts against employers. Which techniques are most likely to be used? Why?
3. Why is it difficult to differentiate between retail shrinkage due to employee theft and shrinkage due to shoplifting? Discuss the similarities in theoretically explaining the two forms of theft.
4. How would the Gottfredson-Hirschi control theory hypothesize the effect of the feminist movement on female rates of theft against employ-

ers and fraud against consumers? How might members of the women's movement respond to your answers?

5. Without giving names, do you personally know anybody who has willfully evaded income tax? Based on what you know about each case, explain the relevance of the theories discussed in Chapter 3.

6. What would you suggest as a feasible plan for the Internal Revenue Service to increase taxpayer compliance? Be sure to consider the financial aspects of your suggestions.

7. What kinds of industry-wide procedural improvements would you suggest to decrease fraudulent odometer rollbacks?

8. Besides overcharging for repairs and used car fraud, what other kinds of consumer frauds can be studied through direct observation? Be sure to include any ethical concerns that may arise in the course of your study.

9. Aside from the cases discussed in this chapter, what other offenses that you know of can be classified as "individual occupational crimes against persons?"

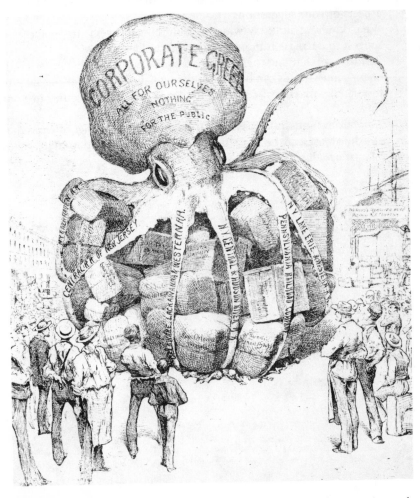

"All for Ourselves and Nothing for the Public" was the *modus operandi* among nineteenth-century railroad tycoons, whose ruthless practices milked stockholders and deprived workers of jobs and security. According to group conflict theory, unethical acts by big business have traditionally been uncensured because of a powerful corporate "grip" on the legislative process. (The Bettman Archive)

EIGHT

SANCTIONING, SOCIAL CONTROL, AND OCCUPATIONAL CRIME

This final chapter of the book will discuss ways to reduce occupational crime.

Three internal personal forces operate to inhibit illegal behavior: (a) fear of formal, officially imposed sanctions (conviction and punishment by the government); (b) fear of informally imposed sanctions (e.g., loss of respectability, loss of job); and (c) the internalization of values that discourage violation of legal codes (see Grasmick and Green, 1980). Sanctioning constitutes the heart of social control not only because threatened formal and informal sanctions can deter, but also because they inculcate pro-legal values through normative validation (Gibbs, 1975; Chapter 3; Andenaes 1974: Chapter 2). Deterrence and morality constitute the reasons why persons refrain from crime voluntarily.

Two other forces generated by formal and informal sanctioning can also inhibit illegal behavior—incapacitation and rehabilitation. Unlike deterrence and morality (which reflect personal choices whether to commit crime), incapacitation is imposed on offenders by others. And rehabilitation efforts can be initiated either from within an offender or imposed from an external source (or both).

Because occupational criminals constitute a diverse lot and because the circumstances surrounding occupational offending are wide-ranging, certain formal and informal sanctions will be more effective in reducing certain crimes. When allocating these diversely effective sanctions, however, one must be careful not to invoke formal or informal punishments that are more severe than the offense and offender warrant. This rule should be followed because when formal and informal sanctions are imposed only on the basis of hoped-for crime reduction, they often exceed being commensurate with the seriousness of the behavior and the culpability of the offender. For instance, deterring employee thieves from stealing a few dollars worth of goods may require a year of imprisonment, which in many cases would be a more serious sanction than is deserved by the offense. Punishment for occupational crime should be allocated under the principle of "parsimony" (Morris, 1974). This means that the least amount of pain should be imposed on offenders as is consistent with crime control concerns, but the punishment should never exceed the upper limit of what might be deserved by the offense and the offender.

It is extremely difficult to determine the exact punishment deserved for a crime or the exact offenders to be sanctioned, especially in cases of organizational occupational crime (see Braithwaite, 1982a). Nevertheless, we at least ought to try to punish offenders equitably (the same kinds of offenders should receive approximately the same sentence) and proportionately (the more serious punishments should be given to the more serious offenders). Of course, as noted in Chapter 2, the "seriousness" of an offense is an evaluation that is relative to the definer. In practice, the concrete meanings of such abstractions as "desert," "equity," "proportionality" and "parsimony" are determined by clashes among parties with differing interests and understandings, and differing power to influence the creation and application of laws.

MORAL EDUCATION AND NORMATIVE VALIDATION

Teaching people that certain behaviors are illegal—and therefore morally inappropriate—is an uncomplicated and extremely effective approach to reducing crime, but it is not easily accomplished. Common sense and differential association tell us that if young children are taught values unfavorable toward the violation of law, they will be unlikely to commit crimes later in life. Control theory (Hirschi, 1969) tells us that children who are taught a greater "attachment" to the feelings of others will be less likely to steal and commit violence. The theory also tells us that the greater one's "belief" in the legitimacy of certain legal rules, the more likely one is to respect those rules (see also Turk, 1969: Chapter 2). Moral teachings about the legitimacy of legal rules, then, should prevent many crimes, including occupational ones. Certainly, perceptions about what constitutes morally appropriate behavior (in occupation and elsewhere) vary among individuals. However, the *moral appropriateness of lawful behavior* can nevertheless serve as the common focus of moral teachings. Durkheim (1961) has discussed moral education extensively.

Moral education that discourages illegal behavior must be continuous. Inculcation must start early in life and be reiterated constantly, because early moral socialization can be mitigated by subsequent pro-criminal associations. Recall the previous discussion about the Harvard Business School professor who trained students to misrepresent their positions in negotiations and other business dealings. Another case in point is the price-fixing offenders who were socialized by their employers to believe that restraining trade was an acceptable "way of life" in the heavy electrical equipment and folding carton industries. These kinds of teachings, having been learned relatively late in life, mitigate previously internalized anti-criminal morality.

Parents, for instance, can teach their children to pay all income taxes due and to respect the property of others. Teachers in business schools can demonstrate to their pupils that it is legally wrong, and therefore morally inappropriate, to fix prices, misrepresent products, pollute the environment, manufacture unsafe products, and exploit labor. Teachers in medical schools can demonstrate that it is legally and professionally inappropriate to split fees, double-bill patients, and commit unnecessary surgery. Correctional officers can be taught that they have a sacred duty to respect citizens' rights. Legal-moral education, then, should not stop in the home, it should continue throughout one's formal education and occupational socialization. Occupational legal morality must be constantly reinforced by educators, firms, industries, and immediate work groups.

Transgressions of criminal laws must be censured and sanctioned in order to promote normative validation. Persons must be informed of the demarcation between criminal and noncriminal behavior so that they can guide their personal demeanor appropriately. If one is told that price-fixing is morally wrong but fails to be formally and informally punished for that behavior, then conflicting signals are sent about the acceptability of price-fixing. The greater and more consistent the censure, the more likely a person is to learn which behaviors are acceptable and which are not. Morality that opposes occupational crime must be validated consistently and constantly. This position assumes a consensual order, which of course is a problematic assumption. Indeed, the lack of such an order is the source of the lack of occupational legal morality.

It would be ideal if everybody practiced the Golden Rule. Unfortunately, because persons are basically pain-avoiding and pleasure-pursuing beings, convincing people that a behavior is simply the "right thing" to do may be insufficient to overcome their pursuit of pleasure. In addition to teaching occupational morality and promoting validation of occupational legal norms, then, there should be some threat of punishment or pain that accompanies the commission of a crime. Such threats are commonly known as "deterrents."

DETERRENCE

Assumptions of the Deterrence Model

Deterrence is based on a general set of assumptions about the way individuals react to sanction threat, although the assumptions are not traceable to a tightly constructed body of theory. Deterrence in criminology is most often associated with "Classical School" writers such as Cesare Beccaria (Monachesi, 1973) and Jeremy Bentham (Geis, 1973b), who wrote at the end of the eighteenth century. Less systematic discussions of deterrence, however, can be traced to much earlier writings, such as Thomas Hobbes's *Leviathan* in the sixteenth century. Even before Hobbes, Lucas de Penna, a fourteenth century Neapolitan legal scholar, anticipated the postulates of Beccaria (Sellin, 1989).

Deterrence theory assumes the same things about human interaction as many economic theories: humans are hedonistically rational in their behavior patterns, seeking pleasure or profit while concomitantly avoiding pain or loss. Quite simply, the assumption of deterrence is that an individual's lawbreaking (or other rule breaking) is inversely related to his or her perceived probability of receiving negative consequences. Deterrence is essentially the same as "operant conditioning" (refer to Chapter 3). Recall that the notion of operant conditioning states that by consistently rewarding persons for appropriate behavior and withholding rewards for inappropriate behavior, they learn to expect positive or negative responses, respectively. Such expectations derive from personal experience and from watching the fates of others. In deterrence theory, the difference between criminals and noncriminals lies in the former's lower fear reaction to perceived formal and informal consequences.

Informal sanctions can often be more feared than formally imposed conviction or punishment. Having been caught for stealing company property may cause an employee thief to: (a) lose his or her job; (b) fail to receive a recommendation for future employment; (c) be removed from his or her social group of co-workers, with whom social activities may have been a source of enjoyment; (d) experience measurable character defamation among family and friends; and (e) experience unmeasurable character defamation as the subject of unknown others' gossip. Informal sanctions such as disbarment and delicensure by professional associations would be perceived as disastrous financially for most potential occupational criminals in the professions. Cameron (1964) found that middle class housewives who were apprehended for shoplifting were more worried about others finding out about their arrests than they were about any fine or jail time. The shoplifters were deeply concerned with the reactions of their husbands, children, friends, and neighbors to their predicament. In another example, one of the convicted electrical equipment conspirators implied that he and his family had undergone tremendous strains because of his involvement in the price-fixing case that were unrelated to his formal sanctioning (Geis, 1968b:114). Informal sanctions often exist without formal ones, but the imposition of formal sanctions will usually trigger additional informal sanctions.

"General" deterrence refers to individuals avoiding a particular behavior because they are aware, through example, that others have experienced negative formal and informal consequences for that behavior. "Specific" (or "special") deterrence refers to individuals avoiding a particular behavior because they have personally experienced negative formal or informal consequences for such behavior in the past, and they fear reexperiencing similar consequences. General and specific deterrence are seperate concepts, but they invariably operate simultaneously—by punishing individual "a," persons "b through z" may be generally deterred and "a" may be specifically deterred.

To deter an individual generally and specifically, his or her probability of receiving negative outcomes need not be realistic, it need only be perceived as realistic. Thus, the most important variable in deterrence is the potential offender's *perception* about the probability of receiving negative consequences. If executions were faked on television, and in fact no person was actually executed, there would still be the possibility of a general deterrent emanating from the program. Or, previously punished persons may believe they will be repunished for committing another offense when in fact that is untrue. Further, there are three dimensions of perceptions about the probability of suffering negative consequences: (a) certainty (whether consequences will occur); (b) celerity (whether consequences will occur swiftly); and (c) severity (extent that consequences are serious for a given individual). When assessing the perceived probability of negative outcomes, beliefs about the certainty, celerity, and severity of the consequences should be considered, although certainty has historically been seen as a greater fear-inducing dimension than either celerity or severity.

It is important that the more severe sanctions must be reserved for the most undesired behaviors. First, as noted, to sanction otherwise would be capricious. Second, purely from a deterrence standpoint, the most serious sanctions should be meted out only for the most harmful behaviors because otherwise, hedonistically rational persons may choose to commit the more harmful crimes because they will not perceive more severe outcomes for them.

Many behaviors are not rational and calculated, however. For instance, persons often do not commit certain behaviors because they are simply morally opposed to them (see previous discussion on moral education). Such persons would not commit proscribed behaviors even in the absence of perceived formal and informal consequences. (We shall call these persons "Group A.") And persons who commit a crime in a heat of passion or who otherwise have no regard for the future personal consequences of such behavior (e.g., political terrorists or "pschopathic offenders") would commit it even if the negative outcome was perceived to be certain, swift, and severe. (We shall call these persons "Group B.") Any amount of fear cannot stop individuals in Group B from committing certain crimes, and it is unnecessary to attempt to coerce those in Group A because they would not commit certain crimes in any case.

Deterrence through fear, then, is only workable among those in a social system who would or would not commit a behavior depending upon the perceived probabilities of the certainty, celerity, and severity of formal and informal personal consequences. (We shall call these persons "Group C.") The extent to which persons in a population are not members of Group C is the extent to which that population will not respond rationally to the pursuit of pleasure and the avoidance of pain (for a discussion of the three groups, see van den Haag, 1985; Green, 1987).

Groups A, B, and C are mutually exclusive and exhaustive. This means that, for a given offense, one cannot be a member of more than one group at one time. For each offense type (e.g., murder, employee theft, forcible rape, unnecessary surgery, insider stock trading), and at a given instant, there are different sizes of Groups A, B, and C. A person may be in Group A for murder (morally opposed to it) but in group C for employee theft (may or may not commit it, depending upon perceived probabilities of punishment). Group sizes are not constant over time, because the infants of today will eventually enter certain groups for certain offenses sometime in the future.

It seems that the size of Group C is larger for occupational crimes than for many "common" crimes, because occupational violations, unlike rape and assault, are most often the result of calculated risks to increase financial benefits. Crimes such as price-fixing, medical insurance fraud, political bribetaking, and unsafe consumer product distribution can hardly be seen as the results of heats of passion or uncontrollable compulsiveness (Group B). While it is true that many occupationally-related behaviors reflect membership in Group A (those who do not commit occupational crime because they believe it is immoral), only a few occupational crimes are the product of membership in Group B (e.g., an employee thief suffering from kleptomania, the alcoholic who drives public transportation while intoxicated, or a sexually compulsive child care worker). At least in the occupational sphere, most persons who commit crimes seem to do so after a rational calculation of the certainty, celerity, and severity of the consequences. Ford's calculated decision not to install safer gas tanks in Pintos because the litigation costs from burn death lawsuits would be less expensive in the long run epitomizes this rationality. Chambliss (1967) points out that occupational crimes are more instrumental and less expressive than street crimes, and therefore can be deterred more readily. Moreover, occupational criminals should perceive a greater severity of punishment for their offenses than do street criminals because occupational offenders usually have more "commitment" to the social order (job, respectability, education, career), and therefore occupational criminals will perceive that they have more to lose if caught (Hirschi and Gottfredson, 1987). If the formal and informal punishment systems can create perceptions among potential occupational criminals in Group C that their contemplated behavior will bring certain, swift, and severe consequences if committed, then deterrence has remarkable promise as a policy to reduce occupational crimes in particular (see also Braithwaite and Geis, 1982). Moreover, threatened punishment for occupational crime not only has the potential to deter persons in Group C, it also can strengthen the size and intensity of Group A through normative validation.

Numerous writers have declared that intentional occupational crimes can be deterred. The three major forms of sanctions advocated as the most effective deterrents are: (a) monetary penalties (Yoder, 1978; Elzinga and Breit, 1976); (b) threats of adverse publicity (Fisse, 1986; Fisse and Braithwaite, 1985; French, 1985); and (c) incarcerating executives (Geis, 1972). Unintentional occupational crimes (e.g., collective knowledge offenses, some strict liability crimes), of course, are not deterrable, because they happen by accident rather than by design (see Cressey, 1989).

Financial Deterrents

Fisse (1986) has argued, contrary to what many believe (e.g., Yoder, 1978; Elzinga and Breit, 1976), that a monetary fine does not always constitute a meaningful formal sanction threat to potential occupational criminals. An initial limitation of monetary punishment is that defendants (individuals and organizations) often do not have the resources to pay fines or monetary penalties in the amount theoretically required for effective general deterrence. Coffee (1981:390) has identified a "deterrence trap" associated with financial penalties, whereby "[t]he maximum meaningful fine that can be levied against any [organization or individual] is necessarily bounded by its wealth." Thus, it would be of no concern to a potential offender whether a threatened fine is $250,000 or $25 million, if both sums are beyond ability to pay. Increasing the monetary penalty, then, sometimes carries no increased deterrent effect.

Allowing the organization or individual to pay off an unaffordable penalty gradually, such as over a period of years, is not feasible, because such a plan would make payment too easy to have any jolting deterrent effect. Additionally, recall from Chapter 4 that complex organizations are highly specialized and that employees' behaviors are often dominated by subunit and personal goals rather than by general organizational goals. As a result, threatened monetary penalties against organizations may have limited deterrent effects against employees' crimes that are motivated nonfinancially. Nonfinancial motivations include the desire for personal power and prestige, the creative urge, and job security (Fisse, 1986).

Stock dilution, an alternative to huge cash fines for convicted organizations, has been proposed by Coffee (1978). Stock dilution (or "equity fining") involves requiring the convicted organization to authorize and issue a certain number of shares to the state (or other entity) which would have an expected market value equal to the cash fine necessary to deter the illegal activity. This alternative mitigates the "deterrence trap" because an organization's ability to pay in fixed assets far exceeds its ability to pay in cash. The state could collect the equity shares and keep them for their future earning power, or sell them for cash. The funds can even be earmarked for the budgets of certain public protection agencies (e.g., labor, environmental, consumer).

Besides lacking the necessary deterrent power in some situations, threatening cash fines as a formal sanction for occupational crime has other conceptual difficulties (Fisse, 1986). First, a money penalty by itself is simply an inappropriately insufficient sanction for offenses that cause serious human harm, because it implies that those harms can be excused on a financial basis. Fisse (1986:29) has noted this lack of normative validation: "Fines do not emphatically convey the message that serious offenses are unwanted. Rather, the impression fostered is that the commission of crime is permissible provided there is willingness to pay the going price." Financial penalties by themselves may be appropriate formal sanctions for relatively minor offenses, but these probably would not have much of a deterrent effect. Second, financial penalties which punish organizations rather than their offending employees tend to blur or eliminate individual accountability for deliberate offenses. Third, if the punishment constitutes only financial penalties, there is no assurance that the organization or individual will reform to avoid committing similar offenses in the future. Fourth, there is often a punishment spillover, by which innocent persons such as stockholders and employees are affected adversely because of the imposition of a severe monetary penalty on an organization. And as

Fisse (1986) points out, while Coffee's "equity fining" may reduce the size of the deterrence trap by increasing an organization's ability to pay higher penalties, equity fining does virtually nothing to overcome the other problems associated with punishing offenders through large cash fines. Monetary penalization by itself is probably not the most viable deterrent to occupational crime (especially serious crime), nor is it always an appropriate punishment by itself for many cases of serious occupational crime.

Adverse Publicity Deterrents

French (1985) has referred to a punishment comprising adverse publicity as the "Hester Prynne Sanction," alluding of course to Hawthorne's character in *The Scarlet Letter* who was forced to wear the letter "A" because she was an adulteress. From a deterrence standpoint, the extent to which adverse publicity is perceived by potential occupational criminals to be harmful is seen as the extent to which they will avoid illegal behavior if adverse publicity is the probable sanction. It should be noted that the stamina of an offender is going to affect its perceptions of the potential consequences of an adverse publicity sanction. Larger organizations have the resources to launch counterpublicity campaigns and legal battles, and can rely on diversified assets to take up any slack in revenue caused by adverse publicity. For them, any negative effects will be temporary in any case. On the other hand, individuals and smaller organizations may not believe that they possess the resources needed to outlive or combat the negative effects of adverse publicity, in which case they may be more deterrable by publicity threats than offenders with greater resources.

Adverse publicity can take two forms, formal and informal. One major generator of informal adverse publicity is the media. The appeal of an occupational crime story relative to other news of the day will determine whether media sources will informally generate varying amounts of adverse publicity about occupational offenses and offenders. Consumer and environmental groups, too, may informally produce certain amounts of adverse information. In the case of localized occupational crime, such as by an attorney or small business owner, gossip constitutes a major form of informal adverse publicity. However, gossip and the news of the day cannot be regulated, so there is no way informal publicity can insure sufficient and truthful coverage. Formal publicity, on the other hand, involves a criminal or administrative sanction requiring an organization or individual to bear the expense of advertising their offense involvements in various media sources which have been carefully selected to reach particular audiences. For instance, a toy manufacturer that is convicted of false advertising could be sentenced to publicize this fact both in general media sources (e.g., weekly and monthly national news magazines) and those with a more specific market (e.g., magazines geared to children and parents). A doctor or business owner convicted of fraud could be required to advertise in their respective trade association publications and the local newspapers.

Adverse Publicity Against Organizations.   Fisse and Braithwaite (1985) have looked extensively at the harms inflicted upon large organizations by informal adverse publicity. On a case-by-case basis, they analyzed the impact of negative publicity on organizations involved in seventeen different well known episodes of wrongdoing (e.g., Allied Chemical and Kepone; Ford and Pinto; Exxon, Lockheed and McDonnell Douglas bribery scandals; General Electric and the electrical equipment price-fix; ITT's covert actions in Chile). The seventeen case studies involved relatively large and powerful conglomerates and some of the most extreme cases of organizational adverse publicity in recent years.

Somewhat surprisingly, overall, the various informal negative publicities had relatively little direct financial impact on the organizations involved. For instance, in only one case was a company's adverse publicity experience exploited by a competitor. Rather than preying on the misfortune, unaffected competitors probably had considerable sympathy for their suffering counterparts. A Ford executive may have epitomized this commiseration when he revealed about the Pinto case that: "[General Motors and Chrysler] were rooting for us on the footing that, but for the grace of God, there go I" (Fisse and Braithwaite, 1985:229). The minimal financial impact of the publicity is also shown in the finding that sales noticeably decreased in only three cases. General Electric, for example, realized no significant loss in sales due to the price-fixing publicity, but Ford Pinto sales declined noticeably.

Legal costs (litigation costs, fines) were significant in about a quarter of the cases (e.g., Ford Pinto, General Electric, Allied Chemical), but such costs are not a direct outgrowth of adverse publicity (except to the extent that the adverse publicity resulted in the matters being brought into the legal system). There were also a few substantial miscellaneous costs, for example: (1) antitrust offenders had to accept lower prices for their products; (2) a drug company's relationship with the FDA deteriorated because of faked drug tests, thereby making future drug marketing more difficult; (3) there were large costs associated with technological solutions to pollution problems for two firms; (4) Allied Chemical incurred costs related to testing those exposed to Kepone contamination; (5) deterioration of worker-management relations as a result of unsafe working conditions for one firm; and (6) a company's loss of steel production because of a mine disaster. Yet, in toto, only four companies suffered a noticeable loss in overall earnings, and only a few companies encountered an adverse stock market reaction to their difficult situation. Most of the top executives of the companies affected by the adverse publicities were unafraid that the overall fiscal strength of their firms would be damaged.

There were many nonfinancial costs to the firms, however. Importantly, in all but two cases, the executives interviewed reported that at the time of the crisis they felt that their corporate image had suffered because of the scandal. And to varying extents, many top management officials perceived a loss of personal prestige in their communities. One of the two companies that denied that its corporate prestige was damaged was ITT, which had launched an intense counterpublicity campaign to combat public disfavor. In the other case denying lower prestige, the organization involved in the scandal (a mine) was a little-known subsidiary, and seldom was the connection made with the parent company, BHP.

Another nonfinancial cost identified by Fisse and Braithwaite, mentioned by fifteen firms, was a decline in their employee morale. Such a decline is viewed as being harmful to a company independent of any effects low morale may have on decreased productivity. Also as a result of the scandals, executives were constantly distracted from the normal duties associated with running their companies. Executives saw this as an important adverse nonfinancial impact. Media attacks and cross-examination by investigators were also viewed by the executives as extremely unpleasant experiences. With regard to nonfinancial impacts, then, Fisse and Braithwaite found a consistent indication of negative consequences for both the company and its employees.

Fisse and Braithwaite found adverse publicity to be a strong impetus for the reformation of organizational procedures, so the most important crime-reducing effect of an organization's public scandal may be rehabilitative rather than deterrent. All seventeen cases demonstrated evidence of at least some procedural changes, and many of the organizational reforms were substantial. In eleven cases, companies increased staff, seniority, or decision-making powers of employees. Eight companies instituted procedures by which management was to provide written certification of adherence to various company rules. Three companies introduced substantial technological changes. In three other cases, adverse publicity led to strong censure of certain middle managers. Four companies cleaned house by accelerating the resignation or retirement of their chief executive officers. Organizational reforms which increase control over employee actions have tremendous potential to reduce future transgressions.

Short-term scandals involving organizational employees may also trigger long-term, industry-wide reforms (e.g., worker safety, organizational procedures and controls, better product design). Some scandals have had far-reaching impact. For instance, Fisse and Braithwaite (1985:236) point out that the Lockheed bribery scandal "cleaned out nests of corruption in a number of foreign governments, brought legislative reforms to tackle corruption in Japan and some Arab countries, strengthened the will of the Securities and Exchange Commission to investigate international bribery . . ., brought the United States the Foreign Corrupt Practices Act of 1977, and gave the world through the United Nations an international agreement on illicit payments." Similarly, scandals involving unsafe working conditions, environmental pollution, dangerous consumer products, price-fixing, and other offenses have stimulated tough regulatory legislation and more vociferous public advocacy.

Informal adverse publicity, then, has been shown to incur substantial nonfinancial costs for organizations. It has also been shown to be a catalyst to various intrafirm and industry-wide reforms. If these are the results from informal publicity, then formally imposed adverse publicity mandates should produce similar results to at least the same degree.

Adverse Publicity Against Individuals.   The most powerful threat associated with adverse publicity against individuals is the loss of self-respect and public repute. Because occupational criminals usually have noncriminal self-images and public reputations, broadcasting their infamous occupational deeds will in most cases embarrass them and their families tremendously. Second, there are financial consequences. Adverse publicity against a small business owner or a professional can cut deeply into the volume of their revenue, if not ruin their business or career entirely. Occupational criminals who do not sell goods or services, such as public servants (e.g., elected officials, public safety workers) will also have their careers adversely affected by negative publicity. And a person's future advancement within the a firm or lateral entry into another firm is inhibited by a personal occupational scandal. Firms are not going to want it known that they promoted known criminals within their ranks (although some have done so), nor is a firm likely to hire one. In fact, one may even lose one's job if too closely identified with a scandal, as did some (but not all) of the executives implicated in the electrical equipment price-fixing conspiracy (Geis, 1968b). Whereas individuals who willfully participate in organizational crime may be immune from civil and criminal actions against the organization, they are not immune from public censure through adverse personal publicity. Targeting organizational individuals for adverse publicity allows a form of punishment and censure sometimes not otherwise available.

Formal adverse publicity sanctions can be instituted only as part of a sentence after conviction by a criminal or administrative court, so there is no danger that the offender (organization or individual) will not receive a fair trial because of a court-imposed publicity provision. Media coverage and gossip, however, may bias the justice process against the accused before he or she gets a day in court, but there is no way to control the damage caused by such informal publicity except to give the defendant a chance to make a statement about offense involvement.

In sum, although court-imposed adverse publicity may sometimes have limited financial impacts on organizations (especially larger ones), it nevertheless has been shown to be a serious sanction to organizations because: (1) the firm loses prestige; (2) the sanction can result in low employee morale; and (3) organizational executives must undergo unpleasant experiences (e.g., media coverage and questions, distraction from normal duties). The court-ordered imposition of adverse publicity against an individual also represents a serious sanction, because it threatens a loss of self-respect, public prestige, and financial security. Moreover, forcing an organization or an individual personally to bear the costs of the adverse publicity adds fitting and stinging dimensions to the sanction. And the fact that adverse publicity tends to instigate procedural safeguards and other reform within organizations and industries is an important positive by-product of the sanction unrelated to its deterrent potential. Another crime-reducing by-product of adverse publicity that is unrelated to deterrence is that it promotes normative validation. By broadcasting the organizational or individual offender's censure, the illegality of the activity is emphasized. Threatening to impose adverse publicity requirements on convicted occupational criminals would seem to offer high potential for general deterrence, given that organizations and individuals perceive the negative ramifications of this sanction to be certain, swift, and severe. Because this is a serious sanction, it should be reserved for serious offenders.

Incarceration as a Deterrent

Threatening to incarcerate individuals who commit occupational crimes can be an extremely potent general deterrent because it should cause the potential offender to imagine all of the unpleasantries associated with modern human captivity, such as living with criminals and suffering the various pains of imprisonment (deprivations of liberty, security, autonomy, heterosexual relationships, and freeworld goods and services) (Sykes, 1958). Beyond these pains, however, incarceration threatens a loss of respectability to an even greater extent than does adverse publicity. Respectable persons care very much about their self-image and public respect, and there is no stronger criminal label than that imposed by incarceration. The threat of imposing an "ex-con" label on a respectable person (and family) seems to be a salient enough deterrent above and beyond any imagined unpleasant incarceration experiences.

Incarceration as a sanction for individuals who willfully commit occupational crime has two other desirable aspects. First, it can be an appropriate punishment. As Geis (1972:377) notes, "[occupational] offenses committed in violation of the criminal law . . . are often of such a severe nature in terms of the physical and fiscal harm they cause others that they clearly deserve severe criminal penalties." Second, incarceration strongly promotes normative validation by sending the message that certain offenses are so serious that they must be punished by the severest penalties. One executive in the electrical equipment conspiracy, for instance, noted that the incarceration visited upon him represented the major reason for a re-evaluation of his actions. The stigma of a jail sentence, he said, had the effect of making people "start looking at the moral values a little bit" (Geis, 1968b:114; 1972:379).

The Efficacy of Deterring Occupational Crime

It was noted previously that, regarding occupational crime at least, many persons are probably in Group C. Being in Group C does not necessarily mean that general deterrence will take place, it means only that the individual may or may not commit an occupational crime, depending upon his or her perceptions of the certainty, severity, and celerity of possible punishment. Therefore, persons must believe that their offenses subject them to punishment, and they must believe that punishments are painful. To create these beliefs among those in Group C, more occupational criminals must be formally censured—caught, convicted and sanctioned. Enforcement levels must be increased for all occupational crimes, from employee theft to price-fixing. Occupational criminals who are apprehended must be charged to the fullest extent of the law rather than handled informally. And when convictions result, the harshest sentences should be imposed for the severest harms. Informal sanctioning must also be increased if it is to act as a general and specific deterrent.

Without these high conviction and punishment rates in our occupational criminal justice system, persons in Group C will not believe that they are subject to harsh punishments. For instance, Pontell, Jesilow and Geis (1986) have noted that many physicians are quite aware that they enjoy almost complete immunity from formal prosecution and punishment for medical insurance fraud. First, there are insufficient investigative resources to ferret out defrauders. Second, many physicians commit fraud by prescribing unnecessary tests and treatments rather than by other means. These physician-criminals are much more difficult to detect than those who double-bill or bill for tests never performed, and even if detected, the physician who orders unnecessary tests and treatment believes the charge will be "abuse" rather than fraud. Third, many doctors who cheat insurance companies are also probably aware that their cases are not generally winnable by the prosecution. It is often quite difficult to prove to a jury that a physician was not acting in his patient's best interest or acting in self-defense against malpractice claims when prescribing allegedly unnecessary tests or treatment. Fourth, for general deterrence to operate, the authority of the law must be seen as legitimate. But because physicians regulate themselves, external judgements by the legal system are accorded little legitimacy. Fifth, the lack of formal prosecution eliminates the threat of any severe informal sanctions which would accompany such a conviction. In short, although many physicians may be in Group C, very few are deterred by the threats of formal and informal sanctions. Apprehension, conviction, and punishment for medical insurance fraud must be increased before society can realistically expect general deterrence to operate for that offense.

In addition to perceiving the certainty of punishment, it is also important that persons in Group C perceive threatened informal and formal sanctions to be painful. The previous discussion emphasized that the most likely sanctions to invoke a fear of severe formal (and informal) sanctions are court-imposed adverse publicity and incarceration. Occupational disqualification, addressed in the following section, is another very serious formal and informal sanction. Given that the offense in question is deserving, punishmnent of occupational criminals must minimally include at least one of these three punishments in order to promote perceptions about sanction severity. A combination of the three, of course, would offer the most severe threat; however, fewer than three may be sufficient for deterrence.

Monetary fines or community service can be parts of a sentence in addition to adverse publicity, incarceration, or occupational disqualification. However, the general deterrence clout carried by fines and community service by themselves is probably small compared to the fears conjured by the other three. And as noted, an affordable fine by itself is often inappropriately lenient and lacks adequate censure for harms inflicted, thereby diminishing normative validation effects. A community service sanction by itself denotes even less censure than a fine because community service has the tendency to paint a positive picture of the offender and often allows him or her to deduct from income tax any community service donations (French, 1985).

Victim restitution should be required for occupational criminals in all cases in addition to other sanctions. Foremost, restitution insures that the victim is compensated financially for the harms suffered. Further, paying restitution precludes the offender from using the gains of the crime to off-set any other sanctions that might be imposed. Restitution would add little deterrent effect unless it were increased, such as if treble (triple) restitution was instituted.

Persons in Group C who are generally deterred need not be specifically deterred. However, those in Group C who are not generally deterred by a threatened formal or informal sanction may nevertheless be specifically deterred by such threats after those sanctions have been imposed. Thus, a person who did not believe that adverse publicity, occupational disqualfi-cation, or incarceration was a certain, swift, or severe punishment may well change his or her mind after being caught and given those sanctions. Of course, general deterrence has the potential to prevent many more crimes among those in Group C than specific deterrence.

Even if general deterrence has been effected in a punishment system, it is difficult to prove that fact. To demonstrate deterrence, one would have to show that crimes that were going to occur did not happen because of a perceived sanction threat, and this is not an easy task. Because deterrence hypothesizes that perceptions of punishment affect behavior, the general deterrence investigator must have an accurate measurement of the crime rate. Chapter 2 has shown that occupational crime and criminal rates gen-erated by official agencies, victims, and criminals are basically invalid be-cause of the large number of offenses and offenders that go unrecorded. The best way to study general deterrence is the controlled field experiment (see Green, 1985b; Jesilow, 1982; Schwartz and Orleans, 1967), in which the researcher unobtrusively observes directly the rate of criminality, in-troduces a threat intervention, and then remeasures the criminality rate to ascertain if the threat had any effect. As noted in Chapter 2, however, oc-cupational offenses are only very rarely observable directly.

There is another problem in evaluating the deterrent effect of increased punishment threat on occupational crime when using agency-generated crime rates. To increase perceptions of punishment, perceptions about the probability of apprehension must first be increased. To increase percep-tions of apprehension, more persons must be caught and those captures must be publicized. However, because agency-generated occupational crime and criminal rates are often based primarily or exclusively on dis-coveries by the agencies (e.g., EPA, FDA, IRS, OSHA), increasing appre-hension will drive up the agency-based crime rate. Thus, attempting to re-duce crime by increasing perceptions of capture will result in an increased recorded crime rate, which will camouflage any true general deterrent ef-fect that may have been in operation.

Using both widespread applicability and potential validity as selection criteria, surveying the general population is probably the best choice for studying the general deterrent effect of sanction threats against occupational crime. This particular method ascertains a respondent's perceptions of the certainty, severity, and celerity of formal and informal sanctions for committing a given occupational crime. This information is compared to the number of such offenses the respondent admits having committed in the past or plans to commit in the future. Assuming that there are valid responses to both items (and this is not always a safe assumption), the researcher can determine whether individuals who perceive that they will be sanctioned are also less likely to commit occupational offenses (see Waldo and Chiricos, 1972; Grasmick and Green, 1980; Tittle, 1980; Paternoster, 1988). Such surveys could include carefully sampled respondents from virtually all occupations (corporate executives, factory workers, police officers, politicians, physicians, small business owners, office personnel, etc.). If lawmakers and law enforcers (and the public) decide to implement more certain, swift, and severe formal and informal sanctions for occupational criminals, then, after those policies are implemented and publicized, perhaps this survey method will help us to evaluate the general deterrent effects.

The specific deterrent effects of sanction might also be studied. Studying longitudinally the future occupational offending of those known to have been formally or informally sanctioned for such crimes will tell us which persons are most likely to be afraid of having the punishment reimposed. Those who re-offend are obviously not specifically deterred. However, the fact that one does not re-offend does not necessarily point to specific deterrence. Persons do not recidivate for many reasons aside from fear of reexperiencing a sanction. It is well known that age is an excellent correlate of criminality, with crime being most prevalent among the young, so nonrecidivism may simply be the product of offender "burn out" associated with advancing age (this is probably not true of organizations, however). Moreover, because much occupational offending goes undetected, those previously punished may recidivate, but the researcher would be unaware of that fact.

INCAPACITATION THROUGH OCCUPATIONAL DISQUALIFICATION

Incapacitation reduces crime by removing the physical opportunities to commit offenses. The criminal justice system incarcerates criminals, thereby physically incapacitating them from committing most offenses. Although prison inmates commit assault and theft against other inmates and guards and have been known to conduct forgery and tax cheating schemes from their jail cells, for the most part, locking someone in prison physically restrains them from preying upon society. Occupational criminals who are incarcerated, then, will have extremely limited opportunities to commit more occupational offenses (though perhaps an inmate paid by the state to work in the kitchen could steal food, etc.).

Unlike "common" crime (such as burglary, robbery, assault, and rape) occupational criminal activity is dependent upon legitimate formalized roles in an economy. Therefore, to incapacitate occupational criminals from opportunities for further occupational crimes, one need only administratively remove or disqualify offenders from their occupational role—removing them from society and putting them in prison is not always necessary. For instance, formal and informal sanctions for criminal doctors and lawyers can include license revocation and disbarment. Formal corporate sanctioning can include dechartering (and divestiture to avoid spilling punishment over to stockholders). Executives and workers can be legally banned from various industries or certain roles within industries, or they can be banned informally. Because of this possibility for administrative removal from occupational roles, Braithwaite and Geis (1982:197) believe that "[administrative occupational] incapacitation . . . can be a highly successful strategy in the control of [occupational] crime."

Legal Precedent for Occupational Disqualification as a Formal Sanction

There is ample legal precedent in various legal statutes and judicial sentences supporting occupatonal disqualification, including both public and private sector occupations (see McDermott, 1982). In most states, there are laws providing that a felony conviction renders one either permanently or temporarily ineligible to pursue certain licensed vocations such as pharmacist, barber, and liquor store or pawn shop owner. And many convicted persons are barred from holding public office and public employment. Among the federal laws, for instance, the Federal Deposit Insurance Act of 1950 (Title 12 U.S.C., Section 1829, amended 1980) prohibits persons convicted of any criminal offense involving dishonesty or breach of trust from serving as director, officer, or employee of a federally insured bank. In another federal example, the Securities Exchange Act of 1934 (Title 15 U.S.C., Section 780 (b)(4)(B)) allows suspension or revocation of the registration of any broker or dealer convicted of a felony or misdemeanor which arises out of the conduct of his business as broker, dealer, or investment adviser. And Section 504(a) of the Labor-Management Reporting and Disclosure Act of 1959 (Title 29 U.S.C., Sections 401-531, amended 1976) forbids convicted felons from holding union office or serving as a labor relations consultant during the five years following conviction for enumerated felonies involving "moral turpitude," including certain occupational offenses (e.g., bribery, embezzlement). Similar statutory provisions (imposed as mandatory or discretionary aspects of sentences) could be put into effect for corporate executives, police officers, day care center workers, or virtually any other occupational criminal convicted of certain crimes. There could also be a similar mandatory or discretionary statutory provision for delicensure (or dechartering) of organizations upon conviction of certain offenses.

In addition to statutory precedent, there is also ample case law precedent for the imposition of occupational incapacitation by judges, in both civil and criminal cases. In the civil area, the Supreme Court, during the appeal of an antitrust case (*U.S. vs. Grinnell Corporation*, 364 U.S. 563, 1966), acknowledged that firing an offending company's employees can occur in the civil antitrust area to protect the general public, but not to protect shareholders. Regarding criminal case law, there is precedent for disqualification particularly in the the area of labor union-related crime. In one California case, later upheld by the U.S. Supreme Court, three defendants were placed on ten-year probation, during which time they could not hold union office, receive a salary for any union services, or participate in union registrations (*People vs. Osslo*, 50 Cal. 2d 75; 357 U.S. 907, 1958). In various federal cases, defendants were forbidden at least from holding union office for varying periods of years (e.g., *Berra vs. U.S.*, 221 F.2d 136, 1955; *U.S. vs. Barrasso*, 372 F. 2d 136, 1967; *Hoffa vs. Saxbe*, 378 F. Supp. 1221, 1974). Professionals have also been subject to occupational incapacitation as a provision of a criminal sentence, independent of any incapacitative intraprofessional sanctions that may also have been imposed, such as delicensure (see, e.g., *People of California vs. Frank*, 94 Cal. App. 2d 740). Another example involved a securities dealer convicted of mail fraud who was prohibited from participating in any securities sales, again independent of any occupational incapacitation to which the offender was subject under the Securities Exchange Act of 1934 (McDermott, 1982).

Formally imposed occupational disqualification is well grounded in our law. To broaden the current scope of this sanction to include other occupations, passage of new statutory penalty provisions is not necessary. Most criminal statutes which include probation as a possible sanction are written in such a way that judges have complete discretion in the imposition of conditions of probation. Although occupational disqualification is not explicitly mentioned in statutes as a condition of probation, it can be imposed through judicial discretion. Under the way laws are currently drafted, in most cases the disqualification could last as long as the statute's provision for the maximum length of probation. Or, disqualification (maybe even for life) could be written into existing statutes.

The Efficacy of Occupational Disqualification

There are two ways to realize crime reduction through incapacitation: (1) attempt to incapacitate only those who you believe will commit future crime if given the opportunity (*selective* incapacitation) and (2) incapacitate all of those convicted in hopes that this group includes recidivists (*collective* incapacitation).

Selective occupational disqualification would involve barring individuals from certain future occupational activities on a case-by-case basis. However, selective incapacitation is predicated upon the idea that one can accurately predict which persons need to be incapacitated. This assumption is often incorrect, and the ramifications of an incorrect prediction are substantial. First, there is the person who is predicted to be a nonrecidivist and is allowed to continue in the same occupational role, who then commits another occupational crime. This person is known as a "false negative" (the offender was predicted to be negative on the future criminality trait, but that prediction was false). An error on the other side would involve the person who is predicted to be an occupational recidivist and is disqualified on that basis, but, had that person not been disqualified by being allowed to continue in occupation, no new crimes would have been committed. This situation represents a "false positive" (the person was predicted to be positive on the future criminality trait, but that prediction was false). The result of the false negative is an additional offense (or several of them). The result of the false positive is the infliction of punishment on persons who need not have received that sanction.

There is another fundamental problem involved with selective incapacitation that goes beyond incompetent predictions. Because incapacitation is rooted in crime control, there will be a tendency to concentrate on the avoidance of false negatives when predicting individual recidivism. This emphasis naturally increases the number of false positives, because when the prognosticator is unsure about whether an offender will commit another crime, recidivism is likely to be overpredicted. In other words, when in doubt, believe the worst, because underestimating recidivism inflicts more crime. Thus, with selective occupational disqualification, there will be a natural tendency for false positives to outnumber false negatives. False positives are particularly likely to increase immediately after a false negative is discovered (parole boards are more cautious in granting paroles after one of their releasees has been involved in a serious crime).

Determining the false negative rate for selective incapacitation is relatively easy. It is the proportion of recidivist individuals and organizations in the group that was not disqualified. Ascertaining this proportion is a fairly simple task, given that one dubiously assumes that all recidivists (false negatives) become known. It is much more difficult to determine false positive rates, because positives, by definition, are disqualified and are not given an opportunity to recidivate. However, false positive rates can be derived under rare circumstances. In a few instances, incarcerative institutions have been ordered by the courts to decarcerate themselves (see, e.g., Van Dine, Conrad, and Dinitz, 1979), which means that persons previously predicted as positive are given a chance to recidivate. To determine the false positive rate for occupational disqualification, disqualified persons and organizations (predicted to be positives) would somehow have to have their occupational opportunities reinstated, after which it could be determined how many, in fact, were incorrectly predicted as a recidivist. However, even if occupational disqualification predictions had extremely low false positive and false negative rates (which is doubtful given our current state of predictive validity), sentences for the same kinds of occupational crimes would be extremely disparate, and they would be based on criteria completely unrelated to the harm and culpability associated with the present offense.

Collective occupational disqualification, on the other hand, makes no attempt to predict which persons or organizations will commit new offenses—all are disqualified if convicted. In theory, collective disqualification does not involve any judicial discretion (although discretion may occur during earlier criminal justice processes, such as in the decision about whether to charge the offender with a crime that includes disqualification as a punishment). The collective disqualification approach assumes that the convictee group comprises at least some future recidivists, and therefore at least some reduction in future crime will result through the disqualification of the entire group. The extent to which convictees constitute future recidivists is the extent to which occupational crime is reduced through collective disqualification. Unlike selective disqualification, collective disqualification does not have the problems associated with inaccurate predictions (i.e., false positives and negatives, disparity in sentences) because no attempts are made to predict and because sentences are equal.

To determine the crime-reducing effectiveness of any collective incapacitation policy, two things must be known (Shinnar and Shinnar, 1975; Green, 1978). First, the researcher must know the average number of crimes that would have been committed by convictees had they been at risk to commit crimes during the period they are incapacitated (F, or future crimes). Second, the researcher must know the average length of time the convictees are incapacitated (S, or sentence). The product FS gives the number of crimes saved per sentenced offender.

Determining S is easy—it represents the average period of occupational disqualification imposed by the courts. Determining F, however, is much more difficult. Because it is generally difficult to predict future criminality, determining the average number of crimes that will be committed sometime in the future by a particular group of convictees (F) is no less problematic, even if accurate information on previous offending is available (and it usually is not). And there may exist a "replacement" effect, through which incapacitated recidivists are replaced by new offenders.

Collective disqualification policies should be preferred over selective ones because of the latter's problems associated with prediction. Because estimating the overall occupational crime-reducing effects of collective disqualification (F) is so difficult, however, such a policy's true effects will be unknown, and therefore it will have to be based on the unverified assumption that convictees constitute a reasonable proportion of all future occupational offenders.

Clearinghouses will have to be set up to keep track of disqualified offenders. In 1986, Congress created a nationwide computer record of complaints against doctors and dentists in order to prevent their escape from "professional rap sheets" by changing localities (AP, 1/1/89). The initial cost was $16 million. The legislation requires state medical licensing authorities to report to the federal file any disciplinary actions taken as well as any malpractice suits lodged against doctors and dentists. Eventually, the data bank is to be expanded to include nurses and other health care providers that must be licensed. Similar national computer files can be instituted for other occupations. For instance, various occupations, such as bank teller or day care worker, might require licensing, and licensing requirements might include a background check through the clearinghouse. Coleman (1985:243) has suggested a licensing system for corporate executives as well. Private industries may have to bear some of the costs associated with maintaining these clearinghouses, but the benefits to them may be worth the investment. There should be a strong concern about limiting the use of such information, because accusations that have not been proved may damage an innocent person. Records should probably be limited to formal disqualifications invoked by courts (civil and criminal) and designated professional organizations. To avoid abuses of the information, records should be treated like a credit report or medical records— they are releasable only with signed permission by the offender. Of course, the offender must allow access to this information upon application for a job within the specified occupation.

Occupational incapacitation, inflicted either mandatorily through statute or through individual conditions of probation, has the potential to be extremely effective (given that occupational incapacitation actually results) and is relatively much less expensive and less personally intrusive than incarceration. This should not imply that incarceration should not be given as a sanction because it is a relatively inefficient incapacitator. The point is simply that the strategy of occupational incapacitation is easy and inexpensive to implement and therefore can readily be imposed. The fact that occupational disqualification acts as a normative validator is not an unimportant consideration. Moreover, because occupational disqualification is a severe sanction (or at least it will probably be perceived as severe), it would seem to hold tremendous promise as a general deterrent threat. It may also act as a potent specific deterrent, given that the disqualified offender is allowed to continue in the occupation sometime in the future. And collective occupational disqualification, by definition, is a certain sanction, and should be perceived by those in Group C as being certain. Perhaps most importantly, it is a severe enough sanction to be appropriate to many different egregious legal violations committed in the course of occupation.

REHABILITATION

Rehabilitation assumes that criminals are in need of correction, and that most offenders are malleable and can be reshaped into productive and law-abiding citizens. Rehabilitation of criminals is founded upon a "medical model"—diagnosis of the problem, prescribed treatment, and ensuing recovery. Unfortunately, as continually high recidivism rates have indicated, the penal system's attempt to rehabilitate traditional criminals (e.g., burglars, robbers, rapists) has failed dismally. Institutional or other rehabilitation programs probably will also have little effect on most occupational criminals. This is true not only because rehabilitation has generally been ineffective (e.g., Martinson, 1974), but also because many occupational offenders (e.g., doctors, executives, factory workers, and politicians) do not need to be rehabilitated, as they are generally law-abiding citizens.

However, there remains the promising possibility of rehabilitating or correcting criminogenic organizations and systems (Braithwaite and Geis, 1972). For instance, poor quality control may be the source of an organization's violation of pure food laws. Inadequate monitoring of promotional material may be the source of a warranty fraud. Police thefts of evidence and inmate property may be encouraged by insufficient documentation procedures. And fee-for-service systems in medicine and law may contribute to fraud and abuse by doctors and lawyers. Thus, although there seems to be little promise for the successful rehabilitation of individuals, organizations and systems may be quite amenable to correctional treatment.

Hopkins (1980) has studied some of the firms convicted under the Australian Trade Practices Act of 1974 to determine the extent to which convicted companies rehabilitated themselves. That law contains two major sets of provisions—one outlaws unfair competition such as price fixing and the other outlaws deceiving consumers. The only defense to violation of the Act is if the defendant can show that it made a reasonable effort to avoid violation, otherwise an offender is guilty regardless of intent to commit the offense. Hopkins identified four basic types of structural defects which were associated with many of the organizations convicted under the Act. By far the most common defect was the failure by management to check adequately promotional literature. A second organizational defect identified by Hopkins was the failure to deal adequately with complaints received from the public after misleading or inaccurate advertisements had appeared. The third defect was the failure of top management to inform sales personnel of all relevant facts about a product. The fourth defect occurred in the case of a used car firm prosecuted for odometer fraud. A speedometer had been replaced on a used car and no attempt was made to make the new odometer accurately reflect the mileage of the car. One or two of these organizational defects were present in about three-quarters (fifteen of nineteen) of the offenders convicted under the consumer fraud provisions at the time of Hopkins's writing. Of the fifteen firms identified as having at least one of these defects, nine made significant procedural changes which would strongly avoid similar future offenses, and two made minor changes which would forestall (but not prevent) recidivism. (Two organizations did nothing and no information was available about the remaining two firms.)

The reforms identified by Hopkins and the previously discussed reforms found by Fisse and Braithwaite (1985) to be associated with adverse publicity were, for the most part, voluntary. There would be an even greater expectation for the rehabilitation of an organizational defect if reform was mandated by a criminal or adminstrative sanction, because such mandates would be unrestricted and comprehensive. This sanction may be particularly effective as a remedy for certain strict liability offenses (e.g., *respondeat superior* and collective knowledge crimes). Hopkins (1980:210) cautions, however, that "the changes made can only have the preventive effect imputed to them if made in good faith, that is, if management sincerely intends to avoid further violations. . . . [The changes] will not be able to prevent offenses which are intended."

INCREASING ENFORCEMENT AGAINST OCCUPATIONAL CRIME

None of the crime control methods we have discussed will work unless offenders are sanctioned. Even if formal and informal sanctions are meted out to occupational offenders, a sufficient number of criminals must be caught in order for the strategies to have any hope of reducing crime in significant proportions. No matter which area of occupational crime is being considered—organizational, state authority, professional, or individual—enforcement levels are unimpressively low.

Braithwaite (1982b: 1470-71) has suggested a novel approach to increasing enforcement against larger organizations in particular; he calls it "enforced self-regulation":

> "Under enforced self regulation, the government would compel each company to write a set of rules tailored to the unique set of contingencies facing that firm. A regulatory agency would either approve these rules or send them back for revision if they were insufficiently stringent. At this stage in the process, citizens' groups and other interested parties would be encouraged to comment on the proposed rules. Rather than having governmental inspectors enforce the rules, most enforcement duties and costs would be internalized by the company, which would be required to establish its own independent inspectorial group. The primary function of governmental inspectors would be to ensure the independence of this internal compliance group and to audit its efficiency and toughness. Such audits would pay particular attention to the number of violators who had been disciplined by each company. Naturally, old-style direct government monitoring would still be necessary for firms too small to afford their own compliance group."

According to Braithwaite's plan, the government would formally sanction violators of the privately written and publicly ratified rules. Regulatory agencies would not accept any set of private rules that was not consistent with minimum requirements set by the legislature. If the internal compliance team does not report discovered violations, then the individual members of that team would be subject to severe sanctioning, including incarceration. The plan is intuitively appealing because it allows a much wider monitoring system without the tremendous governmental expenditure needed to achieve that level of enforcement. The approach has other advantages as well: (1) complex rules which attempt to apply to all organizations would not be necessary, since rules would be tailored to match each organization; (2) rules would be capable of quick adjustment in the face of changing business environments; (3) rules would be more comprehensive in their coverage, usually going beyond the minimum standards; and (4) organizations would probably be more committed to the rules they wrote themselves. And of importance to crime control, more offenders would be caught more often.

Those caught would be subject to severe informal and formal sanctions. Formal sanctions would be easier for courts to mete out under self-regulation because it would be easier for government prosecutors to obtain organizational crime convictions. More certain and severe informal sanctions would also be forthcoming, because the organizational punishment system for violation of internal rules is farther-reaching than its punishment system for violation of governmental regulations. And according to Braithwaite (1982b: 1482), "Compliance would become the path of least [organizational] resistance."

Braithwaite presents several current examples of enforced self-regulation or variants of it. For one, the private airline industry has long been involved in making their own routes, rules, and regulations within the mandates of governmental standards. The Federal Aviation Administration, of course, has monitored airline companies' compliance with their personal sets of rules. Braithwaite also points to the Toxic Substance Control Act of 1976, which authorizes the EPA to order manufacurers to test suspect chemical substances, to monitor internally compliance with Act procedures, and to indicate proposed quality control protocols. The EPA can also revise any procedures found to be inadequate. The FTC has long had the authority to insititute new internal organizational policies and establish internal monitoring systems for firms convicted of misrepresentation in advertising.

Braithwaite is aware of problems inherent in policies of enforced self-regulation, such as the increased cost to regulatory agencies associated with approval procedures for a vast number of rule sets and revisions each year. Moreover, there would be a danger of worsening the cooptation of the regulatory process by business, because there would be a tendency to overparticularize government-business relationships. There may also be a problem concerning whether Western jurisprudence would be able to accomodate publicly enforced private rules. Further, government bureaucracies being what they are, organizations would probably bear increased costs due to delays and red tape associated with getting new company rules approved. Braithwaite also points out that companies would write their rules in ways which would assist them to evade the spirit of the law. And to what extent can we expect the internal compliance monitoring group to be completely honest, given that to do its job properly it must bite the hand that feeds it? One way to get around this problem, at least in the area of occupational safety and health, is to construct the team with both management and labor reporesentatives. By placing these two groups on the compliance team, corporate-employed team members will not be able to hide occupational safety violations from the union members on the team. In spite of its inherent potential problems, Braithwaite's ideas about enforced self-regulation may go far to increase enforcement levels against both organizations and its criminal employees, while at the same time increasing thresholds of voluntary compliance.

To increase enforcement levels against state authority criminals, consideration should be given to broadening the staff of the Federal Bureau of Investigation, which is the primary federal agency responsible for enforcing laws against political bribetaking and civil right violations. Locally, public safety agencies, such as police and correctional departments, can institute strict operating procedures which discourage theft and violence opportunities for its officers and employees. The internal investigatory branches of various public safety departments and the armed forces—internal affairs divisions—represent a type of self-regulatory structure. Indeed, the public trust vested in public agencies demands their vigorous self-regulation.

Increasing enforcement against professional occupational criminals may be more problematic, however, because the professions have already demonstrated that they cannot be trusted to monitor themselves adequately. The public is forced to allow professionals to regulate themselves because professional standards are often complicated, rendering them too difficult for the lay person to understand. As noted in Chapter 5, the "professional dominance" tends to protect the image of a profession from outside criticisms, and in so doing a large number of professional violations are handled discreetly through intraprofessional channels. Of the approximately 320,000 physicians in the United States in the early 1970s, 16,000 were believed incompetent or unfit, but on the average only seventy-two licenses were revoked each year (using data for the years 1971-1974) (Rensberger, 1976 in Coleman, 1989). Lawyers, too, are reluctant to police themselves, at least according to the American Bar Association's Special Committee on Evaluation and Disciplinary Enforcement. That body found that "Disciplinary action is practically non-existent in many jurisdictions; practices and procedures are antiquated; many disciplinary agencies have little power to take effective steps against malefactors" (cited by Garbus and Seligman, 1976 in Coleman, 1989). Moreover, the fact that professionals are quite unwilling to report a colleague's misconduct severely hampers the external investigation of professional crime. Coleman (1989:156) sums it up nicely:

"Ironically, the same professional organizations that claim to be watching out for the public's best interest have themselves been involved in repeated criminal activities [such as antitrust violations]. . . . Together with lax enforcement practices, these repeated criminal activities clearly indicate that the agencies of professional self-regulation are primarily concerned with the interests of professionals, not with those of the public, and cannot be considered important agents for the control of [professional occupational] crime."

Professional occupational criminals will probably continue to enjoy immunity from prosecution. Hence, they are unlikely to be deterred by sanction threat and are unlikely to be formally disqualified by their professional organizations. They will therefore feel and be free to continue or begin their criminal activities.

Individual occupational crimes comprise many different kinds of offenses and offenders, so it would be difficult to find an enforcement strategy that would work in most cases. Employer-victims can play an important part in increasing enforcement of occupational crime laws, such as by turning employee thieves over to the authorities rather than handling them informally. The Internal Revenue Service can beef up its auditing programs to find more tax cheaters. Consumers can be informed about fraudsters' schemes and encouraged to report them to the police or the local Better Business Bureau. Increasing victim reporting to the authorities and increasing enforcement agency budgets seem to be the most obvious ways to enhance enforcement levels against individual occupational criminals.

A CONCLUDING NOTE

The purpose of this book has been to bring together under the single rubric of occupational crime several criminological literatures which have heretofore been either disparately or differently categorized. In so doing, the book has tried to familiarize the student with a variety of historical, theoretical, legal, and empirical perspectives on the problem of occupational crime.

The reduction and control of occupational crime is a formidable task, but it can be a doable one. Iconoclastic approaches to enforcing occupational crime laws—such as Braithwaite's enforced self-regulation, Coffee's equity fining, and Fisse's adverse publicity mandates—are sorely needed. Refreshing suggestions such as these should not be rejected out of hand simply because they appear to be too radical or currently lack the political and organizational support necessary for their successful implementation. Disallowing these novel ideas simply because they are currently impractical or simply unfamiliar will cause us to inch along in mire, rather than rapidly move forward against these often very harmful kinds of actions.

We cannot lose sight of the fact that the powerful and respectable positions of many occupational offenders promote a lack of formal and informal censures against them. This state of affairs cannot be allowed to continue if sanctioning is to have any effect on controlling their offenses. Punishing these elite would also be more equitable.

QUESTIONS FOR DISCUSSION

1. Explain the basic differences among: normative validation, deterrence, incapacitation, and rehabilitation.
2. What are the assumptions of the general deterrence model? What are the assumptions of the specific deterrence model?
3. Explain the "deterrence trap" in relation to punishing occupational criminals.
4. How can crime control rationales lead to punishments greater than those deserved by the offender?
5. How did informal adverse publicities affect the large firms in the Fisse and Braithwaite (1985) study?
6. Under which conditions should incarceration be imposed for occupational crimes?
7. What are the methodological problems associated with studying the general and specific deterrent effects of sanctions against occupational criminals?
8. Describe the practical implementation of occupational disqualification programs for executives, college teachers, and police officers involved in occupational crime.
9. Why does rehabilitation have a greater potential to help organizations rather than individuals?
10. Explain and critique Coffee's "equity fining" and Braithwaite's "enforced self-regulation" in terms of practicality and potential effectiveness.
11. Why do professions have such poor self-regulation records?

REFERENCES

Adler, Jerry
   1977   "Employee Thievery: A $6 Billion Hand in the Till." *New York Sunday News Magazine* (September 11): 6+.

Akers, Ronald, Marvin Krohn, Lonn Lanza-Kaduce, and Marcia Radosevich
   1979   "Social Learning and Deviant Behavior." *American Sociological Review* 44: 636-55.

Albanese, Jay
   1987   *Organizational Offenders.* Niagara Falls, NY: Apocalypse.

Allman, William F.
   1989   "Cooking the Paleontological Books." *U.S. News and World Report* (May 8):61.

Altick, Richard D.
   1951   *The Scholar Adventurers.* New York: Macmillan.

Amnesty International
   1975   *Amnesty International Report on Torture.* New York: Farrar Straus, and Giroux.

Andenaes, Johannes
   1974   *Punishment and Deterrence.* Ann Arbor: University of Michigan Press.

Asch, Peter and J. J. Seneca
   1976   "Is Collusion Profitable?" *Review of Economics and Statistics* 58:1-12.

Associated Press
   5/29/87   "Bus Driver Given 20 Years." *Evansville Courier*: 30.

   6/4/87   "Firm to Pay $25 Million Insider Penalty." *Evansville Courier*: 12.

   6/10/87   "Sex Charge Filed Against Therapist." *Evansville Courier*:16.

   6/30/87   "Local Attorney Indicted on Theft Charges." *Evansville Courier*:1.

   11/29/87 "Fraud Discovered Among Research." *Albany Herald*:6B.

   12/18/87 "Boesky Handed 3 Years." *Albany Herald*:11A+.

   2/16/88   "Engineer Enters Guilty Plea to Manslaughter in Accident." *Albany Herald*:1A+.

4/16/88	"Former Teacher Convicted." *Albany Herald*:1A+.
4/20/88	"Postal Workers Charged in Fraud." *Albany Herald*:1A.
5/13/88	"Gynecologist Guilty of Improper Exams." *Albany Herald*:6A.
7/1/88	"Pentagon Bribery Detailed." *Albany Herald*:1A+.
8/24/88	"Chrysler Odometer Settlement Reached." *Albany Herald*:6B.
9/2/88	"OSHA Enforcement of Job-Safety Law Ripped." *Albany Herald*: 8A.
9/23/88	"Georgia Preacher Convicted." *Albany Herald*:5A.
9/24/88	"Instructor Convicted in Recruit's Death." *Albany Herald*:3A.
9/29/88	"Tax Shelter Promoter Gets 27 Years in Scam." *Albany Herald*: 6A.
10/15/88	"Funeral Director Charged." *Albany Herald*:1A+.
12/6/88a	"Steinberg Rebuffed in Insanity Defense." *Albany Herald*:5A.
12/6/88b	"Bakker, Former Aide Indicted on 24 Counts of Fraud." *Atlanta Constitution*:1A+.
12/17/88	"LaRouche Convicted of Fraud." *Albany Herald*:1A+.
12/25/88	"Drexel Decided Against the Risk." *Albany Herald*:4B.
1/1/89	"Feds Set Up Nationwide Rap Sheet for Doctors." *Albany Sunday Herald*:4B.
1/14/89	"Seven Enter Innocent Pleas in Pentagon Bribery Case." *Atlanta Constitution*:14A.
1/28/89	"LaRouche Gets 15-Year Sentence." *Albany Herald*:1A.
2/2/89	"Request Denied." *Albany Herald*:1B.
2/14/89	"Union Carbide to Pay $470 Million." *Albany Herald*:1A.
2/17/89	"Baptist Minister Convicted." *Albany Herald*:5A.
6/17/89a	"Shield Victims Awarded Cash." *Albany Herald*:4B.
6/17/89b	" 'Robin HUD' Says Others Took Money Too." *Albany Herald*:6A.

Bancroft, Tom
1989   "Two Minutes." *Financial World* (June 27): 28–32.

Barker, Thomas
1978   "An Empirical Study of Police Deviance Other than Corruption." *Journal of Police Science and Administration* 6:264-77.

Becker, Howard, B. Greer, E. Hughes, and A. Strauss.
1961   *Boys in White: Student Culture in Medical School*. Chicago: University of Chicago Press.

Benson, Michael L.
    1985   "Denying the Guilty Mind: Accounting for Involvement in White Collar Crime." *Criminology* 23:585-607.

Berg, Eric
    1989   "46 Indicated in Commodities Probe." *Los Angeles Daily News.* (August 3): Business 1.

Berger, Stuart M.
    1988   *What Your Doctor Didn't Learn in Medical School.* New York: William Morrow and Company.

Biderman, Albert and Albert J. Reiss, Jr.
    1980   *Data Sources on White-Collar Law-Breaking.* Washington, D.C.: U.S. Government Printing Office.

Binder, Arnold, Gilbert Geis, and Dickson Bruce
    1988   *Juvenile Delinquency.* New York: Macmillan.

Black, Donald
    1979   "Common Sense in the Sociology of Law." *American Sociological Review* 44:18-27.

Blau, Peter and W. Richard Scott
    1962   *Formal Organizations.* San Francisco: Chandler.

Blumberg, Abraham S.
    1984   "The Practice of Law as a Confidence Game: Organization Cooptation of a Profession." In George Cole (ed.) *Criminal Justice: Law and Politics* (4th ed.). Monterey, CA: Brooks/Cole.

Blumenthal, Ralph
    1979   "Automobile Repair is Due for a Major Overhaul Soon." *New York Times* (June 4):E9.

Blumrich, Chris
    1986   "Call the Feds." *Newsweek* (December 22):42.

Box, Steven
    1983   *Power, Crime, and Mystification.* New York: Tavistock.

Bradley, Craig
    1988   "Mail Fraud After *McNally* and *Carpenter:* The Essence of Fraud." *Journal of Criminal Law and Criminology* 79:573–622.

Braithwaite, John
    1979   "An Exploratory Study of Used Car Fraud." In Paul R. Wilson and John Braithwaite (eds.) *Two Faces of Deviance.* Queensland, Australia: University of Queensland Press.
    1982a   "Challenging Just Deserts: Punishing White-Collar Criminals." *Journal of Criminal Law and Criminology* 73:723-64.
    1982b   "Enforced Self-Regulation: A New Strategy for Corporate Crime Control." *Michigan Law Review* 80:1466-1507.

1984   *Corporate Crime in the Pharmaceutical Industry*. London: Routledge and Kegan Paul.

1985   *To Punish or Persuade*. Albany, NY: State University of New York Press.

Braithwaite, John and Gilbert Geis
1982   "On Theory and Action for Corporate Crime Control." *Crime and Delinquency* 28:292-314.

Brenner, S.N. and E.A. Molander
1977   "Is the Ethics of Business Changing?" *Harvard Business Review* 55 (January-February):59-70.

Broy, Anthony
1974   "The Big Business Rip-Off." *Finance* (November): 42-45.

Bulmer, M.
1982   "The research Ethics of Pseudo-patient Studies: A New Look at the Merits of Covert Ethnographic Methods." *Sociological Review* 30:627-47.

Bureau of Justice Statistics
1979   *Computer Crime*. Washington, D.C.: U.S. Government Printing Office.

1981   *Dictionary of Criminal Justice Data Terminology* (2nd ed.). Washington D.C.: U.S. Government Printing Office.

Burgess, Ann
1981   "Physician Sexual Misconduct and Patients' Responses." *American Journal of Psychiatry* 13:1335-42.

Burgess, Ernest W.
1950   "Comment to Hartung." *American Journal of Sociology* 56: 25-34.

Burgess, Robert L. and Ronald L. Akers
1968   "A Differential Association—Reinforcement Theory of Criminal Behavior." *Social Problems* 14:128-47.

Cameron, Mary Owen
1964   *The Booster and the Snitch*. New York: Free Press.

Carlin, Jerome E.
1966   *Lawyers' Ethics: A Survey of the New York City Bar*. New York: Russell Sage Foundation.

Carter, Danny
1988   "Warning: Odometer Tampering Said 'Cottage Industry' in Georgia." *Albany Herald* (May 25):3A.

Caudill, Harry M.
1988   "Manslaughter in a Coal Mine." In Stuart L. Hills (ed.) *Corporate Violence: Injury and Death For Profit*. Totowa, NJ: Rowman and Littlefield.

Cauley, Leslie
1986 " 'Stock Watch' Blows Whistle on Inside Deals." *Washington D. C. Times* (November 25):B5.

Chambliss, William
1967 "Types of Deviance and the Effectiveness of Legal Sanctions." *Wisconson Law Review* (Summer): 703–719.

Chase, Stuart and F. J. Schlink
1927 *Your Money's Worth*. New York: Macmillan.

Clark, John P. and Richard Hollinger
1977 "On the Feasibility of Empirical Studies of 'White-Collar Crime'." In Robert F. Meier (ed.) *Theory in Criminology*. Beverly Hills, CA: Sage.

Clark, John P. and Larry L. Tifft
1966 "Polygraph and Interview Validation of Self-Reported Delinquent Behavior." *American Sociological Review* 31:516–523.

Clinard, Marshall B.
1946 "Criminological Theories of Violations of Wartime Regulations." *American Sociological Review* 11 (June): 258-70.
1953 *"Other People's Money*—A Critique." *American Sociological Review* 18:362–363.

Clinard, Marshall B. and Richard Quinney
1973 *Criminal Behavior Systems* (2nd ed.). New York: Holt, Rinehart and Winston.

Clinard, Marshall B. and Peter Yeager
1980 *Corporate Crime*. New York: Free Press.

Clinard, Marshall B., Peter Yeager, Jeanne Brissette, David Petrashek, and Elizabeth Harris
1979 *Illegal Corporate Behavior*. Washington, D.C.: U.S. Government Printing Office.

Coffee, John C., Jr.
1981 " 'No Soul to Damn; No Body to Kick': An Unscandalized Inquiry into the Problem of Corporate Punishment." *Michigan Law Review* 79:386-459.

Cohen, Albert K.
1955 *Delinquent Boys: The Culture of the Gang*. New York: Free Press.

Coleman, James William
1985 *The Criminal Elite*. New York: St. Martin's Press.
1987 "Toward an Integrated Theory of White-Collar Crime." *American Journal of Sociology* 93 (2):406-39.
1989 *The Criminal Elite* (2nd ed.). New York: St. Martin's Press.

Commodity Futures Trading Commission
　　1988　　　*Annual Report 1987*. Washington, D.C.: U.S. Government
　　　　　　　Printing Office.

Comstock, Anthony
　　1880　　　*Frauds Exposed*. Reprinted by Patterson Smith, Montclair,
　　　　　　　NJ (1969).

Conklin, John E.
　　1977　　　*Illegal But Not Criminal: Business Crime in America*. Engle-
　　　　　　　wood Cliffs, NJ: Prentice-Hall.

Crane, Diana
　　1975　　　*The Sanctity of Social Life: Physicians' Treatment of Criti-
　　　　　　　cally Ill Patients*. New York: Russell Sage Foundation.

Cressey, Donald
　　1953　　　*Other People's Money: A Study in the Social Psychology of
　　　　　　　Embezzlement*. Glencoe, IL: Free Press.

　　1989　　　"The Poverty of Theory in Corporate Crime Research." In
　　　　　　　William Laufer and Freda Adler (eds.) *Advances in Crimino-
　　　　　　　logical Theory* (Vol. 1). New Brunswick, NJ: Transaction
　　　　　　　Publishers.

Cullen, Francis, Gregory Clark, Bruce Link, Richard Mathers, Jennifer Niedos-
pial, and Michael Sheahan
　　1985　　　"Dissecting White-Collar Crime: Offense Type and Punitive-
　　　　　　　ness." *International Journal of Comparative and Applied
　　　　　　　Criminal Justice* 9 (Spring):16-27.

Cullen, Francis, Bruce Link, and Craig Polanzi
　　1982　　　"The Seriousness of Crime Revisited." *Criminology* 20:83-
　　　　　　　102.

Cullen, Francis, William Maakestad, and Gray Cavender
　　1987　　　*Corporate Crime Under Attack*. Cincinnati, OH: Anderson.

Cullen, Francis, Richard Mathers, Gregory Clark, and John Cullen
　　1983　　　"Public Support for Punishing White-Collar Crime: Blaming
　　　　　　　the Victim Revisited?" *Journal of Criminal Justice* 11:481-
　　　　　　　93.

Daly, Kathleen
　　1986　　　"White-Collar Crime and Gender." Paper presented to the
　　　　　　　American Society of Criminology, Atlanta, Georgia, Octo-
　　　　　　　ber.

DeMott, John
　　1984　　　"Light Fingers." *Time* (December 31):35.

Douglas, Jack and John Johnson (eds.)
　　1977　　　*Official Deviance: Readings in Malfeasance, Misfeasance,
　　　　　　　and Other Forms of Corruption*. Philadelphia: J.B. Lippin-
　　　　　　　cott.

Dowie, Mark
1977   "Pinto Madness." *Mother Jones* 2 (September/October):18-22.
1988   "Pinto Madness." In Stuart L. Hills (ed.) *Corporate Violence: Injury and Death For Profit.* Totowa, NJ: Rowman and Littlefield.

Downs, Robert B.
1964   "Afterword." In Upton Sinclair's *The Jungle.* New York: New American Library of World Literature.

Downs, Anthony
1967   *Inside Bureaucracy.* Boston: Little, Brown.

Dubin, Robert
1958   *The World of Work.* Englewood Cliffs, NJ: Prentice-Hall.

Durkheim, Émile
1961   *Moral Education.* New York: Free Press.

Eckert, David
1980   "Sherman Act Sentencing: An Empirical Study, 1971-1979." *Journal of Criminal Law and Criminology* 71 (3): 244-54.

Edelhertz, Herbert
1970   *The Nature, Impact and Prosecutioon of White-Collar Crime.* Washington, D.C.: U.S. Government Printing Office.

Eisenhauer, Paul
1981   "Genocide." In Marvin Wolfgang and Neil Weiner (eds.) *Surveying Violence Across Nations.* Unpublished Manuscript. Philadelphia: Center for Studies in Criminology and Criminal Law, University of Pennsylvania.

Elliott, Delbert S.
1982   "Review Essay: *Measuring Delinquency.*" *Criminology* 20: 527-37.

Elliott, Delbert S., S. Ageton, D. Huizinga, B. Knowles, and R.J. Canter
1983   *The Prevalence and Incidence of Delinquent Behavior: 1976–1980.* Boulder, CO: Behavioral Research Institute.

Elzinga, Kenneth and William Breit
1976   *The Antitrust Penalties: A Study in Law and Economics.* New Haven, CT: Yale University Press.

Ennis, Phillip H.
1967   *Criminal Victimization in the United States: A Report of a National Survey.* Washington, D.C.: U.S. Government Printing Office.

Environmental Protection Agency
1988a   *Summary of Enforcement Accomplishments, Fiscal Year 1987.* Washington, D.C.: U.S. Government Printing Office.
1988b   *Summary of Criminal Prosecutions Resulting From Environmental Investigations.* Washington, D.C.: U.S. Government Printing Office.

Ermann, M. David and Richard Lundman (eds.)
    1978   *Corporate and Governmental Deviance: Problems of Organizational Behavior in Contemporary Society.* New York: Oxford.

Esper, George
    1988   "My Lai." *Albany Sunday Herald* (March 13): 2C.

Federal Trade Commission
    1986   *Annual Report of the Federal Trade Commission, Fiscal Year 1987.* Washington, D.C.: U.S. Government Printing Office.

Festinger, Leon
    1957   *A Theory of Cognitive Dissonance.* Stanford, CA: Stanford University Press.

Figlio, Robert M.
    1978   "A Note on the Endpoint Truncation Effect of a Category Scale." Paper presented to the American Society of Criminology, Dallas, Texas, November.

Fisse, Brent
    1984   "The Duality of Corporate and Individual Criminal Liability." In Ellen Hochstedler (ed.) *Corporations as Criminals.* Beverly Hills, CA: Sage.

    1986   "Sanctions Against Corporations: Economic Efficiency or Legal Efficacy?" In W. Byron Groves and Graeme Newman (eds.) *Punishment and Privilege.* Albany, NY: Harrow and Heston.

Fisse, Brent and John Braithwaite
    1985   *The Impact of Publicity on Corporate Offenders.* Albany, NY: State University of New York Press.

Flaherty, Robert J. and Tedd A. Cohen
    1979   "Rascality Springs Eternal." *Forbes* (April 20):87-8.

Fleischman, Paul R.
    1973   "Letter." *Science* 180 (April 27):356.

Fletcher, G. P.
    1968   "Legal Aspects of the Decision Not to Prolong Life." *Journal of the American Medical Association* 203:119-22.

Folsom, R.
    1974   "A Randomized Response Validation Study: Comparison of Direct and Randomized Reporting in DUI Arrests." Research Triangle Park, NC: Research Triangle Institute.

Folsom, R., B. Greenberg, D. Horvitz, and J. Abernathy
    1973   "The Two Alternative Questions Randomized Response Model for Human Surveys." *Journal of the American Statistical Association* 68:525-30.

Fox, James A. and Paul E. Tracy
 1986   *Randomized Response*. Beverly Hills, CA: Sage.

Frank, Nancy
 1988   "Murder in the Workplace." In Stuart L. Hills (ed.) *Corporate Violence: Injury and Death For Profit*. Totowa, NJ: Rowman and Littlefield.

Franklin, Alice P.
 1976   *Internal Theft in a Retail Organization*. Unpublished Ph.D. dissertation. Columbus, OH: The Ohio State University.

Freidson, Eliot
 1970a   *The Profession of Medicine*. New York: Dodd and Mead.
 1970b   *Professional Dominance*. New York: Atherton Press.

French, Peter A.
 1985   "Publicity and the Control of Corporate Conduct: Hester Prynne's New Image." In Brent Fisse and Peter French (eds.) *Corrigible Corporations and Unruly Law*. San Antonio, TX: Trinity University Press.

Garbus, Martin and Joel Seligman
 1976   "Sanctions and Disbarment: They Sit in Judgement." In Ralph Nader and Mark Green (eds.) *Verdicts on Lawyers*. New York: Thomas Crowell.

Geis, Gilbert
 1968a   "Introduction." In Gilbert Geis (ed.) *White-Collar Criminal*. New York: Atherton Press.
 1968b   "The Heavy Electrical Equipment Antitrust Cases of 1961." In Gilbert Geis (ed.) *White-Collar Criminal*. New York: Atherton Press.
 1972   "Corporate Penalties for Corporate Criminals." *Criminal Law Bulletin* 8 (5):377-92.
 1973a   "Deterring Corporate Crime." In Ralph Nader and Mark Green (eds.) *Corporate Power in America*. New York: Grossman.
 1973b   "Jeremy Bentham." In Hermann Mannheim (ed.) *Pioneers in Criminology* (2nd ed.). Montclair, NJ: Patterson Smith.
 1974   "Avocational Crime." In Daniel Glaser (ed.) *Handbook of Criminology*. Chicago: Rand McNally
 1988   "From Deuteronomy to Deniability: A Historical Perlustration on White-Collar Crime." *Justice Quarterly* 5 (March):7-32.

Geis, Gilbert and Colin Goff
 1982   "Edwin H. Sutherland: A Biographical and Analytical Commentary." In Gilbert Geis *On White-Collar Crime*. Lexington, MA: Lexington Books.

1983   "Introduction." In Edwin H. Sutherland *White Collar Crime: The Uncut Version*. New Haven, CT: Yale University Press.

Geis, Gilbert, Paul Jesilow, Henry Pontell, and Mary Jane O'Brien
1985   "Fraud and Abuse of Government Medical Benefit Programs by Psychiatrists." *American Journal of Psychiatry* 142 (2): 231-34.

Geis, Gilbert, Henry Pontell, Constance Keenan, Stephen Rosoff, Mary Jane O'Brien, and Paul Jesilow
1985   "Peculating Psychologists: Fraud and Abuse Against Medicaid." *Professional Psychology: Research and Practice* 16:823-32.

Gibbons, Don C.
1969   "Crime and Punishment: A Study of Social Attitudes." *Social Forces* 47:391-97.

1973   *Society, Crime and Criminal Careers*. Englewood Cliffs, NJ: Prentice-Hall.

Gibbs, Jack P.
1975   *Crime, Punishment and Deterrence*. New York: Elsevier.

1985   "The Methodology of Theory Construction in Criminology." In Robert F. Meier (ed.) *Theoretical Methods in Criminology*. Beverly Hills, CA: Sage.

1987   "The State of Criminological Theory." *Criminology* 25:821-40.

Giordano, Peggy, Sandra Kerbel, and Sandra Dudley
1981   "The Economics of Female Criminality: An Analysis of Police Blotters." In Lee Bowker (ed.) *Women and Crime in America*. New York: Macmillan.

Gold, Martin
1966   "Undetected Delinquent Behavior." *Journal of Research in Crime and Delinquency* 3:37-46.

Gottfredson, Michael and Travis Hirschi
1989   "A Propensity-Event Theory of Crime." In William Laufer and Freda Adler (eds.) *Advances in Criminological Theory* (Vol. 1). New Brunswick, NJ: Transaction Publishers.

in press   *A General Theory of Crime*. Stanford, CA: Stanford University Press.

Gottfredson, Stephen, K. Young, and William Laufer
1980   "Additivity and Interactions in Offense Seriousness Scales." *Journal of Research in Crime and Delinquency* 17:4-25.

Grasmick, Herold and Donald Green
1980   "Legal Punishment, Social Disapproval, and Internalization as Inhibitors of Illegal Behavior." *Journal of Criminal Law and Criminology* 71: 325-35.

Green, Gary S.
1978   "Measuring the Incapacitative Effectiveness of Fixed Punishment." In James Cramer (ed.) *Preventing Crime.* Beverly Hills, CA: Sage.

1981a   *Citizen Reporting of Crime to the Police.* Unpublished Ph.D. Dissertation. Philadelphia: University of Pennsylvania.

1981b   "Torture." In Marvin Wolfgang and Neil Weiner (eds.) *Surveying Violence Across Nations.* Unpublished manuscript. Philadelphia: Center for Studies in Criminology and Criminal Law, University of Pennsylvania.

1985a   "The Representativeness of the *Uniform Crime Reports:* Ages of Persons Arrested." *Journal of Police Science and Administration* 13 (March):46-52.

1985b   "General Deterrence and Television Cable Crime: A Field Experiment in Social Control." *Criminology* 23:629-45.

1987   "Citizen Gun Ownership and Criminal Deterrence: Theory, Research, and Policy." *Criminology* 25:63-81.

Green, Mark J.
1973   "The Corporation and the Community." In Ralph Nader and Mark J. Green (eds.) *Corporate Power in America.* New York: Grossman.

Greenberg, B., R. Kuebler, J. Abernathy, and D. Horvitz
1971   "Application of the Randomized Response Technique in Obtaining Quantitative Data." *Journal of the American Statistical Association* 66:243-50.

Greenberg, David F.
1981   "Delinquency and the Age Structure of Society." In David F. Greenberg (ed.) *Crime and Capitalism.* Palo Alto, CA: Mayfield.

Greene, Robert W.
1981   *The Sting Man: Inside Abscam.* New York: E.P. Dutton.

Gross, Edward
1979   "Organizations as Criminal Actors." In Paul R. Wilson and John Braithwaite (eds.) *Two Faces of Deviance.* Queensland, Australia: University of Queensland Press.

1980   "Organization Structure and Organizational Crime." In Gilbert Geis and Ezra Stotland (eds.) *White-Collar Crime: Theory and Research.* Beverly Hills, CA: Sage.

Gross, M. L.
1967   *The Doctors.* New York: Dell.

Groves, Harold M.
1958   "An Empirical Study of Income-Tax Compliance." *National Tax Journal* 11 (December):241-301.

Guarasci, Richard
    1988   "Death by Cotton Dust." In Stuart L. Hills (ed.) *Corporate Violence: Injury and Death For Profit*. Totowa, NJ: Rowman and Littlefield.

Hagan, Frank
    1986   *Introduction to Criminology*. Chicago: Nelson-Hall.

Hall, Jerome
    1952   *Theft, Law, and Society*. Indianapolis, IN: Bobbs-Merrill.

Hall, Richard
    1969   *Occupations and the Social Structure*. Englewood Cliffs, NJ: Prentice-Hall.

Hamilton, Walton H.
    1931   "The Ancient Maxim of Caveat Emptor." *Yale Law Journal* 40: 1133-87.

Hanley, John
    1973   "Letter." *Science* 180 (April 27):360.

Harding, T. Swann
    1935   *The Popular Practice of Fraud*. New York: Longmans, Green and Company

Harris, Louis
    1969   "Changing Morality: The Two Americas." *Time* (June 6):26-7.

Henderson, Charles R.
    1901   *Introduction to the Study of the Dependent, Defective and Delinquent Classes* (2nd ed.). Boston: D.C. Heath.

Hindelang, Michael J.
    1976   *Criminal Victimization in Eight American Cities*. Cambridge, MA: Ballinger.

    1978   "Race and Involvement in Common Law Crimes." *American Sociological Review* 43:93-109.

    1979   "Sex Differences in Criminal Activity." *Social Problems* 27: 143-55.

Hindelang, Michael J., Travis Hirschi, and Joseph Weis
    1981   *Measuring Delinquency*. Beverly Hills, CA: Sage.

Hirschi, Travis
    1969   *Causes of Delinquency*. Berkeley: University of California Press.

Hirschi, Travis and Michael Gottfredson
    1987   "Causes of White-Collar Crime." *Criminology* 25:949-74.

    1989   "The Significance of White-Collar Crime for a General Theory of Crime." *Criminology* 27:359-72.

Hirst, Paul
  1975   "Marx and Engels on Law, Crime, and Morality." In Ian
            Taylor, Paul Walton, and Jock Young (eds.) *Critical Crimi-
            nology*. London: Routledge and Kegan Paul.
Hollinger, Richard and John Clark
  1983   *Theft by Employees*. Lexington, MA: Lexington Books.
Hopkins, Andrew
  1980   "Controlling Corporate Deviance." *Criminology* 18:198-
            214.
Horning, Donald M.
  1979   "Blue Collar Theft: Conceptions of Property Attitudes To-
            ward Pilfering and Work Group Norms in a Modern Indus-
            trial Plant." In Erwin Smigel and H. Lawrence Ross (eds.)
            Crime Against Bureaucracy. New York: Van Nostrand
            Reinhold.
Hughes, Everett C.
  1965   "The Study of Occupations." In R. Merton, L. Broom, and L.
            Cottrell (eds.) *Sociology Today*. New York: Harper and Row.
Inciardi, James
  1987   *Criminal Justice* (2nd ed.). San Diego, CA: Harcourt Brace
            Jovanovich.
Internal Revenue Service
  1988   *Annual Report* 1987. Washington, D. C.: U.S. Government
            Printing Office.
Jaspan, Norman
  1974   *Mind Your Own Business*. Englewood Cliffs, NJ: Prentice-
            Hall.
Jesilow, Paul
  1982   *Deterring Automobile Repair Fraud: A Field Experiment*.
            Unpublished Ph.D. Dissertation. Irvine, CA: University of
            California.
Jesilow, Paul, Henry Pontell, and Gilbert Geis
  1985   "Medical Criminals: Physician and White-Collar Offenses."
            Justice Quarterly 2 (2):151-65.
Johnston, Michael
  1982   *Political Corruption and Public Policy in America*. Belmont,
            CA: Brooks/Cole.
Kallett, Arthur and F. J. Schlink
  1933   *100,000,000 Guinea Pigs*. New York: Vanguard Press.
Kardner, S. H., M. Fuller and I. N. Mensh
  1973   "A Survey of Physicians' Attitudes and Practices Regarding
            Erotic and Nonerotic Contact With Patients." *American
            Journal of Psychiatry* 130:1077-81.

Karnofsky, D. A.
    1960   "Why Prolong the Life of a Patient with Advanced Cancer?"
            CA Bulletin of Cancer Progress 10 (January-February):9-
            11.

Keisling, P.
    1983   "Radical Surgery: Let's Draft the Doctors." *The Washington
            Monthly* 14 (February):26-34.

Kidd, Roobert F.
    1979   "Crime Reporting: Toward a Social Psychological Model."
            Criminology 17:380-94.

Klockars, Karl
    1974   *The Professional Fence.* New York: Free Press.

Knapp, Whitman
    1973   *The Knapp Commission Report on Police Corruption.* New
            York: George Brazziler.

Kramer, Ronald C.
    1988   "Organizational Crime by State Agencies: The Space Shuttle
            Challenger Disaster." Paper presented to the American Soci-
            ety of Criminology, Chicago, Illinois, November.

Lader, L.
    1965   "The Scandal of Abortion Laws." *New York Times Maga-
            zine* (April 25):30-35.

Lane, Robert E.
    1953   "Why Businessmen Violate the Law." *Journal of Criminal
            Law, Criminology and Police Science* 44:151-65.

Lanza-Kaduce, Lonn
    1980   "Deviance Among Professionals: The Case of Unnecessary
            Surgery." *Deviant Behavior* 1:333-59.

Laub, John
    1983   *Criminology in the Making: An Oral History.* Boston:
            Northeastern University Press.

Lemert, Edwin
    1951   *Social Pathology.* New York: McGraw-Hill.

Leonard, William N. and Marvin G. Weber
    1970   "Automakers and Dealers: A Study of Criminogenic Market
            Forces." *Law and Society Review* 4:407-24.

Lewis, H. and M. Lewis
    1970   *The Medical Offenders.* New York: Simon and Schuster.

Litman, Richard C. and Donald S. Litman
    1981   "Protection of the American Consumer: The Muckrakers
            and the Enforcement of the First Federal Food Drug Law in
            the United States." *Food Drug Cosmetic Law Journal* 36:
            647-68.

Loeffler, Robert
    1974   *Report of the Trustee of Equity Funding Corporation of America Pursuant to Section 167(3) of the Bankruptcy Act.* United States Bankruptcy Court, Los Angeles (November 1).

Lombroso, Cesare
    1911   *Crime: Its Causes and Remedies.* Boston: Little Brown.

Lombroso-Ferrero, Gina
    1972   *Lombroso's Criminal Man.* Montclair, NJ: Patterson-Smith.

Lyons, R.D.
    1984   "Cheating on Exams for Doctors Causes Alarm." *New York Times* (April 3).

Mannheim, Hermann
    1965   *Comparative Criminology.* London: Routledge and Kegan Paul.

Mars, Gerald
    1974   "Dock Pilferage: A Case Study in Occupational Theft." In Paul Rock and Mary McIntosh (eds.) *Deviance and Social Control.* London: Tavistock.

Mason, Robert and Lyle Calvin
    1978   "A Study of Admitted Income Tax Evasion." *Law and Society Review* 12:73-89.

Matza, David
    1964   *Delinquency and Drift.* New York: John Wiley and Sons.

Martinson, Robert
    1974   "What Works—Questions and Answers About Prison Reform." *Public Interest* 35:22-54.

McCaghy, Charles and Janet Nogier
    1982   "A Pilot Survey on Exposure, Victimization, and Susceptibility to Consumer Fraud." Paper presented to the American Society of Criminology, Toronto, Ontario, November.

McCleary, R., M.J. O'Neil, T. Epperlein, C. Jones, and D. H. Gray
    1981   "Effects of Legal Education and Work Experience on Perceptions of Crime Seriousness." *Social Problems* 28:276-89.

McDermott, Martin F.
    1982   "Occupational Disqualification of Corporate Executives: An Innovative Condition of Probation." *Journal of Criminal Law and Criminology* 73:604-41.

Merton, Robert K.
    1942   "Science and Technology in a Democratic Order." *Journal of Legal and Political Sociology* 1:115-26.
    1968   "Social Structure and Anomie." In Robert K. Merton *Social Theory and Social Structure.* New York: Free Press.
    1973   "Priorities in Scientific Discovery." In Robert K. Merton *The Sociology of Science.* Chicago: University of Chicago Press.

Merton, Robert K. and Harriet Zuckerman
1973   "Age, Aging, and Age Structure in Science." In Robert K. Merton *The Sociology of Science*. Chicago: University of Chicago Press.

Milgram, Stanley
1963   "Behavioral Study of Obedience." *Journal of Abnormal and Social Psychology* 67:371-78.
1965   "Some Conditions of Obedience and Disobedience to Authority." *Human Relations* 18:54-74.

Miller, Walter B.
1958   "Lower-Class Culture as a Generating Milieu of Gang Delinquency." *Journal of Social Issues* 14:5-19.

Minor, W. William
1981   "Techniques of Neutralization: A reconceptualization and Empirical Verification." *Journal of Research in Crime and Delinquency* 18:295-318.

Mintz, Morton
1988   "At Any Cost: Corporate Greed, Women, and the Dalkon Shield." In Stuart L. Hills (ed.) *Corporate Violence: Injury and Death For Profit*. Totowa, NJ: Rowman and Littlefield.

Monachesi, Elio
1972   "Cesare Beccaria." In Hermann Mannheim (ed.) *Pioneers in Criminology* (2nd ed.). Montclair, NJ: Patterson Smith.

Moors, J.
1971   "Optimization of the Unrelated Question Randomized Response Model." *Journal of the American Statistical Association* 66: 627-29.

Morison, R.
1971   "Death: Process or Event?" *Science* 173 (August 20):694-98.

Morris, Albert
1968   "Criminals of the Upperworld." In Gilbert Geis (ed.) *White-Collar Criminal*. New York: Atherton Press.

Morris, Norval
1974   *The Future of Imprisonment*. Chicago: University of Chicago Press.

Murton, Tom and Joe Hyams
1969   *Accomplices to the Crime*. New York: Grove Press.

Nader, Ralph
1965   *Unsafe at Any Speed: The Designed-in Dangers of the American Automobiles*. New York: Grossman.

Nader, Ralph and Mark Green
1972   "Crime in the Suites: Coddling the Corporations." *New Republic* (April 29):17-21.

Needleman, Martin and Carolyn Needleman
1979   "Organizational Crime: Two Models of Criminogenesis."
          The Sociological Quarterly 20: 517-39.
Nettler, Gwynn
1974   "Embezzlement Without Problems." *British Journal of Crim-
          inology* 14:70-77.
Newsweek
1985a   "Murder in the Front Office." (July 8):58.
1985b   "Child Abuse at the Point." (July 8):45.
New York Times
1939   "Hits Criminality in White Collars." (December 28): 12.
Newman, Donald J.
1968   "Public Attitudes Toward a Form of White-Collar Crime." In
          Gilbert Geis (ed.) *White-Collar Criminal*. New York: Ather-
          ton Press.
Noonan, John
1984   *Bribes*. New York: MacMillan.
O'Brien, Robert M.
1985   *Crime and Victimization Data*. Beverly Hills, CA: Sage.
O'Malley, Pat
1986   "Marxist Theory and Marxist Criminology." *Crime and So-
          cial Justice* 29:70-87.
Occupational Health and Safety Administration
1988   *Report of the President to the Congress on Occupational
          Safety and Health for Calendar Year 1987*. Washington,
          D.C.: U. S. Government Printing Office.
Ostow, Mortimer
1973   "Letter." *Science* (April 27):361-62.
Oxford American Dictionary
1980   New York: Oxford University Press.
Packer, Herbert L. and Ralph J. Gampell
1959   "Therapeutic Abortion: A Problem in Law and Medicine."
          Stanford Law Review 11:417-37.
Paltrow, Scot
1989   "6 Found Guilty of Racketeering and Securities Fraud." *Los
          Angeles Times* (August 1): IV-1 + .
Parisi, Nicolette
1984   "Theories of Corporate Criminal Liability." In Ellen Hoch-
          stedler (ed.) *Corporations as Criminals*. Beverly Hills, CA: Sage.
Paternoster, Raymond
1988   "Examining Three-Wave Deterrence Models: A Question of
          Temporal Order and Specification." *Journal of Criminal
          Law and Criminology* 79:135-79.

Pearce, Frank
    1976   *Crimes of the Powerful: Marxism, Crime, and Deviance.* London: Pluto.

Pennsylvania Crime Commission
    1980   *A Decade of Organized Crime: 1980 Report.* St. Davids, PA: Pennsylvania Crime Commission.

Perrow, Charles
    1961   "The Analysis of Goals in Complex Organizations." *American Sociological Review* 26:854-65.

Philadelphia Inquirer
    1939   "Poverty Belittled as Crime Factor." (December 28):17.

Pierce, David
    1987   " 'Exterminator' to be Charged in Death of Mitchell Infant." *Albany Herald* (November 6):1A.

    1989   "Sentencing Set Friday in Americus." *Albany Herald* (September 13): 2A.

Pontell, Henry
    1984   *A Capacity to Punish.* Bloomington, IN: Indiana University Press.

Pontell, Henry, Daniel Granite, Constance Keenan, and Gilbert Geis
    1985   "Seriousness of Crimes: A Survey of the Nation's Chiefs of Police." *Journal of Criminal Justice* 13:1-13.

Pontell, Henry, Paul Jesilow, and Gilbert Geis
    1982   "Policing Physicians: Practitioner Fraud and Abuse in a Government Medical Program." *Social Problems* 30:117-25.

    1984   "Practitioner Fraud and Abuse in Medical Benefit Programs: Government Regulation and Professional White-Collar Crime." *Law and Policy* 6:405-24.

    1986   "Physician Immunity from Punishment." In W. Byron Groves and Graeme Newman (eds.) *Punishment and Privilege.* Albany, NY: Harrow and Heston.

Pontell, Henry, Paul Jesilow, Gilbert Geis, and Mary Jane O'Brien
    1985   "A Demographic Portrait of Physicians Sanctioned by the Federal Government for Fraud and Abuse Against Medicare and Medicaid." *Medical Care* 23 (8):1028-31.

Pope, Leroy
    1978   "Surveys Say White Collar Crime Growing Threat." *Atlanta Journal* (July 16):4J.

President's Commission on Law Enforcement and Administration of Justice
    1968   *Challenge of Crime in a Free Society.* New York: Avon Books.

Quételet, Adolphe Jacques
    1972   "Treatise on Man." In Sawyer F. Sylvester, Jr. *The Heritage of Modern Criminology.* Cambridge, MA: Schenkman Publishing.

Quinney, Richard
  1964   "The Study of White-Collar Crime: Toward a Reorientation
            in Theory and Research." *Journal of Criminal Law, Crimi-
            nology, and Police Science* 55:208-14.
  1968   "Occupational Structure and Criminal Behavior: Prescrip-
            tion Violations by Retail Pharmacists." In Gilbert Geis (ed.)
            White-Collar Criminal. New York: Atherton Press.
  1970   *The Social Reality of Crime.* Boston: Little, Brown.

Reiman, Jeffery
  1979   *The Rich Get Richer and the Poor Get Prison: Ideology, Class,
            and Criminal Justice.* New York: John Wiley and Sons.

Rensberger, Boyce
  1976   "Few Doctors Ever Report Collegues' Incompetence." *New
            York Times* (January 29):1.

Reiss, Albert J., Jr.
  1968   "Police Brutality: Answers to Key Questions." *Society* 5 (8):
            10-19.

The Reporters
  1988   "See No Evil, Hear No Evil." Fox Television Network (De-
            cember 10).

Reutter, Mark
  1988   "The Invisible Risk. . . ." In Stuart L. Hills (ed.) *Corporate
            Violence: Injury and Death for Profit.* Totowa, NJ: Rowman
            Littlefield.

Richter, Paul
  1989   "Latest Black Eye Brings On a Crisis in Confidence." *Los An-
            geles Times* (August 4): IV–1 + .

Roe, Anne
  1956   *The Psychology of Occupations.* New York: John Wiley and
            Sons.

Roebuck, Julian and Stanley C. Weeber
  1978   *Political Crime in the United States: Analyzing Crime By and
            Against Government.* New York: Praeger.

Rogers Commission
  1986   *Report of the Presidential Commission on the Space Shuttle
            Challenger Accident.* Washington, D.C.: U.S. Government
            Printing Office.

Rosenhan, D. L.
  1973   "On Being Sane in Insane Places." *Science* 179 (January 19):
            250-58.

Ross, Edward Alsworth
  1968   "The Criminaloid." In Gilbert Geis (ed.) *White-Collar Crimi-
            nal.* New York: Atherton Press.

Ross, Irwin
    1980   "How Lawless Are Big Companies?" *Fortune* (December
                1):55-61.

Rossi, Peter, Emily Waite, Christine Bose, and Richard Berk
    1974   "The Seriousness of Crimes: Normative Structure and Indi-
                vidual Differences." *American Sociological Review* 39:224-
                37.

Ruff, Charles
    1977   "Federal Prosecution of Local Corruption: A Case Study in
                the Making of Law Enforcement Policy." *Georgetown Law
                Journal* 65:1171-1213.

Russell, Bertrand
    1929   *Our Knowledge of the External World.* New York: W. W.
                Norton.

Sanders, Joseph
    1969   "Euthanasia: None Dare Call it Murder." *Journal of Crimi-
                nal Law, Criminology, and Police Science* 60:351-59.

Schafer, Charles and Violet Schafer
    1974   *Breadcraft.* San Francisco: Yerba Buena Press.

Schmidt, Franz
    1973   *A Hangman's Diary.* Montclair, NJ: Patterson-Smith.

Schrager, Laura S. and James F. Short, Jr.
    1980   "How Serious a Crime? Perceptions of Organizational and
                Common Crimes." In Gilbert Geis and Ezra Stotland (eds.)
                White-Collar Crime: Theory and Research. Beverly Hills,
                CA: Sage.

Schur, Edwin
    1965   *Crimes Without Victims.* Englewood Cliffs, NJ: Prentice
                Hall.

Schwartz, Richard and Sonia Orleans
    1967   "On Legal Sanctions." *University of Chicago Law Review*
                34: 274-90.

Sebba, Leslie
    1984   "Crime Seriousness and Criminal Intent." *Crime and and De-
                linquency* 30 (2):227-44.

Securities and Exchange Commission
    1987   "The Insider Trading Act of 1987." Report submitted to the
                United States Senate, Subcommittee on Securities (August 7).

    1988   *Fifty-Third Annual Report, 1987.* Washington, D. C.: U.S.
                Government Printing Office.

Seidler, Lee, Frederick Andrews, and Marc Epstein
    1977   *The Equity Funding Papers.* New York: John Wiley and
                Sons.

Sellin, Thorsten
 1938 *Culture Conflict and Crime.* New York: Social Science Research Council.
 1951 "The Significance of Records of Crime." *Law Quarterly Review* 67:489-504.
 1989 "Book Review of Hans Schneider's *Kriminologie.*" *Journal of Criminal Law and Criminology* 79:1377-81.

Sellin, Thorsten and Marvin E. Wolfgang
 1964 *The Measurement of Delinquency.* New York: John Wiley and Sons.

Shapiro, Susan
 1984 *Wayward Capitalists.* New Haven, CT: Yale University Press.

Sheridan, John H.
 1979 "Is There a Computer Criminal Working for You?" *Industry Week* (January 8):69-77.

Shinnar, R. and S. Shinnar
 1975 "The Effects of the Criminal Justice System on the Control of Crime: A Quantitative Approach." *Law and Society Review* 9: 581-611.

Short, James F., Jr. and F. Ivan Nye
 1957 "Extent of Unrecorded Juvenile Delinquency: Tentative Conclusions." *Journal of Criminal Law, Criminology, and Police Science* 49:296-302.

Short, James F., Jr. and Fred L. Strodtbeck
 1965 *Group Process and Gang Delinquency.* Chicago: University of Chicago Press.

Shover, Neal
 1976 "Organizations and Interorganizational Fields as Criminogenic Behavior Settings: Notes on the Concept of Organizational Crime." Unpublished manuscript, Department of Sociology, University of Tennessee.

Sigelman, Carol K. and Lee Sigelman
 1976 "Authority and Conformity: Violation of a Traffic Regulation." *Journal of Social Psychology* 100:35-43.

Silverman, Milton and Phillip Lee
 1974 *Pills, Profits, and Politics.* Berkeley, CA: University of California Press.

Simon, David R. and D. Stanley Eitzen
 1982 *Elite Deviance.* Boston: Allyn and Bacon.

Simon, Rita J.
 1981 "American Women and Crime." In Louise I. Shelley (ed.) *Readings in Comparative Criminology.* Carbondale, IL: Southern Illinois University Press.

Sinclair, Upton
 1906 *The Jungle.* New York: Vanguard Press.

Skolnick, Jerome
 1966 *Justice Without Trial: Law Enforcement in a Democratic Society.* New York: John Wiley and Sons.

Smigel, Erwin O.
 1970 "Public Attitudes Toward Stealing as Related to the Size of the Victim Organization." In Erwin Smigel and H. Lawrence Ross (eds.) *Crime Against Bureaucracy.* New York: Van Nostrand Reinhold.

Steffensmeïer, Darrell
 1980 "Sex Differences in Patterns of Adult Crime, 1965-77: A Review and Assessment." *Social Forces* 58:1080-1108.

 1987 "Update on Male/Female Arrest Patterns." Paper presented to the American Society of Criminology, Montreal, November.

 1989 "On the Causes of 'White-Collar Crime': An Assessment of Hirschi and Gottfredson's Claims." *Criminology* 27:345-58.

Stevens, S.
 1957 "On the Psychophysical Law." *Psychology Review* 64:153-81.

Stone, Christopher
 1975 *Where the Law Ends: The Social Control of Corporate Behavior.* New York: Harper and Row.

 1988 "A Slap on the Wrist for the Kepone Mob." In Stuart L. Hills (ed.) *Corporate Violence: Injury and Death For Profit.* Totowa, NJ: Rowman and Littlefield.

Storer, Norman
 1967 "The Hard Sciences and the Soft: Some Sociological Observations." *Bulletin of the Medical Library Association* 55:75-84.

Stroman, D.
 1979 *The Quick Knife: Unnessesary Surgery U.S.A.* Port Washington, NY: Kennikat.

Strumpel, Burkhard
 1969 "The Contribution of Survey Research to Public Finance." In Alan T. Peacock (ed.) *Quantitative Analysis in Public Finance.* New York: Praeger.

Sutherland, Edwin H.
 1940 "White-Collar Criminality." *American Sociological Review* 5: 1-12.

 1945 "Is 'White-Collar Crime' Crime?" *American Sociological Review* 10:132-39.

1949   *White Collar Crime.* New York: Holt, Rinehart and Winston.

1983   *White Collar Crime: The Uncut Version.* New Haven, CT: Yale University Press.

Sutherland, Edwin H. and Donald R. Cressey
1974   *Criminology* (9th ed.). Philadelphia: J.B. Lippincott.

Sykes, Gresham
1958   *The Society of Captives.* Princeton, NJ: Princeton University Press.

Sykes, Gresham and David Matza
1957   "Techniques of Neutralization: A Theory of Delinquency." *American Sociological Review* 22:667-70.

Tallmer, Matt
1988   "Chemical Dumping as a Corporate Way of Life." In Stuart L. Hills (ed.) *Corporate Violence: Injury and Death For Profit.* Totowa, NJ: Rowman and Littlefield.

Tappan, Paul
1947   "Who is the Criminal?" *American Sociological Review* 12:96 102.

Thornberry, Terence
1987   "Toward and Interactional Theory of Delinquency." *Criminology* 25:863-92.

Thornton, Mary
1984   "Computer Crime." *Washington Post* (May 20):A1 + .

Time
1986   "Light-fingered Work Ethic." (June 23):34.

1989a   "Prestige." (July 31):50.

1989b   "Doing the Crime, Not the Time." (September 11):81.

Tittle, Charles R.
1980   *Sanctions and Social Deviance: The Question of Deterrence.* New York: Praeger.

Tracy, Paul E. and James A. Fox
1981a   "The Validity of Randomized Response for Sensitive Measurements." *American Sociological Review* 46:187-200.

1981b   "The Randomized Response Approach to Criminological Surveys." In James A. Fox (ed.) *Methods in Quantitative Criminology.* New York: Academic Press.

1989   "A Field Experiment on Insurance Fraud in Auto Body Repair." *Criminology* 27:589–603.

Tullock, Gordon
1965   *The Politics of Bureaucracy.* Washington, D.C.: Public Affairs Press.

Turk, Austin T.
1969   *Criminality and Legal Order.* Chicago: Rand McNally.
U. S. Attorney
1985   "Press Release on PHARMONEY". United States Attorney's Office, Northern District of Georgia (July).
U. S. Attorney General
1955   *Report of the Attorney General's National Committee to Study the Antitrust Laws.* Washington, D. C.: U.S. Department of Justice.
1987   *Annual Report of the Attorney General of the United States, 1986.* Washington, D. C.: U.S. Government Printing Office.
U. S. Department of Labor
1987   *Seventy-Fifth Annual Report, 1987.* Washington, D. C.: U. S. Government Printing Office.
U. S. News and World Report
1982   "What Americans Think of Business Leaders." (September 6):29
1988a   "News You Can Use: Shrinks' Secrets." (March 21):73.
1988b   "Throwing the Book at Drexel." (September 19):41.
United Nations
1975   *Torture and Other Cruel, Inhuman, or Degrading Treatment or Punishment in Relation to Detention and Imprisonment.* New York: The United Nations (General Assembly, 30th Session, October 3).
van den Haag, Ernest
1985   "The Neoclassical Theory of Crime Control." In Robert F. Meier (ed.) *Theoretical Methods in Criminology.* Beverly Hills, CA: Sage.
Van Dine, Stephen, John P. Conrad, and Simon Dinitz
1979   *Restraining the Wicked.* Lexington, MA: Lexington Books.
Vaughan, Diane
1979   *Crime Between Organizations.* Unpublished Ph.D. dissertation. Columbus, OH: The Ohio State University.
1982   "Toward Understanding Unlawful Organizational Behavior." *Michigan Law Review* 80:1377-1402.
1983   *Controlling Unlawful Organizational Behavior.* Chicago: University of Chicago Press.
Vogel, Joachim
1974   "Taxation and Public Opinion in Sweden: An Interpretation of Recent Survey Data." *National Tax Journal* 27:499-510.
Vold, George B.
1958   *Theoretical Criminology.* New York: Oxford University Press.

Vold, George B. and Thomas J. Bernard
    1986   *Theoretical Criminology* (3rd ed.). New York: Oxford University Press.

Waldo, G. P. and T. G. Chirikos
    1972   "Perceived Penal Sanction and Self-Report Criminality: A Neglected Approach to Deterrence Research." *Social Problems* 19:522-40.

Wallerstein, James, S. and Clement J. Wyle
    1947   "Our Law-Abiding Law-Breakers." *Probation* 25:107-12.

Weaver, Paul
    1975   "The Hazards of Trying to Make Consumer Products Safer." *Fortune* (July):133–140.

Williamson, Oliver
    1970   *Corporate Control and Business Behavior: An Inquiry into the Effects of Organization Form on Enterprise Behavior.* Englewood Cliffs, NJ: Prentice-Hall.

Whitman, H.
    1953   "Why Some Doctors Should Be in Jail." *Collier's* (October 30):23-27.

Wilson, Paul, Gilbert Geis, Henry Pontell, Paul Jesilow, and Duncan Chappell
    1985   "Medical Fraud and Abuse: Australia, Canada, and the United States." *International Journal of Comparative and Applied Criminal Justice* 9:25-34.

Wolfgang, Marvin, Robert Figlio, and Terence Thornberry
    1978   *Evaluating Criminology.* New York: Elsevier.

Wolfgang, Marvin, Robert Figlio, Paul Tracy, and Simon Singer
    1985   *The National Survey of Crime Severity.* Washington, D. C.: U. S. Government Printing Office.

Work, Clemens
    1986   "What You Can Do if Your Broker Did You Wrong." *U.S. News and World Report* (December 1):51.

Wright, Erik Olin
    1973   *The Politics of Punishment.* New York: Harper and Row.

Wright, Vernon .L.
    1980   "Use of Randomized Response Technique to Estimate Deer Poaching." In K. Beattie (ed.) *Environmental Law Enforcement Theory and Principles: A Sourcebook* (Vol. 2). Stevens Point, WI: College of Natural Resources, University of Wisconson.

Yoder, Steven A.
    1978   "Criminal Sanctions for Corporate Illegality." *Journal of Criminal Law and Criminology* 69:40-58.

Zeitlin, Lawrence R.
    1971   "A Little Larceny Can Do a Lot for Company Morale." *Psychology Today* 14 (June):22-26, 64.
Zeitz, Dorothy
    1981   *Women Who Embezzle or Defraud: A Study of Convicted Felons.* New York: Praeger.
Zimbardo, Philip
    1972   "Pathology of Imprisonment." *Society* 9:4-8.
Zuckerman, Harriet
    1977   "Deviant Behavior and Social Control in Science." In Edward Sagarin (ed.) *Deviance and Social Change.* Beverly Hills, CA: Sage.

INDEX

Abernathy, J., 43
Abortions, nonspontaneous, 189
ABSCAM, 45, 57, 172-75
Absorbine Jr., 105
Accum, Frederick, 210
Adler, Jerry, 203, 205
Administrative law violations, 8
Adverse publicity, 237-41
  against individuals, 240-41
  against organizations, 238-40
  court-imposed, 241
Advertising, misrepresentations in,
  105-6, 111, 120-21
Agency-based records
  assumptions about, 25-26
  improving, 29-30
  of occupational crimes and crimi-
    nals, 24-30
  problems with, 26-29
Ageton, S., 38
Agob, Sembat, 138
Akers, Ronald, 76
Albanese, Jay, 12
Alcmaenoid family, 3
Allied Chemical, 112, 136, 238
Allman, William F., 214
Altick, Richard D., 213
Amerada Hess, 112
American Airlines, 112, 141, 142
American Bakeries, 112
American Bar Association's Special
  Committee on Evaluation and
  Disciplinary Enforcement, 255
American Beef Packers, 112
American Brands, 112, 139
American Can, 112
American Chiclets, 142

American Cyanamid, 112
American Export Industry, 112
American Sugar Refining, 103, 104
American Tobacco, 103, 104
Amin, Idi, 154
Amnesty International, 154, 155
Andenaes, Johannes, 229
Anderson, Warren, 136
Andrews, Frederick, 214
Anheuser-Busch, 112, 142
Anomie, 73
Antitrust actions, 66
Antitrust violations, 121-24
"Appeal to higher loyalties" neutrali-
  zation technique, 208
Archer-Daniels-Midland, 112
Arden, Elizabeth Cosmetics, 105
Arden-Mayfair, 112, 142
Armco, 112
Armour & Co., 103, 104, 105
Asch, Peter, 110
Ashland Oil, 112, 141
Associated Milk Producers, 112,
  139
Australian Trade Practices Act
  (1974), 252
Authority leakage, 98, 100

Baggett, Eugene, 138
Bakker, Jim, 211-12
Baltimore study, 54, 55
Bancroft, Tom, 145
Bank Secrecy Act, 217-18
Barker, Thomas, 160
Bayer Aspirin, 105
Beatrice Foods, 112, 142
Beccaria, Cesare, 232

285